THE MAKING OF MODERN

CORPORATE FINANCE

THE
MAKING
OF
MODERN
CORPORATE
FINANCE

A HISTORY OF THE IDEAS
AND HOW THEY HELP BUILD
THE WEALTH OF NATIONS

DONALD H. CHEW, JR.

Columbia Business School
Publishing

Columbia University Press
Publishers Since 1893
New York   Chichester, West Sussex
cup.columbia.edu

Library of Congress Cataloging-in-Publication Data
Names: Chew, Donald H., author.
Title: The making of modern corporate finance : a history of the ideas and how they
    help build the wealth of nations / Donald H. Chew.
Description: New York : Columbia University Press, [2025] | Includes index.
Identifiers: LCCN 2024024433 | ISBN 9780231211109 (hardback) |
    ISBN 9780231558747 (ebook)
Subjects: LCSH: Corporations—Finance.
Classification: LCC HG4026 .C467 2025 | DDC 658.15—dc23/eng/20240923
LC record available at https://lccn.loc.gov/2024024433

Printed in the United States of America

Cover design: Noah Arlow
Cover image: Shutterstock

GPSR Authorized Representative: Easy Access System Europe—
Mustamäe tee 50, 10621 Tallinn, Estonia, gpsr.requests@easproject.com

With love to my wife, Susan Emerson . . .
and to our Emily, Michael, and Ben

With gratitude to Carl Ferenbach, longtime business partner and
patron . . . and to my associate editor John McCormack and all the
people at Stern Stewart & Co. and Morgan Stanley I've had the good
fortune to work with for the past 45 years

CONTENTS

PROLOGUE

The Magic of Finance Capitalism

American-style corporate finance—a phrase that combines two if not three of the most vilified words in today's English-language media, social and otherwise—has for the past 40 years been one of the world's remarkable success stories. It's right up there with widely recognized and much-heralded advances in medical and information technology, advances often made possible by corporate finance. The principles and methods of finance that continue to be taught in business schools around the world have played a critical role in the productivity of the U.S. private sector—a group, it's important to keep in mind, that encompasses not only profit-seeking commercial enterprises, but also America's many well-run nonprofits.

Like Adam Smith in the opening pages of *The Wealth of Nations*, this book will propose that U.S. private-sector productivity is the fundamental source of U.S. (and a great deal of global) economic and social wealth. For as Smith suggested nearly 250 years ago, it is the efficiency gains from finding commercial uses for new technologies—some developed, to be sure, with government oversight and tax dollars—by mostly *private* enterprises that end up footing the bill for the health, education, and other forms of general well-being that most of us value most.

THE CONGLOMERATE MOVEMENT AND "OLD-FASHIONED" CORPORATE FINANCE

But why focus on just the past 40 years? We begin with the premise that corporate America was *failing* during the 1970s, when the prospects for U.S.

public companies had become so bleak that the S&P 500 at one point lost almost half its value. Few will dispute the role of U.S. government policy in the "stagflation" of the 1970s, when wage and price controls, the War on Poverty, and other well-intended social programs led to an unprecedented mix of high unemployment and runaway inflation. But the most direct and visible contributor to the bear market of the 1970s was the collapse of U.S. corporate profitability. This collapse, together with the weakness of the dollar, made U.S. stocks much less valuable to the many overseas as well as American investors who normally line up to buy them.

By the end of the '70s, many if not most of the largest U.S. public companies had become bloated "conglomerates" by paying huge sums for unrelated businesses their top management teams knew little or nothing about, and with predictably little to show for it. The managements of such companies assumed they could satisfy their shareholders simply by "buying earnings"—that is, by acquiring other businesses with the aim of reporting steadily rising *earnings per share*. And by diversifying the *corporate* "portfolio" of businesses in much the same way as individual investors diversify their own holdings of stocks and bonds, corporate strategists told themselves (and their boards) that they had achieved a fool-proof way of cushioning their shareholders and employees from the painful effects of the business cycle. When one business was struggling, others would take up the slack.

Take the case of General Mills, which during the '70s transformed itself from the maker of Cheerios and other breakfast foods into what it proudly proclaimed to be "the all-weather growth company." To supplement the earnings from its core cereals business, the company bought large operations that produced Play-Doh, Star Wars toys, and even small submarines—all businesses that, while having a certain appeal for a CEO who was a retired former general, failed to prosper and ended up being sold off in the 1980s.

But to understand the spread and popularity of conglomerates, it's important to see their attraction for their CEOs and top managements. Conglomerate CEOs, although handsomely rewarded in the form of salary and bonuses, seldom owned much of the companies' stock themselves, so their personal fortunes were not much affected by their companies' success (or lack thereof). Sure, it would be nice if the new businesses worked out; but if not, the CEOs' professed commitments to growth and full employment ensured their own continuing status as pillars of the community.

In this book, we call such an approach "old-fashioned corporate finance." Its hallmark is the largely unquestioned and undisciplined pursuit of growth and diversification as corporate ends in themselves. Success was demonstrated by a company's ability to report steadily rising earnings per share, or EPS, throughout the ups and downs of the business cycle. (Jack Welch, to the extent that earnings "management" played a role in his remarkable 20-year run as CEO of General Electric, is held up in these pages as perhaps the most successful and preeminent practitioner of *old-fashioned, not* modern, corporate finance.)

Along with its reliance on diversification and the conglomerate form, old-fashioned corporate finance also typically involved at most modest use of debt financing. For top management, the requirement to service a heavy debt load during downturns could imperil the smooth ascent of the reported EPS stream. And a large debt load would also likely be viewed with misgivings by corporate strategists, community planners, and any others predisposed to welcome the conglomerate form's assurances against the inevitable downturns in the business cycle.

In sum, corporate America of the 1970s was designed to perpetuate what corporate law and governance expert Adolf Berle—and its most famous policy architect—hailed as "controlled capitalism." In that system, shareholders were only one among a number of major corporate constituencies top management must consider when making its strategic and financial decisions. Changes that impose significant costs on any member of the corporate "family" were simply off the table. And the barriers erected by U.S. business law and custom to hostile takeovers not only enabled but encouraged the CEOs of U.S. conglomerates to amass and continue to preside over these sprawling corporate empires. Shareholders were largely powerless; when dissatisfied with management, their only recourse was to sell their shares.

At the end of the '70s, two University of Rochester finance professors, Michael Jensen and William Meckling, found the state of the U.S. economy and corporate governance bleak enough that they wrote an article called "Can the Corporation Survive?"[1] In that article, Jensen and Meckling identified the shareholders of U.S. public companies as "the *only* corporate constituency with no serious representation in corporate boardrooms."

In the 1980s, however, the situation changed dramatically. In response to massive losses in the values of their holdings—and the growing perception of a widening gulf between the actual and potential value of the conglomerates (if and when dismantled)—the shareholders of U.S. companies began to assert their long dormant control rights. Thanks in large part to the passage of the Glass-Steagall Act in 1933, these rights had been unexercised and allowed to atrophy since the first decades of the 20th century. Those were the days when bankers like J.P. Morgan had large debt as well as equity stakes in public companies and helped make strategy while sitting on their boards.

In the '80s, as we shall see, these shareholder rights were reinvigorated and reasserted with a vengeance.

THE RISE OF MODERN CORPORATE FINANCE (AND THE CONVERGENCE OF THEORY AND PRACTICE)

So, again, it was in the 1980s, in response to the corporate failings of the '70s, that what we are calling modern corporate finance was born—or, in some important ways, rediscovered. But what exactly do we mean by *modern* corporate finance, and how is it different from what came before?

In 1982, I joined a handful of others then working at the Chase Manhattan Bank in following two University of Chicago MBAs named Joel Stern and Bennett Stewart to become partners in starting a New York-based corporate finance consulting firm. The main activity of the firm, which later became known as Stern Stewart & Co., was helping companies to estimate—and find ways to increase—the going-concern values of their operations using a discounted free cash flow method that Stern and Stewart adapted from their University of Chicago business school training.[2] In a direct challenge to corporate America's preoccupation with reporting steadily rising EPS, Stern Stewart's guiding principle was summed up in Stern's favorite statement, "Earnings per share don't count." As we told our corporate clients, what really mattered to the world's most sophisticated and influential investors—Stern liked to call them "lead steers"[3]—was the ability of companies to earn consistently high rates of return on their investors' capital, and the more such high-return investments the better.

With that insight as starting and vantage point, it was fairly straightforward to see and show why corporate shareholders place little if any value on *corporate* diversification. The ability, and clear tendency, of most shareholders to diversify their own holdings meant that the widespread conglomerate practice of paying hefty premiums to get into unrelated businesses, however tempting the near-term boost to reported EPS, was likely to reduce longer-run operating efficiency and value.

Which brings us to Stern Stewart's most controversial message for corporate executives in the early '80s: in the eyes of their shareholders, *not all growth is good*. All corporate capital, whether it takes the form of debt or equity, comes with a cost. For corporate managements, the "cost of capital" is a critically important variable. It represents their investors' required rate of return on the capital they are committing to the company when buying its shares. And viewed as such, the cost of capital provides both the benchmark for evaluating current corporate performance and the hurdle rate for most new projects or investments.

To sum up, then, companies increase their own values by earning—or showing clear promise of earning—operating returns on capital that are higher than their cost of capital, regardless of their reported EPS. Among the most dramatic illustrations of this principle is the remarkable increase in the market cap of Amazon.com, which for decades has invested in promising growth opportunities while reporting as little earnings as it can get away with. By contrast, companies that find ways to "engineer" their reported EPS while failing to earn their cost of capital have almost invariably ended up reducing efficiency and value. Along with GE in the post-Jack Welch era, this group includes most of the conglomerates assembled in the '60s and '70s, which ended up being dismantled and sold off in pieces by the active investors who emerged in the 1980s.

So, to repeat what may well be the most important, and counter-intuitive message, of modern corporate finance, *not all growth is good for shareholders*. And to that I would add the following precept: growth that is not good for shareholders is not likely to be *good for the economy at large*. The importance of this lesson will become especially clear in later chapters, when we contrast the success of the U.S. corporate sector with the failure of Japanese and Chinese public companies to provide competitive returns to their shareholders over most of the last three decades.

CORPORATE WASTE AND THE RISE OF THE MARKET FOR CORPORATE CONTROL

The competitive failures of corporate America in the '70s were deep and pervasive enough to provoke what Michael Jensen has described as the "reemergence of active investors." Such investors have been the main participants in reinvigorating what financial economists like Jensen have taken to calling "the market for corporate control."[4] Starting in the early 1980s, and for the first time in postwar corporate America, unaffiliated investors that were identified as "corporate raiders" began launching unsolicited, or "hostile," takeover bids financed heavily by debt—in a remarkable number of cases backed by "highly confident letters" from Drexel's Michael Milken—to acquire control of large public U.S. companies.

The eventual success of such transactions ended up shedding considerable light on the extent of corporate America's failings. After reviewing the findings of a large body of academic studies, Jensen concluded that corporate conglomerates had been "allowed to destroy 50 percent or more of the operating value of their franchises" before outside investors became willing and able to raise the funding to intervene. That was the verdict, for example, of a postmortem of the highly publicized leveraged buyout of RJR Nabisco, by far the largest LBO of the 1980s, by Kohlberg Kravis and Roberts (now known as "KKR"). In that transaction, a handful of professionals lined up over $25 billion of mostly debt financing to acquire control of a company that, under CEO Ross Johnson, was valued by the market at only about $12 billion, or under half the price eventually paid to close the deal.

It's important to keep in mind that RJR at the time was a company whose businesses were generating hundreds of millions of dollars in cash and that, when judged by conventional EPS standards, appeared to be doing just fine. But when KKR looked under the hood of RJR, what they saw was corporate mismanagement and waste on a colossal scale. As reported in *Barbarians at the Gate*, Bryan Burrough and John Helyar's bestselling account of the deal, Johnson instructed the head of the firm's tobacco operations to spend a couple hundred million dollars on extra promotions to *conceal* the firm's profit potential from the suitors who were then circling. As Jensen later put it, "The real barbarians turned out to be *inside* the gates!"

But Jensen himself was arguably the last person who should have been surprised by this revelation of corporate waste. Some 15 years earlier he and Rochester colleague Bill Meckling published what was to become by far the most cited article in the corporate finance "literature." Appearing in the prestigious *Journal of Financial Economics* in 1976, and thus exactly 200 years after *The Wealth of Nations*, this article—which has now been cited well over 100,000 times by other finance and economics scholars—begins with an epigraph taken from Smith's most famous book, one that does not augur well for the "joint-stock companies" run by "professional" (that is, non-owner) managers that had begun to sprout in Smith's day.

Noting the natural tendency of such managers to "fail to exercise the vigilance in managing other people's money they would accord their own," Smith warns us that "negligence and profusion . . . must ever prevail in the management of the affairs of such companies." In other words, the universality of self-interest, however enlightened, suggested to arguably the world's greatest spokesman for private enterprise that outside investors were unlikely *ever* to feel confident enough to commit their funds to such an arrangement in *any* undertaking involving significant amounts of managerial discretion and autonomy. Joint-stock companies might continue to work in "turn-key" operations such as utilities and banks with asset restrictions, and in collecting tolls for and maintaining canals and bridges—all activities where the joint-stock form was then commonly observed. But any commercial enterprises involving greater uncertainty and risk-taking requiring decentralization and large amounts of capital seemed bound, in Smith's cautious view of things, to end up organized and operated as *closely held* partnerships of owner-managers.

And, so, with Smith's warning prominently displayed and in full view, Jensen and Meckling's famous article set out to explain the same conundrum that Smith raised two centuries earlier:

> How does it happen that millions of individuals are willing to turn over a significant fraction of their wealth to organizations run by managers who have so little interest in their welfare?

The answer provided by Jensen and Meckling, which is discussed at length in chapter 4, was reassuring in one sense, but also hinted at trouble ahead. Most important for our purposes, however, their explanation of how U.S. corporate governance works (and could fail to work) ended up revolutionizing the theory of corporate finance.

Up to this point, the mountain of studies produced by finance scholars rested heavily on the assumption that the managers of publicly traded companies were reasonably effective "agents" for their shareholders, committed to serving their interests by aiming to maximize long-run firm value. Jensen and Meckling were the first to explore in a systematic way the major potential conflicts of interests and incentives between the top managements and shareholders of public companies—conflicts that, unless managed effectively, could wipe out much of their value to investors as "going concerns."

What kind of conflicts? The corporate jets and other well-known perks of office were the most visible and obvious. But much more subtle, and far more costly, was a deep fundamental disagreement about the size and extent of risk-taking by public companies. As Jensen and Meckling saw the problem, the natural tendency of resourceful, enterprising corporate CEOs *without* significant equity stakes and presiding over large, mature businesses was to seek out and pay up for growth in other areas—in other words, corporate diversification and empire-building. And so, to make the public corporation a viable form that could continue to be able to go to outside investors for *equity* capital—which, unlike debt, has few strings attached—such investors needed assurances. More specifically, some combination of *internal* corporate control systems and *outside* "market" forces would have to prove effective in restraining management's "natural" preferences for growth and diversification. And keep in mind that back in the '70s, there were as yet few signs of a functioning corporate control market, much less the hostile takeovers that were about to break out in the '80s.

* * *

Now, as even many finance scholars seem to have forgotten, the Jensen and Meckling story has a happy ending, in the following sense: In the best tradition of descriptive economics, they interpreted the continuing dominance of the corporate form, not only in the U.S. but in all developed economies, as the best proof of its success, at least up until that point.

But this happy ending was also tempered by their expressed misgivings about their inability to explain a remaining puzzle: the apparent success of large public companies run by top executives with *minimal equity ownership*. And in closing, Jensen and Meckling go so far as to suggest that many of these same public companies might be made much more efficient and valuable by taking the following steps: Raise enough debt to buy back 99 percent of the outstanding stock, and then keep (or purchase) the remaining 1 percent for themselves, thereby making themselves 100 percent owners! What this suggestion amounted to, as finance specialists will recognize, is a rough template of the leveraged buyouts that were soon to materialize.

THE MAGIC OF FINANCE CAPITALISM

Sure enough, as we recount in the pages that follow, then came the 1980s, and the wave of hostile takeovers and other leveraged "corporate control transactions" that ushered in this new era that we are calling "modern corporate finance." During the next 40 years, after U.S. public companies had lost much of their efficiency and nearly half their market value, the principles and methods of corporate finance played a major role in the continuous restructuring and increases in the long-run efficiency and value of corporate America.

And in so doing, they contributed to the rising social wealth of a great many—though by no means all—American citizens. As Adam Smith promised they would, the enormous increases in productivity and value resulting from such restructuring have translated fairly directly into other forms of national and social well-being. Together with the resources needed to maintain a strong military, the U.S. private sector has continued to address the challenges of climate change and poverty that are central concerns of today's sustainability and ESG advocates (the main focus of this book's closing chapter). And without minimizing today's threats and challenges, this book aims to show how financial markets encourage effective (or long-run value-increasing) corporate investments in environmental and social progress, while discouraging others.

In the story we are about to tell, the predictability with which private profit-seeking translates into social gains depends in large part on what might be called the "magic of finance capitalism." And at the risk of getting too deep into the weeds too soon, that magic can be seen at work most directly in the success of the U.S. corporate finance and governance system in giving investors the confidence to assign valuations (or "market capitalizations") to public corporations that would have dazzled not only Smith, but post-War investors in U.S. companies up until the 1960s.

One of the most important—and encouraging—messages of this book is the ability of so many U.S. companies to transform $1 of current earnings into anywhere from $15 to $30 or more of market value, as compared to the average of roughly $6 to $10 of yesteryear, which continues to be the norm in most developed economies—and the enormous social benefits that come with this feat. Corporate stock prices, however volatile and subject to downturns and bad public policy, represent real transactions between buyers and sellers, and hence become sources

THE MARKET'S TESTIMONY TO THE MAGIC

It was not until 1958 that investors felt comfortable raising the prices of U.S. public companies to the point where the average dividend yield dropped below the yield on corporate bonds. For example, in an era when investment grade corporations issued bonds with a coupon rate of about 4 percent, few companies' stock prices would trade above the level that would be required to provide their shareholders with dividends yields of 5 percent or 6 percent or more. For aspiring "growth" companies in those days, this constraint likely meant that, for all practical purposes, a company earning $10 per share, and faced with enough growth opportunities to want to limit its dividend payout to 50 percent, or $5 a share, was also effectively limiting its share price to $100, or roughly ten times earnings. In today's U.S. stock markets, by contrast, only companies in the most mature sectors—think banks, utilities, and energy companies—trade below ten times their normalized earnings. At the same time, today's growth companies, many of which have never paid a cash dividend, trade at P/E multiples ranging from the high 20s (like Apple and Merck) to as high as 80 to 100 (like Amazon.com and Salesforce.com at the end of 2023).

of real wealth—a reality that seems to have escaped the notice of most public policymakers (and, as we will see in chapter 12, a surprising number of macroeconomists). Think of the major role of capital gains taxes in recently helping the State of California refill its pandemic-depleted coffers. Or the $3.3 billion in federal corporate income taxes that Warren Buffett proudly proclaimed was paid in 2021 by Berkshire Hathaway—or the record-high corporate income taxes of over $400 billion paid by all U.S. companies in 2023 (even after the corporate tax rate was cut in 2018 from 35 percent to 21 percent).

These kinds of payments, on top of all the jobs and other taxes and community support provided by profitable and profit-seeking companies, represent the social payoff from a healthy and efficient private sector. The big ideas that underlie and inform the practice of corporate finance described in the chapters that follow—among them an "efficient" market that produces stock prices that, though by no means infallible, are reliable enough to help guide corporate investment decisions, and a vigorous market for corporate control that disciplines underperforming corporate managers—are seen as contributing directly to what one Nobel Prize-winning economist has described as a "mass flourishing."[5]

To the extent there have been negative consequences of corporate activity, as there no doubt have been and will continue to be, the thesis of this book is that such social costs are dwarfed by the social benefits. Yes, we need to think harder and better about limiting the negative consequences and ensuring that as few people as possible are left behind—but in ways that also ensure that modern corporate finance can continue to work its magic.

THE MAKING OF MODERN
CORPORATE FINANCE

CHAPTER 1

INTRODUCTION TO CORPORATE FINANCE

What Is It, and Why Does It Matter?

But what exactly, you might be asking yourself at this point, do we mean by *corporate finance*? How do we distinguish matters of *corporate finance* from those we encounter in our own personal investing—say, when choosing whether to hold mainly stocks or bonds—and from the questions and decisions that come up in strategic planning, marketing, and all the other activities going on inside companies, industrial as well as financial?

The main premise of this book is the significant potential of the corporate finance function to increase the efficiency and value of all kinds of organizations, from publicly traded companies to nonprofit institutions and state-owned enterprises. Thanks to technological advances and the globalization of business during the past 50 years, the scope of the finance function has expanded well beyond its traditional funding and accounting responsibilities. Today's financial executives often play important roles in developing business strategy and designing the organizational structure to help carry out the strategy.

TOWARD A WORKING DEFINITION OF CORPORATE FINANCE

Corporate finance can be seen as providing a framework for addressing four key sets of questions that confront all business enterprises:

- The corporate *investment* decision: What is our business plan and its requirements for capital? And how do we evaluate investment opportunities, including acquisitions and other strategic investments?

- The corporate *financing* decision: Should we fund the investment required by our business plan mainly with equity—or with significant amounts of debt? More broadly, how do we address questions of capital structure, financing and securities innovation, and the distribution of excess capital through stock repurchase and dividends?
- Enterprise *risk management*: Are there major risks to our ability to execute our business plan and, if so, how do we limit them to acceptable levels? This involves strategic decisions to retain or transfer major corporate risks as well as tactical issues such as the use of "derivatives" to manage such risks.
- Corporate *governance* and investor *communication*: How do we organize the business to motivate our people to carry out the plan? Besides determining who reports to whom and gets to make what decisions, how do we set goals, measure performance, and design incentive pay—and then communicate these corporate policies and goals not only to our employees, but to our investors and other key stakeholders?

In the chapters of this book that follow, we explore each of these four "core subjects" by focusing on the research and writings of a single financial economist—or, in some cases, *pairs* of economists—whose work best represents the insights and accomplishments of the academic finance profession in that area. For example, after chapter 2 uses "the cautionary tale of Japan Inc." to reinforce the link between corporate productivity and social wealth, chapter 3 begins with the corporate investment decision and theory of business valuation by looking back at the pioneering work of Merton Miller (much of it with Franco Modigliani) in developing the famous "capital structure and dividend irrelevance" propositions in the late 1950s and early '60s. The core insight of the "M&M theorems," as they came to be called, is that the market values reflected in public companies' stock prices depend first and foremost on corporate investments of capital in people and their ideas as well as physical capital goods—and *not* on the mix of stocks, bonds, and other instruments used to finance those investments. For M&M—and in what we refer to throughout this book as "the Chicago School theory of value"—the corporate challenge of creating value for investors has little to do with establishing and maintaining a track record for uninterrupted increases in reported earnings per share, as GE's Jack Welch and his many management disciples seemed to believe. What it involves instead is management's commitment to the continuous building of what Miller himself called corporate "earnings power." How do public companies build earnings power? By investing in all projects that promise to earn at least their cost of capital, communicating corporate plans and policies as clearly and forthrightly as possible, and then trusting in a reasonably sophisticated and far-sighted market to recognize and reward such an approach. (The remarkable success of Amazon.com over the past three decades is offered as testimony to the viability of this approach.)

Chapter 4 moves from valuation to Michael Jensen's formulation (with his University of Rochester colleague William Meckling) of the theory of "agency costs"—the conflicts of interests and incentives between corporate managers and their shareholders that, unless addressed effectively, reduce the value of public companies. Consideration of such agency conflicts and costs in turn leads to a focus on the critical social role of the "market for corporate control," which is seen at work in both friendly and hostile takeovers, with the latter relying heavily on debt financing. One major aim of this chapter is to show how the active functioning of this market helps public corporations and their managers gain the trust and commitment of outside investors—something that, as noted earlier, not even Adam Smith foresaw happening.

Chapter 5 takes us more deeply into the corporate financing decision by focusing on the work of the MIT Sloan School of Management's Stewart Myers (revered by many as the world's most accomplished living finance scholar). Along with his "trade-off" theory that continues to be the point of departure for most discussions of corporate capital structure, one of Myers's most important contributions is his view of corporate market valuations as deriving from and reflecting two fundamentally different sources: (1) the mostly tangible "assets in place" that produce current earnings and cash flow; and (2) the often intangible "growth options" reflected in companies' future growth values—loosely speaking, the parts of their current market capitalizations that cannot be explained just by applying a market-wide multiple to their current earnings. Using elements of the option pricing model pioneered by his MIT colleagues (and Nobel laureates) Bob Merton, Fischer Black, and Myron Scholes, Myers is shown developing both a method of valuing corporate real options and a set of financing prescriptions to go with it. Those rules boil down to the simple rule of financing tangible assets in place primarily with debt to limit corporate "overinvestment," and funding intangible growth options with equity, mainly to avoid the "debt overhang" and "underinvestment" problems that Myers (and many other finance scholars) spend a good deal of time worrying about.

The focus of chapter 6 is *corporate* risk management, and some notable differences in its underlying principles and methods from those used by investors and individuals. The main theorists here are the University of Rochester's Clifford Smith and his one-time Rochester colleague René Stulz, who is viewed as extending and enlarging Smith's work on the corporate demand for insurance into a progressively more realistic theory that explains how and when the management of corporate exposures to changes in currencies, interest rates, or commodity prices can be expected to increase the long-run value of public companies. This theory, like modern corporate finance in general, has little if anything to do with the inflating or smoothing of earnings per share associated with old-fashioned GAAP-driven finance—but everything to do with helping companies carry out their long-run business plans.

The main subject of chapter 7 is effective internal corporate governance, as reflected in and demonstrated by the remarkable rise and success of U.S. private equity. In trying to explain this success, we rely heavily on a corporate governance framework provided by Jensen and Meckling in a lesser-known article called "Specific and General Knowledge and Organizational Design."[1] In that article well-designed companies are identified as those having a coherent business strategy with two main supports: (1) an effective allocation of "decision rights" in which decision making-authority rests with those with the relevant "specific knowledge" (about, say, products or local markets); and (2) a performance measurement and corporate reward system that works to reinforce this kind of decentralization and empowerment.

Our guide to the accomplishments of private equity is the University of Chicago's Steve Kaplan (a former student of Jensen's at Harvard), whose research has attested to significant improvements since the 1980s in the governance and performance of U.S. *public* companies—improvements that Kaplan attributes to strengthened equity incentives for top managers in combination with pressure from capital markets. But for all their success in outperforming their European and Asian competitors, the record of U.S. public companies also continues to be overshadowed by the remarkable accomplishments of private equity. While Jensen himself was the first to recognize leveraged buyouts as "a new organizational form," the work of Kaplan and others is seen as tracking the evolution of PE into what has become America's most productive asset class—one that has succeeded for the past 40 years in providing returns to its limited partners that have consistently exceeded the shareholder returns to public companies in the U.S., and increasingly throughout Europe and Asia as well.

Chapter 8 describes the efforts of corporate finance consulting firm Stern Stewart & Co. (where I was one of seven founding partners) to incorporate the principles, insights, and methods of modern corporate finance into real-world corporate decision-making at mostly publicly traded companies. Reflecting the University of Chicago training of Joel Stern and Bennett Stewart, the firm's practice was premised on an efficient-markets view of the world projected by Stern's trademark statement, "Earnings per share don't count." Although often called on to serve as valuation experts providing estimates of the market values of companies or their divisions, most Stern Stewart assignments involved helping our corporate clients design performance measurement and incentive pay systems based on the use of a new measure we called "Economic Value Added," or "EVA" for short. *Fortune Magazine* featured EVA on its front cover in 1993, and the likes of Peter Drucker and Michael Jensen flattered us by calling it "the best single-period measure" and "the first measure of total factor productivity."

Like chapter 8, the subjects of chapters 9–12 are not academics, but *practitioners* working in different areas of corporate finance. Chapter 9, for example, explores with my former Stern Stewart colleague Steve O'Byrne the longstanding controversy over U.S. CEO pay, along with Steve's career-long quest to develop what he calls "the perfect pay plan." Though the goal of his quest has yet to be realized, we learn what some of us have long suspected—that although many American public company CEOs have been egregiously overpaid, the total compensation of the *best* CEOs has not kept pace with the valuation increases of the companies they manage. All of which, as Steve suggests, goes a long way in explaining why U.S. private equity has outperformed its public counterparts for the past 40 years.

In chapter 10, we examine the remarkable and greatly underappreciated accomplishments of the U.S. high-yield bond market, from its first billion-dollar issuance year in 1977 to over $400 billion in 2020 alone. This success story is told from the vantage point of Marty Fridson, former director of high-yield research at Morgan Stanley and later at Merrill Lynch. While ensuring that "junk bond king" Michael Milken gets his well-deserved due, Fridson also ends up defending modern portfolio and corporate finance theory in ways that lead him to question some (though, in my view, relatively minor) aspects of the Milken-Drexel high-yield success story.

The subject of chapter 11 is the Chinese government's failure since the early '90s to develop the well-functioning Western-style capital markets its reformers once envisioned and hoped for. In the telling of Carl Walter, former head of JP Morgan Chase's and then Morgan Stanley's China operations in Beijing, what China has succeeded in producing is mostly the trappings of American-style capitalism, along with lots of artificial GDP growth—but almost none of the substance in the form of productive and profitable listed enterprises. The recent stunning failures of China Evergrande, one of the world's largest real estate companies, and the finance company China Huarong (whose CEO ended up convicted of and executed for "treasonous" fraud) are seen as the predictable outcome of a failing corporate finance as well as public finance system. And it's important to keep in mind that Walter's writings were pointing to this outcome long *before* the outbreak of COVID, in fact pretty much since his first major book, *Red Capitalism: The Fragile Foundations of China's Rise to Power*, was published in 2010.

One big reason why Chinese authorities have been able to distract attention from their failing publicly traded corporate sector for so long has to do with the limitations of macroeconomic statistics like GDP in reflecting underlying "micro" economic realities. Chapter 12 showcases the efforts of James Sweeney, former chief economist of Credit Suisse, to make macro measures do a better job of reflecting two critically important variables: inflation and productivity. One of Sweeney's main messages is that because conventional macro measures like real GDP growth do such a bad job of capturing these two highly important determinants of social wealth, business economists and policymakers might be better served by paying more attention to measures—including, notably, stock prices—that do tend to reflect such important variables.

The book's Epilogue addresses the current controversy over today's beleaguered ESG (short for "Environmental, Social, and Governance") and sustainability movements by holding up a model of financial management that Michael Jensen has called "enlightened value maximization." Along with and in much the spirit of Jensen, this book ends by viewing the long-run success of corporate America as depending on its effectiveness in making commitments to and gaining the support of *all* its major stakeholders, from representatives of the environment and local communities to employees, suppliers, and customers. The challenge for public companies and their managements lies in committing to and carrying out the right kinds and levels of investment in all these stakeholders—not too little, but not too much. This is the most reliable, if not indeed the only, way for shareholders and their companies (and their nations) to prosper in the long run.

SOME "COUNTERINTUITIVE" LESSONS FROM MODERN CORPORATE FINANCE

Although today's academic corporate finance is by no means a monolith, and has its share of vigorous dissenters, there is nevertheless a remarkable degree of consensus—enough that I feel justified in ending this chapter with a list of nine "lessons"—or perhaps "propositions" is the better word—from modern corporate finance scholarship. Many of them run counter to statements that appear regularly, even to the point of seeming axiomatic, in the pages of venerable publications like *The New York Times*, *The Washington Post*, and even *Harvard Business Review*.

* * *

Lesson #1: The core social mission of public companies is to continue to increase their own long-run productivity and value.

For the past 40 years, the U.S. and other developed economies have succeeded in creating a form of capitalism with enough dynamism and resilience to provide jobs for ever growing numbers of the two or three billion relatively unskilled workers spawned by the globalization of the world economy. The American private sector, after having lost much of its efficiency—and, at one point, half its market value—in the 1970s, has used the principles of continuous restructuring and improvement to produce enormous increases in productivity and value. And the still-growing U.S. lead in corporate productivity and wealth creation over continental Europe and Asia has spilled over into other forms of national and social well-being, including military strength and standard measures of "human" and "natural" capital of central concern to today's sustainability and ESG advocates.

● ● ●

Lesson #2: U.S. capital markets, far from being short-sighted, are by far the most growth-oriented in the world, especially when taking account of U.S. venture capital markets.

Up until the late 1950s, the stocks of U.S. companies had dividend yields that were higher than the interest rates the companies paid on their bonds. Such pricing of stocks reflected investors' insistence on such payouts to ensure that corporate profits were real and sustainable, and that excess capital wouldn't be wasted on uneconomic investments. By contrast, many U.S. companies today pay no dividends—and their stocks trade at multiples of earnings (if they have any earnings at all) and sales that were once unthinkable. These multiples reflect both the legal protections afforded minority investors—many of them foreigners with no other legal recourse or standing in the U.S.—as well as pressures for efficiency exerted by U.S. institutional investors and shareholder activists to increase long-run value.

● ● ●

Lesson #3: Contrary to conventional wisdom, not all growth is good—and not all debt financing is bad—for the economy.

The technological advances that drive growth in the U.S., and in any relatively free market, economy also tend to create overcapacity in the industries made obsolete. And because such excess capacity becomes an impediment to future growth, accomplishing the "efficient exit" of failing industries and companies is an important function in a thriving economy. Debt financing and dividend payouts (and much-maligned stock buybacks) play a critically important role in the U.S. economy of channeling excess capital from companies with limited growth opportunities to companies with lots of them. Seen in this light, debt, dividends, and buybacks are all part of the capitalist process of recycling capital and resources from mature or declining sectors into more promising areas.

● ● ●

Lesson #4: America's CEO pay system, while admittedly providing excessive rewards for many of its worst performers, has contributed significantly to the increases in the efficiency and long-run value of U.S. public companies during the past 40 years.

CEO pay and equity incentives play a critical role in the U.S. corporate governance system and have been a major contributor to the productivity and superior stock performance of U.S. companies over the past 40 years. But for all the benefits of CEO pay, the rise of so-called "competitive pay" practices since World War II has had the unintended (and largely unrecognized) effect of *reducing* pay-for-performance at U.S. public companies from their pre-War levels. As a consequence, the rewards of many of America's best public company CEOs have long fallen short of the payoffs for success to their private-equity counterparts.

* * *

Lesson #5: Even as U.S. public companies continue to outperform their international counterparts, they have long and consistently been outshone by the companies owned or controlled by U.S. private equity firms.

Thanks in large part to private equity's highly concentrated ownership and governance structure, in which a company's largest investors sit on its board, the top-tier PE firms have been remarkably successful in improving the long-run operating efficiency of their portfolio companies. Studies have long shown, and continue to show, PE funds providing their limited partners with annual net returns that consistently outperform the S&P 500 by 300–500 basis points, and the top-tier PE funds by considerably more. And the success of the U.S. PE market has also gone global, with high returns reported throughout Europe and Asia. Much of the recent experience of companies in Eastern Europe and Asia suggests that PE may be the *only* way for companies and investors to prosper in less developed economies with limited legal and governance protections for minority investors.

* * *

Lesson #6: Contrary to the widespread view that companies are stuck with their existing shareholders, well-run public companies can increase their own market values by attracting more sophisticated, longer-term investors.

Research has shown that although about 60 percent of U.S. institutional investors are short-term momentum investors (or "transients"), the other 40 percent are either "indexers" (with very small, long-term holdings in lots of companies) or "dedicated holders" (with a small number of very large, long-term positions). Companies with lots of dedicated holders (think Warren Buffett) have been shown to have less volatile stock prices and are more likely to make value-increasing long-run investments that require some sacrifice of near-term earnings.

The presence of such sophisticated and far-sighted investors gives companies greater opportunity to create a more strategic dialogue between managers and shareholders that focuses less on quarterly EPS and more on longer-run corporate goals and policies. When the late CEO of Sealed Air, Dermot Dunphy, declared and paid out a special dividend that was almost equal to the firm's market cap before the announcement, not only did Sealed Air's market cap (adjusted for the dividend) jump, but the large numbers of widows and orphans and momentum investors in the shareholder base were replaced by active value-based investors like Julian Robertson of Tiger Management, leading to larger efficiencies and value increases.

* * *

Lesson #7: The theory of stock market efficiency does not say that current prices are always right, nor does it tell investors that beating the market is impossible. What it says is that stock prices are "unbiased estimates" of future values—and that even competitive markets provide a payoff to investors and analysts in the form of above-market returns for providing valuable information.

Market regulators and many observers have accused the theory of efficient markets of contributing significantly to the Global Financial Crisis of 2008, reinforcing regulatory and corporate complacency about current economic prices and conditions that caused them to miss important warning signs. But efficient markets theory does not say that current prices are the right prices, only that that they are *unbiased*—that is, neither too high nor too low, on average. What's more, active investors—a group that includes the top-tier PE firms and hedge funds as well as the Warren Buffetts of the world—who uncover and bring to the table valuable information end up earning returns that justify their efforts to discover the underlying or potential value of the companies they follow, and sometimes even try to influence.

* * *

Lesson #8: Corporate risk management models and policies, when designed and carried out properly, work to preserve and increase corporate values by

protecting the ability of companies to keep investing in their futures and carry out their business plans.

Enterprise-wide risk management systems should be designed not to boost or smooth earnings, but rather to limit major "tail risks" that can disrupt the enterprise and jeopardize execution of the investment plan. This is a lesson that even America's best-managed companies—think of the not-so-distant Whale-trading fiasco at JPM Chase—have had to learn the hard way. The main motive for and most visible outcome of effective corporate risk management is to persuade longer-run investors to reduce their risk-adjusted required rates of return, or cost of capital, thereby increasing the P/E multiples the market assigns their current earnings and expanding the company's access to capital.

* * *

Lesson #9: Corporate reputation and ethics matter.

In the popular view, the Global Financial Crisis left in tatters the reputations of investment bankers and other financial intermediaries, such as commercial banks and rating agencies and auditors. But especially in human-capital-intensive businesses like investment banking, where value depends on the expectation of repeat business, a reputation for fair dealing with clients has always been among the most valuable assets, a major source of franchise value. Consistent with and reinforcing this argument, recent evidence associated with today's ESG movement suggests that market investors reward ethical behavior by assigning higher P/E multiples to companies they perceive to be "virtuous"—if only because such companies are seen as less subject to future political and regulatory risks.

CHAPTER 2

THE CAUTIONARY TALE OF JAPAN INC.— AND THE LINK BETWEEN CORPORATE FINANCE AND SOCIAL WEALTH

Our story begins on May 11, 1993 in Tokyo's famed Ryogoku Sumo Hall, where this writer, though far from a knowledgeable or committed fan of sumo wrestling, is watching the annual tournament of champions. Sitting next to me is an exceptionally animated gray-haired American, shouting the names of the favorites and, in keeping with Japanese custom, casting fistfuls of salt on fellow spectators to express approval.

The sumo enthusiast is Merton Miller, the University of Chicago finance professor whose research and writings have recently won him a Nobel Prize in Economics. At this point in his career, and nearing 70, Miller is a familiar figure on the university lecture circuit, recognized by many colleagues and former students as the "Father of Modern Corporate Finance." Along with his humor-leavened proselytizing about the social virtues of well-functioning financial markets, he is well known for requesting—and being granted—a meeting with the head football coach as partial payment for his services.

But at this moment in Tokyo, having published a dozen of Miller's articles (in an obscure publication I'd then been editing for over a decade (and still do) called the *Journal of Applied Corporate Finance*)—and taken in even more of his public lectures—I was thinking to myself, "Why is Mert in such good spirits; there isn't a football coach within a thousand miles for him to charm or be photographed with?"

A couple hours earlier Miller had delivered a speech in a debate of sorts before hundreds of Japanese corporate executives at a gathering of the Keidanren, the Tokyo counterpart of the U.S. Business Roundtable in Washington. The speech was titled "Is American Corporate Governance Fatally Flawed?," and it was billed and received as the main event of a University of Michigan-sponsored symposium called "Corporate Governance in Japan and the United States." The other two main speakers—the warm-up acts, if you will—were Joichi Aoi, the highly regarded Chairman of Toshiba, the Japanese multinational conglomerate, and well-known U.S. corporate strategist C.K. Prahalad. Both men were vigorous and vocal critics of the *shortsightedness* of the U.S. corporate finance and governance system.

In the early 1990s, with the global economy deep in recession, there was no shortage of critics of U.S. "short termism." But nor was there much new about such claims. Throughout the 1980s, the *Harvard Business Review* and other popular business publications were routinely chastising U.S. companies for falling ever farther behind their Japanese and other global competitors, even as U.S. stock prices were climbing steadily. And providing some support for these widespread claims of U.S. corporate "myopia," Japanese corporate market shares and stock prices in those days were climbing even faster—until they suddenly stopped. On December 29, 1989, the Nikkei 225, the Japanese equivalent of the S&P 500, reached a new peak of just under 39,000 that, after a 60 percent plunge in the 1990s, it did not see again until February of 2024, and thus over 35 years later.

In 1992, lending considerable authority to this charge of American shortsightedness, a group of 25 academics under the leadership of Harvard Business School's strategy guru Michael Porter went so far as to sign a statement asserting that U.S. companies were systematically "underinvesting," thereby jeopardizing not only their own future, but that of the entire U.S. economy. We were warned that the U.S. corporate restructuring movement of the 1980s, with its wave of leveraged takeovers and buyouts, had compounded the American competitiveness problem by pressuring companies for distributions of cash and cutbacks in capital spending. At the same time, Japanese companies like Toshiba and Toyota were being declared the victors in the competitive wars, and U.S. managers and investors were urged to cultivate the "patience" of their Japanese counterparts.

In a spirit largely consistent with this accepted wisdom, Toshiba's Chairman Aoi launched the symposium at the Keidanren by offering an attractive vision of a new "information age" in which the keys to corporate success were said to be "continuous technological advance" supported by "an unwavering commitment to human resource development." To help accomplish these goals, Aoi called for a "new metric" of corporate performance—one that, instead of profits or other standard financial measures, would aim to reflect and balance the entire range of social benefits from corporate activity against its social costs. In such a reckoning, things like safety and environmental records, and corporate taxes and wages paid, were all to be assigned equal if not greater weighting than corporate net income and returns to stockholders.

After Chairman Aoi sat down, Michigan's strategist C. K. Prahalad reinforced Aoi's message by focusing on what he viewed as the most important challenge facing large corporations: ensuring "continuous renewal" through the discovery of new growth opportunities based on, and designed to make the most of, corporate competitive advantages or "core competencies." With this end in view, Prahalad issued a call to corporate America to "balance its single-minded commitment to shareholder interests" with greater concern for other corporate "stakeholders."

THE CASE FOR (LONG-RUN) VALUE MAXIMIZATION

Professor Miller (and since we're going to be spending much of the next two chapters with him, let's call him "Mert"—he wouldn't have minded in the least) responded to both speakers with a forceful restatement of what he called the "shareholder-value principle." Repeating a message delivered with much more fanfare (and provoking far more controversy) nearly 20 years earlier by his University of Chicago colleague (and fellow Nobel laureate) Milton Friedman, Mert told his Japanese audience that the social mission of public corporations is to increase their own long-run profit and value to their investors.

Under most circumstances, he went on to say, the managers of U.S. companies that aim to increase their own long-run value face no serious conflicts between the interests of their shareholders and the *long-run* interests of their customers, employees, suppliers, and other major stakeholders. In a system (or a national economy) made up of as many companies as possible dedicated to making large enough profits to provide their investors with competitive returns, the companies' customers, employees, and local communities should *all* end up better served.

Now it's true, of course, that during economic downturns (like the one in the early '90s that was then weighing down the global economy), the pursuit of profit will reduce employment for a while. But when and as conditions show signs of turning up, something critically important happens: the investors' *expectations* of *future* corporate profits that are built into *today's* stock prices end up stimulating more corporate investment. And it is this *market-stimulated* and *-rewarded* investment that makes possible and works to maintain the expected profit stream that in turn ensures the return and expansion of jobs.

To Pay Out or Not to Pay Out. Mert uses a wonderfully simple demonstration to show how investors' expectations and the "signals" sent by stock prices help U.S. companies make farsighted investment decisions. In the example, a company's managers are deciding how much of its $10 million profit earned in the past year to retain and possibly reinvest, as opposed to paying it out to shareholders as a dividend.

The decision comes down to what management—and, possibly even more important, stock market investors—*expect* the company to accomplish with the $10 million by keeping it. If the $10 million is paid out as dividends, the shareholders have the cash to reinvest or spend as they please. "Suppose, however," Mert goes on say,

> . . . that the $10 million is not paid out but used instead for investment in the firm—buying machinery, expanding the factory, setting up a new branch, or what have you. The stockholders now do not get the cash, but they need not be disadvantaged thereby. That will depend on how the stock market values the proposed new investment projects.[1]

And from there, the story then turns into an exemplum on the value of good management:

> If the market believes the firm's managers have invested wisely, the value of the shares may rise by $10 million or even more. Stockholders seeking to convert this potential consumption into actual consumption need only sell the shares and spend the proceeds. But if the market feels that the managers have spent the money foolishly, the stock value will rise by less than the forgone dividend of $10 million—perhaps by only $5 million, or possibly not at all. Those new investments may have expanded the firm's market share; they may have vastly improved the firm's image and the prestige of its managers. But they have not increased shareholder wealth and potential consumption. They have reduced it.

In those cases when keeping and reinvesting the cash is expected to reduce value—and with the critical proviso that management has provided its investors with good information about its intended use of the cash—the moral of the story is that the company should pay out the cash it has no profitable uses for.

But ambassador of goodwill that he invariably was (and constantly surrounded by admirers throughout his stay in Tokyo), Miller then concedes that such heavy reliance on the stock market as a guide to corporate investment decision-making

> may strike many here in Japan as precisely the kind of short-termism that has led so many American firms astray. Let it be clearly understood . . . that, in a U.S.-style stock market, focusing on current stock prices is not short-termism. Focusing on current earnings might be myopic, but not so for stock prices, which reflect not just today's earnings, but the earnings the market expects in all future years as well.

And after pointing to the substantial body of academic studies suggesting that U.S. stock prices tend to function as "unbiased"—though by no means perfect—indicators of future performance, Mert left his standing-room-only audience with an unambiguous message:

> That U.S. managers are more concerned than Japanese managers about stock prices is not a flaw, but rather one of the primary strengths of the U.S. economy.

As for the charge of "myopia" or underinvestment that then as now continues to be leveled against U.S. companies and managers, Miller pointed out that

> Myopia is not the only disease of vision afflicting business managers. They may suffer from astigmatism or even from excessive far-sightedness or hyperopia. Over the last 20 years, one will find cases in which American firms facing strong stockholder pressures to pay out funds invested too little. But many Japanese firms, facing no such pressures, have clearly overinvested during the same period.

But having said as much, Mert then went on to sympathize with, if not actually condone, such widespread "overinvestment" by Japanese companies by noting that Japanese stock prices tend to offer far less reliable guides than U.S. prices to corporate investment decision-making. In Miller's words,

> given the heroic scale of financial intervention by the Ministry of Finance, Japanese managers can be pardoned for wondering whether the stock market

may be just a Bunraku theater, with the bureaucrats from MOF backstage manipulating the puppets.

By the end of the 1980s, such "manipulative" practices by the Ministry of Finance, when combined with bans on short-selling and extensive Japan bank and cross-stock holdings, had allowed the valuations of Japanese companies to reach levels well above those of U.S. companies. At a time when the most highly valued U.S. growth companies were trading at roughly three times book value, many Japanese companies had price-to-book ratios as high as ten. And when priced at such levels, Japanese companies were effectively being expected to produce what Mert described as "centuries of well-above-market earnings growth."

THE HIDDEN COSTS OF JAPANESE SUCCESS—AND THE LOST DECADES THAT FOLLOWED

What we now know, of course, with the benefit of three decades of hindsight, is that Japanese companies were in fact wildly overvalued at the end of the '80s. And although recently (in mid 2023) attracting interest from the likes of Warren Buffett, Japanese companies and the Japanese economy itself *still* appear to be recovering from the "farsightedness" that Miller cautioned against 30 years ago.

In an article published in my *Journal of Applied Corporate Finance* in 1991 (and thus a few years before Miller's speech) called "The Hidden Costs of Japanese Success,"[2] the author pointed to a fundamental problem with Japanese corporate governance that was being masked by their gains in market share, by the alleged (and we now suspect greatly exaggerated) benefits of having Japanese banks as major shareholders, and by the growing Japanese trade surplus. The crux of the problem, which had already been identified and given a name— "the agency costs of free cash flow"—by Michael Jensen, was the inability of Japanese (or any outside) investors to force large, mature Japanese companies to return their excess capital through dividends or stock buybacks. Corporate profits and cash that could not be profitably reinvested in the business were effectively "trapped" inside the firm—a condition made worse by the propensity of the Japanese legal system to view corporate assets as the "property" of employees as well as shareholders. Having accumulated ever larger hoards of cash, Japanese managers found it increasingly difficult to resist two major temptations: to make ill-advised investments in gaining market share in industries already weighed down by massive overcapacity; or, often inflicting even more damage on their own shareholders, diversifying through overpriced acquisitions into unfamiliar industries where they had no comparative advantage.

Consistent with Miller's warnings, Toshiba's Chairman Aoi began his speech at the Keidanren that day by citing the two main findings of a report on Japanese corporate performance during the early 1990s by the highly regarded Nomura Research Institute (NRI):

> Declines in Japanese corporate earnings and share prices far exceeded those that would have been expected in a purely "cyclical" downturn . . . [which] NRI has attributed to a "structural" overcapacity stemming from lax investment criteria employed by Japanese companies.
>
> In addition to denying shareholders any means of effective oversight or control over their investment policies, Japanese companies also tend to compound the problem by retaining excess capital rather than returning it to shareholders in the form of higher dividends or share repurchases. Failure to pay out excess capital leads to inefficiency.[3]

In view of today's conditions, and with nearly 30 years of hindsight, the concerns expressed by Miller, Jensen, and the NRI have been more than amply vindicated. As noted earlier, after losing as much as 80 percent of its value in the 1990s and 2000s, the Nikkei 225 has only recently returned to its 1989 peak. And even if one recognizes that Japanese stock prices were absurdly inflated by the MOF and Japanese policies, both Japanese corporate performance and economic growth since then have been so anemic as to merit the designation "lost decade" for the 1990s—followed by another in 2000, making it "lost decades." And the 2010s, despite some limited improvements associated with "Abenomic" reforms, arguably constitute a third.

The bottom line, then, is that Japan, although reportedly showing signs of promise from recent (2023) corporate governance reforms, has experienced what amounts to a 30-year recession. And macro economists, and the policymakers who look to them for answers, have continued to find themselves at a loss for either a plausible macro-based explanation of the Japanese economic malaise or an effective policy response.[4] Heroic efforts at fiscal and monetary stimulus—including those overseen by Milton Friedman and a team of Chicago School monetarists during the early 2000s—have all largely failed to improve Japanese corporate performance and revive economic growth. And perhaps even more alarming, Japanese policymakers have proved unable to reverse a downward trend in the Japanese population itself that was first reported in 2013.

MORE EVIDENCE THAT NOT ALL ECONOMIC GROWTH IS GOOD

All this gives rise to a disturbing—some economists might call it "Malthusian"— possibility: Could a flawed corporate governance system in one of the world's most developed, and at one time most productive and widely admired, economies end up producing investor returns and economic growth so disappointing as to *reduce its population*?

Jay Ritter, a University of Florida finance professor best known for his work on IPO markets, shed some light on this question in a *JACF* article we ran in 2012 with the title, "Is All Economic Growth Good for Investors?"[5] Following Jensen's diagnosis over two decades earlier, Ritter identified Japan as having a "massive corporate overinvestment problem." After reviewing the stock returns and growth in GDP per capita and dividends per share for the past 112 years of the world's 19 developed nations (all those with stock markets in continuous operation since 1900), Ritter noted that the average real growth rate in per share dividends of Japanese companies was the *lowest* of the 19 countries—in fact a *negative* 2.4 percent per year—and this was happening even as the Japanese economy itself was achieving the *highest rate of growth* (2.7 percent) *in per capita GDP*. Like other high-GDP growth economies such as Italy and China, Japan also found itself among the group of countries with the *lowest* (2–4 percent) overall average annual stock returns. (And China's stock returns since reopening its markets in 1993, as we come back to in chapter 11, have actually been a *negative* 5.5 percent!)

For U.S. companies, by contrast, Ritter estimates the effective real growth rate of dividends at a positive 2.8 percent (when also including payouts in the form of stock buybacks). And the U.S. is identified as the leader of a small group of countries with average annual per capita GDP growth rates *less than* 2 percent—one that includes the UK, Canada, and Australia. These relatively low-growth stock markets, perhaps somewhat surprisingly, have produced average annual real equity returns in the range of 5 percent to 7 percent.

As Ritter explains these findings,

> Japanese policymakers have long professed their commitment to growth and
> full employment—when necessary, at the expense of corporate profitability—
> and this commitment is reflected in the negative dividend growth and, until
> 1994, a ban on corporate repurchases of stock. In this sense, Japanese com-
> panies' reluctance to pay out corporate cash reflects what has amounted to a
> national policy goal of using corporate assets to preserve growth and employ-
> ment. But, as policymakers have begun to recognize, the shareholder losses
> resulting from this pursuit of growth at all cost *have arguably played a major
> role in the country's relatively poor economic performance since 1990.*[6]

More generally, and in some ways equally puzzling, Ritter reports finding for
his entire sample of 19 developed economies a *negative* correlation (of roughly
-0.4 percent) between per capita GDP growth and equity returns over the entire
112-year period. Loosely speaking, each tenth of a percentage point-increase in a
country's GDP tends to be accompanied by an average *reduction* of annual stock
market returns of some 40 basis points. And this in turn suggests that investors
in 1900 would actually have been better off investing in the companies of nations
that ended up experiencing *lower* per capita growth. (Indeed, the "sweet spot"
appears to have been between 1.5 and 1.75 percent per annum.)

And Ritter finds much the same for *developing* economies. For a group of
15 emerging markets that includes the "BRIC" countries of Brazil, Russia, India,
and China, the correlation during the 24-year period 1988 to 2011 was a strikingly
similar -0.41. And China, with the highest growth rate of all—in excess of 9 percent—
has the lowest stock returns, the *negative* 5.5 percent mentioned earlier.

So what is all this telling us? Surely not that economic growth per se is bad.
There is no shortage of evidence that people who live in countries with higher
incomes have higher standards of living and longer life spans. But even though
consumers and workers typically benefit from general economic growth, the
owners of capital do not always and necessarily benefit. Countries can grow
rapidly, and for considerable periods of time, simply by supplying more labor
and capital *without* the owners of capital earning high returns.

But the question is: For how long? Can this growth-at-all costs be sustained
indefinitely?

Ritter's findings—and most of the thinking and evidence summarized in this book—suggest that the answer is probably no. And such findings thus bring into focus a major conundrum facing today's public policymakers: *Can any nation succeed in creating long-run growth and jobs without the help of a productive corporate sector, one that uses capital efficiently enough to create competitive returns for its shareholders?*

U.S. PRODUCTIVITY AND THE WEALTH OF NATIONS

Some of the most suggestive analysis bearing on this question has been provided by a series of studies conducted by the consulting firm McKinsey & Co. on U.S. and global productivity since World War II. Such studies have continued to provide a clear and consistent demonstration of the long-run association between corporate productivity and job growth. The McKinsey study conducted in 2012, for example, reported a significant productivity gap between U.S. companies and their European and Asian counterparts, with a significant advantage for American companies that was evident as early as the 1950s (when the data started being produced and collected) and has only continued to grow over the last 70 years.[7]

One of the main questions posed by this analysis is this: Though it's not hard to see how corporate productivity benefits corporate shareholders, what are its long-run effects on employment and labor? The good news from the 2012 study is that the relationship between U.S. corporate productivity and job growth has proved to be positive in all but one of the 72 rolling ten-year periods from 1929 through 2009. In other words, in virtually every ten-year period of U.S. economic history in which productivity increased, American jobs increased along with it—and in the minority of periods in which productivity fell, so did total employment.

And the performance of the U.S. economy since the Global Financial Crisis in 2008 suggests much more of the same. Throughout the crisis and ensuing recession, the U.S. corporate sector proved remarkably effective in preserving its profitability and value. And the growth of U.S. GDP and jobs in the aftermath of the crisis, while clearly disappointing, ended up looking pretty good to most European and Asian policymakers.

What's more, whereas the Nikkei 225 has only recently managed a return to its 1989 peak, the past three decades have seen a total return to U.S. S&P 500 companies of over 3,000 percent, or roughly 10.5 percent a year. To be sure, the fact that the *number* of U.S. public companies has fallen in half during the past 25 years has alarmed some economists and policymakers. But it's important to recognize that, along with the remarkably vibrant U.S. private equity market (where many once public companies are now flourishing), the increase in the market cap of today's remaining public companies has far more than made up for the companies that have disappeared—or become part of now much larger corporate acquirers.

And one final note in closing: During the period of slow growth that followed the Global Financial Crisis, the growth of U.S. jobs—except for the sharp drop during the COVID pandemic—has been remarkably robust, including even the long-awaited jump in wages. And as of this writing (in the spring of 2024), the U.S. corporate sector, stock market, and economy at large have all exhibited remarkable resilience in weathering over 500 basis points of Federal Reserve interest rate hikes, an outcome that macro pundits (and even most Fed policymakers) were saying a year or two ago could never happen—and are still struggling to produce a plausible explanation for.[8]

The rest of this book might be viewed as providing the most plausible explanation for this U.S. corporate resilience that has puzzled our macro and policy types.

CHAPTER 3

MERTON MILLER AND THE CHICAGO SCHOOL THEORY OF VALUE

F inance scholars might be surprised to learn that Merton Miller, the father of modern corporate finance, did not take (much less teach) his first course in corporate finance until he was a 33-year-old associate professor in the economics department at Carnegie Mellon (then called Carnegie Tech). In fact, the courses Miller taught back then—economic history and public finance—were pretty far afield from what most people now think of as *corporate* finance.

As Peter Bernstein tells the story in his wonderful book, *Capital Ideas: The Improbable Origins of Modern Wall Street*, Miller was asked in the fall of 1956 to consider filling a vacant spot in corporate finance in the Business School to "help build the school's flagship program."[1] His initial response was to reject the offer, which he chalked up to economists' well-known "snobbishness" about business schools and, truth be told, most forms of commercial activity. But when the Dean pointed out to him the substantial difference between econ department and business school salaries, Mert said that images of his wife and second child on the way flashed before his eyes—and before he knew it, he was taking a course in corporate finance.

The following spring, the man who over the next 40 years was to become the most venerated scholar and sought-after lecturer in his field—and the Robert H. McCormick Distinguished Service Professor of Finance at the University of Chicago's Graduate School of Business—*taught* his first classes in corporate finance. But not without supervision. The most notable among the Carnegie senior faculty assigned to keep "an avuncular eye" on Mert was a somewhat older (five years to be exact), Italian-born macroeconomist named Franco Modigliani, who like Miller, ended up with a Nobel Prize in Economics (awarded in 1985, five years before Mert's). Along with Franco's five-year head start, and what some have identified as quasi-Marxist leanings, Mert pointed to another difference between the two Nobel laureates:

> On an ebullience scale of 1 to 10, most economists would rank Franco as at least a 9 and a half, and possibly even higher in his younger days. I think they would rate me no better than a 6.[2]

But before making too much of such differences, it's good to keep in mind that Mert offered most of his sayings with more than a grain of salt. As he was fond of telling people—and I'm sure I heard this one more than once during visits to his office in Chicago—"Beware of averages, Don. You might be impressed when I tell you that Harry Markowitz and I run an *average* of five miles a day. But I should also mention that while Harry usually runs ten miles, I seldom leave this chair!"[3]

TOWARD THE NEW "SUB-SCIENCE" OF CORPORATE FINANCE

During their last five years together at Carnegie Mellon, Mert and Franco worked in adjoining offices and soon discovered they were thinking about much the same problem. Franco's main focus, as a highly regarded macroeconomist, was understanding fluctuations in business investment and the broader economy, and how both depended on changes in financial variables like interest rates. Mert found himself asking somewhat related, but more "micro"-focused questions. What kinds of securities should public companies issue when funding their capital investments—mostly equity with minimal debt financing, or significant amounts of debt? And is there likely to be such a thing as an *optimal* capital structure, a ratio of debt to total capital that—if not for *all* companies under *all* conditions and circumstances, then at least for certain kinds under certain conditions—can be *expected* to maximize what people refer to as the *total enterprise value* of the firm, the value of its debt plus its equity? And if the answer is yes, how should corporate managers think about finding it?

In the late 1950s, there was no broadly accepted theory and set of principles informing the teaching of finance in business schools or guiding corporate practice. As Mert told Peter Bernstein, the business community seemed to be running on a set of unorganized rules-of-thumb . . . there were no systematic guidelines that would tell a corporate financial officer how deeply to go into debt—whether going into debt would matter at all.[4]

The overarching ambition of "M&M" (as Modigliani and Miller soon became known) turned out to be no less than to transform the entire discipline of corporate finance from "a mixture of seat-of-the-pants decision-making by accountants and Wall Street bankers into a structured theory and set of practices that would produce a better outcome."[5]

In what we earlier identified as "old-fashioned corporate finance," corporate treasurers and CFOs viewed their mission as helping the company produce enough operating cash flow—that is, earnings before interest but after taxes—to be able to report smoothly rising *earnings per share*, pretty much every quarter year in and year out. They also counted on financial markets to reward their success (and consistency) by "capitalizing" their EPS at the same stock price-to-earnings (or P/E) "multiples" assigned companies in the same industry or "risk class." So, for example, if management succeeded in increasing the company's EPS by 10 percent every year, its stock price was also expected to grow by roughly 10 percent. The P/E multiple itself was effectively viewed as a "given" that was determined by "the market," and about which few questions were asked.

Corporate treasurers also believed in a kind of "magic in leverage" that was understood to work as follows: Companies could raise their reported EPS simply by choosing to fund new investment with more debt (instead of equity or retained earnings) as long as the expected return on the new investment was at least equal to the (after-tax) rate of interest on the debt—which, as we will see later, is far from an acceptable standard of profitability. Though the higher interest payments reduced the earnings left over for shareholders, replacing equity with debt meant that the somewhat lower earnings would now be spread over a smaller number of shares outstanding.

The expected outcome of such "financial engineering" was higher reported EPS—and, as long as the P/E multiples stayed the same, higher stock prices. Presto! Such was the magic that continued to be practiced by veteran CFOs after conferring with their time-tested bankers, who in turn claimed to divine the mysterious workings of capital markets.

But, as Franco and Mert began to ask themselves: where do these P/E multiples come from—and are they affected in any systematic or predictable way by corporate decisions to use debt instead of equity? They also questioned the plausibility of highly sophisticated investors consistently being taken in by this pretty simple and transparent financial sleight of hand. Why didn't investors intent on understanding companies' underlying profitability see *through* such "cosmetic" financing differences among otherwise similar companies and focus on the *entire* (again, pre-interest, but after-tax) operating earnings stream? Why didn't the markets capitalize *these* similarly sized and risky expected earnings at the same P/E or valuation multiples?

EARNINGS POWER AND THE LAW OF CONSERVATION OF INVESTMENT VALUE

As it turns out, a Harvard finance scholar named John Burr Williams was thinking in much the same way some two decades before M&M. By the time he enrolled in the Harvard Ph.D. program in the early 1930s, Williams was already a wealthy man thanks to a successful career as an investor during the 1920s. His motive for going back to the academy was to find answers to questions like the following: What had gone so wrong with the U.S. economy during and after the Great Stock Market Crash of 1929, and how could so much wealth have been destroyed in such a short period of time? And, perhaps most important of all, what was the underlying, or *fundamental*, basis for this kind of wealth that could be created, and then disappear, so quickly?

Williams's Ph.D. dissertation was directed by the legendary Austrian-school economist Joseph Schumpeter, who spent the last two decades of his life at Harvard fleshing out his concept of the capitalist process he famously identified as "creative destruction." At Schumpeter's suggestion, and with his full encouragement, Williams devoted his efforts to developing both a theory of and practicable method for estimating "the intrinsic value" of common stocks. In so doing, Williams, who was not a particularly modest man, saw himself as creating a "new sub-science that shall be known as the Theory of Investment Value." *The Theory of Investment Value* was the title of Williams's book—a book that, when it came out in 1938, had already been accepted and was being readied for publication by Harvard University Press, even before his dissertation had been signed off on by the Harvard faculty!

But if Williams's name for his own undertaking never caught on, his method, and the basic insights underlying its use, clearly did. Virtually all stock analysts in those days spent much of their time—and many still do—predicting a company's next quarter's and full year's earnings per share, and then applying an industry-wide P/E multiple to that EPS to come up with their price targets. Williams's ambition was to identify—and then capture in his valuation method—the fundamental source of the value produced by stocks for their investors.

Almost 40 years earlier, renowned Yale economist Irving Fisher had demonstrated that the value of a government (or a corporate) bond, with its contractually spelled-out series of semi-annual coupon payments, could be calculated by discounting each payment at the appropriate "market rate of interest," and then adding up the sum of the discounted payments. The equation—and, I promise you, this is the first of what will be at most a half dozen throughout the rest of this book—looks like this:

$$V = CP_1 / (1 + r) + CP_2 / (1 + r)^2 + CP_3 / (1 + r)^3 + \ldots CP_n / (1 + r)^n$$

where CP is the coupon payment and r the market rate of interest.

In the special case of "perpetual" bonds such as British consols, the formula collapses into this simple form:

$$V = CP / r,$$

Such a formula would tell us, for example, that a consol issued by the UK government today promising to pay its holder 100 pounds a year *forever*, and assuming today's market rate of interest for such bonds is 5 percent, would be worth (100 / .05), or 2,000, pounds.

Williams's innovation was to extend to the world of *corporate* finance, with its considerably greater "uncertainties," essentially the same discounting procedure when estimating the intrinsic values of common stocks. As Williams saw it, the only truly reliable way to think about and understand a stock's fundamental value was to try to capture the series of payments that stockholders could expect to receive over the entire *life of the company*—and then discount each of those payments for risk and the time value of money.

But that begged the question: what exactly were these expected payments to stockholders? And how might one go about estimating their present values?

For most stockholders of going concerns, as Williams began by reasoning, dividend payments were the only ones they were likely to see (unless and until they sold their shares). And by simply extrapolating, or projecting forward, past dividend payments and their rates of growth into the future, Williams came up with a "Dividend Discount Model" that effectively rolls up the entire series of future payments into a single equation with just three variables that looks like this:

$$\text{Stock Price} = \text{Dividends per share} / \text{Required market rate of return} - \text{Dividend growth rate, or}$$
$$V = D / r - g$$

The beauty of the DDM was that two of its three main variables—current dividends and their recent growth rates—are fairly straightforward and easy to come by. As for the required rate of return, analysts in a hurry could just fall back on the rule of thumb of 10 percent for U.S. stocks of average risk, which has turned out to be remarkably close to estimates of the historical average total returns (dividends plus price appreciation), some going as far back as 1890, that cluster around 9 percent.

So, for example, if Company ABC was earning $2 per share with steady growth of 5 percent while paying out half of its earnings (or $1) as a dividend—and assuming the company's required rate of return (or cost of equity capital) was 10 percent, a back-of-the-envelope calculation using Williams's DDM would have shown us the following:

$$\text{Stock Price} = \$1 / (.10 - .05) = \$20$$

With an EPS of $2 and a stock price target of $20, analysts could have given their calculations a quick "reality check" just by noting that Company ABC's P/E of 10 times was pretty much in line with the average multiples of U.S. stocks back then, a reality of corporate valuation that, as we saw earlier, didn't begin to change until the late 1950s.

But as Williams was well aware, the dividend payments themselves were clearly *not* the underlying source or driver of these values. That source was the company's expected future operating earnings or *cash flows*—those cash flows from which a company's dividends, as well as the interest payments on any debt, would have to be paid.

Which brings us to Williams's two main contributions to the theory of modern corporate finance. The first was to identify a company's "earnings power"—a term Franco and Mert reinvigorated 20 years later—as the fundamental determinant of its market value. The second, which he called "The Law of the Conservation of Investment Value," stated simply that a company's earnings power, and hence its intrinsic value, does not depend on *how it chooses to fund* its investment and operations. William reasoned as follows:

> Clearly, if a single . . . institutional investor owned all the bonds, stocks, and warrants issued by a corporation, it would not matter to this investor what the company's capitalization was . . . it would be perfectly obvious that [the company's] total interest- and dividend-paying power was in no wise dependent on the kinds of securities issued to the company's owner.[6]

What mattered most to investors looking at companies was their "total interest- and dividend-paying power." Such earnings power was at the core of Williams's theory of investment value. And it was the critical variable in the discounted cash flow methods that M&M proposed two decades later when putting into practice their own theory of value.[7]

FROM EARNINGS POWER TO THE M&M PROPOSITIONS

In 1958, and thus 20 years after publication of Williams's *Theory of Investment Value*, Modigliani and Miller came out with the path-breaking *American Economic Review* article they called "The Cost of Capital, Corporation Finance and the Theory of Investment"—and which introduced their soon-to-become famous capital structure irrelevance propositions.[8]

M&M began the article by asking us to imagine what Miller himself liked to call "the economist's frictionless dreamworld"—a world without taxes or transactions costs, where financially troubled companies are quickly reorganized without much loss of operating value, and reliable information about a company's plans and future operating profits is freely available. It's thus effectively a world without uncertainty; everyone is assumed to know everything of much importance, even about the corporate future. And almost equally implausible (but of critical importance to M&M's agenda), Franco and Mert ask us to envision corporate managers who are "perfect agents" for their shareholders, investing in all positive-NPV projects and walking away from all others.

M&M's Proposition I starts by asserting that, in this world of "perfect markets," a company's market value is "completely independent of its capital structure"—and then it goes on to say that that market value can be estimated by "capitalizing" the firm's expected operating earnings stream "at a rate appropriate to its risk class." Prop I, as Franco and Mert concede in the article, is not much of a departure from Williams's concepts of earnings power and Conservation of Value.

But Prop II was something new. Contrary to the message investment bankers had long been giving their clients about the magic of leverage, Prop II told companies that "the expected yield on their stocks"—and thus their cost of equity capital—should be seen as containing a "premium related to financial risk." In other words, investors should be seen as demanding not lower, but *higher*, returns for bearing the financial risk associated with corporate leverage. And Prop II also identifies the mechanism that makes Prop I work. It says in effect that investors' buying and selling of the shares of otherwise comparable (or at least same-industry) companies with different leverage ratios ends up reversing or "undoing" any effects, positive or otherwise, of debt financing on reported EPS.

More specifically, Franco and Mert described investors as engaged in a process of continuous "arbitrage," buying the shares of companies they perceive to be undervalued—or trading at below-market multiples of their operating earnings—and selling shares trading at above-market multiples. Thanks to such buying and selling, the P/E multiples of companies whose financial risk might have been obscured by, say, their rising EPS are adjusted downward—while the multiples of companies with less debt whose greater earnings stability might have gone unappreciated go up. In both cases, the net effect of such adjustments is to transmit the greater financial risk stemming from higher leverage into somewhat lower total earnings capitalization multiples, while ensuring that the total value of the firm remains unaffected, as Prop I tells us it should, by such "cosmetic" increases in EPS.

THE EVIDENCE ("SKIMPY" AS IT IS) FOR PROPS I AND II

The "perfect markets" assumptions set out by Franco and Mert as the necessary conditions for their capital structure irrelevance propositions made them impossible to subject to direct empirical testing. Where in the world does one find economic regimes without taxes or transactions costs, or with a preponderance of farsighted managers overseen by wise and omniscient investors? In the absence of such a laboratory, M&M, after describing the empirical evidence in support of their propositions as "amazingly skimpy," go on to cite a pair of existing studies by others, along with a brief follow-on test of their own.

The two studies by others—the first of 43 U.S. electric utilities during the two-year period 1947–48 and the second of 42 U.S. oil companies in 1953—were designed to detect any effect of differences in corporate debt ratios on the companies' (implied) cost of *total* capital, debt as well as equity. To the extent they were influenced by the corporate conventional wisdom of the day, the researchers conducting the studies might have expected to find somewhat *lower* costs of total capital associated with higher leverage ratios, thereby confirming the perceived "magic in leverage." This would show up as a *negative* correlation between debt and the actual returns. But M&M's Props I and II predicted a correlation coefficient of *zero*, which would show up on a scatterplot diagram as a more or less random assortment of leverage ratios, valuation multiples, and their implied costs of capital.

Both studies estimated the companies' costs of *total* capital by dividing their *total* net returns to investors during the periods in question—that is, interest payments, any preferred dividends, and after-tax net income—by their total debt, preferred, and market equity capitalization at the ends of the periods. The finding of both studies was a quite small, though in fact *positive*, relationship between corporate leverage ratios and their proxy for cost of capital—a finding that might be interpreted as the market's even imposing a small cost-of-capital *penalty* for debt financing.

Lending further credence to these findings, the regressions reported by the two studies were consistent with average total returns to the utilities running around 5.3 percent (derived from an average valuation multiple close to 18, or 1/.053), as compared to total returns to riskier oil companies that clustered around 8.5 percent (reflecting a considerably lower average

(continued on next page)

(*continued from previous page*)

multiple of around 12, or 1/.085). But the main point here again is that, in both studies, the franchise valuation multiples and implied costs of total capital were largely unrelated to the debt ratios, providing no support for the conventional wisdom that higher leverage causes the cost of capital to fall.

To the findings of these two studies Franco and Mert then added those of their own "experiment." Using the same sets of companies and much the same data as the two just mentioned, M&M ran a series of regressions of the *common stock* "*yield*"—that is, after-tax net income divided by total equity market cap—on corporate debt-to-equity ratios for the same two-year period 1947–48. What they found, consistent with the prediction of Prop II, is that the common stock yield, and hence the implied cost of equity, rises in pretty much linear fashion with increases in the debt ratios and financial risk.

This, in short, is how a sophisticated market would be expected to "price" differences in leverage—namely, by raising investors' expected or required returns to reflect their greater financial risk. And what such findings leave us with, then, is a tantalizing suggestion of the plausibility of the M&M view of capital markets. It's a view that sees investors' continuous buying and selling as working to ensure that U.S. companies with comparable earnings power end up with shares trading at roughly the same market valuation multiples, regardless of differences in their capital structures or the kinds of securities they use to fund their activities.

THE PRESCRIPTIVE IMPORT OF THE M&M PROPOSITIONS

After Prop I tells us that corporate market values are independent of the firm's capital structure, and Prop II describes the basic adjustments by which this independence is accomplished by investors, Proposition III turns to the implications for corporate investment decision-making.

Here again M&M's message is a simple one: because a company's cost of capital is unaffected by its capital structure, management's strategic investment and operating choices—which are referred to collectively as "the corporate investment decision"—can and should be made without taking account of the company's existing capital structure, or any new securities that might be used to finance them.

In other words—and with the important proviso that the contemplated capital projects do not involve new and unusually high levels of risk—management should pursue all opportunities that promise to earn the company's total cost of capital, but with little or no consideration of the specific securities or kinds of financing that might be expected to fund (or even be made possible by) the investment.

Or as this message gets hammered home to MBA students in their first corporate finance class, "the corporate investment decision comes *first*—and thus *before* the financing decision." And as corporate strategists like to point out, it's the corporate investment and operating decisions, not the financing decisions, that end up producing the lion's share of the value that corporations create for their investors.

BACK TO THE DIVIDEND QUESTION

In the first of their two famous M&M articles, Franco and Mert dismissed the question of dividends and their possible effects on corporate market values as "a mere detail." The irrelevance of dividends to total shareholder returns seemed almost self-evident. Any earnings paid out today in the form of dividends (or stock buybacks) would be expected to reduce the "remaining" value of the company by roughly the same amount—which is pretty much what happens when stocks begin to trade "ex-dividend." Like corporate financing decisions, decisions about whether or how to distribute cash to shareholders were seen as little more than different ways of repackaging for investors the corporate operating earnings that were the main driver of value.

But when Mert himself came in 1988 to write his retrospective account of "The Modigliani-Miller Propositions After Thirty Years," he told a somewhat different story about the origins of the M&M "dividend-irrelevance" proposition, which did not appear formally until three years later in 1961. When looking back after nearly three decades, Mert described the capital structure and dividend irrelevance concepts as "Siamese-twin MM propositions, joined together at birth, but soon parted and living separate lives thereafter."[9]

The article that announced and accomplished this separate existence was called "Dividend Policy, Growth, and the Valuation of Shares."[10] And it came out in the *Journal of Business*, then housed at the University of Chicago—where Mert had recently moved from Carnegie Mellon, and where he was to serve on the finance faculty for the next nearly 40 years until his death in 2000.

But why should Franco and Mert feel compelled to revisit the dividend question after having so long viewed the matter as if not settled, at most a "second order" concern? After all, as Mert wrote when looking back in 1988, "the essential content of the dividend-'irrelevance' argument was already in hand at the time of the original leverage paper." And as he went on to say,

> The dividend invariance proposition stated only that, given the firm's investment decision, its dividend decision would have no effect on the value of the shares. The added cash to fund the dividend payout must come from somewhere . . . and with investment fixed, that somewhere could only be from selling off part of the firm. As long as the securities sold could be presumed sold at their market-determined values . . . the whole operation of paying dividends . . . could just be seen as a wash—a swap of equal values not much different from withdrawing money from a passbook-book savings account.[11]

And to the extent finance scholars have found ways to test the dividend-irrelevance proposition in real-world capital markets, Mert and Franco's reasoning and intuition appear to have been borne out.

A QUICK LOOK AT THE EVIDENCE ON DIVIDEND IRRELEVANCE

The most important empirical study of the effect of corporate dividend policy on company market values was published in the *Journal of Financial Economics* in 1974. The authors of the study were Myron Scholes (another Nobel laureate) and Fischer Black (whose work with Scholes on the Black-Scholes option pricing model would surely have been recognized by the Nobel committee had he lived past his mid-fifties). The aim of Black and Scholes in this study was to determine the relationship, if any, between both the dividend yields and payout ratios of U.S. companies and their total stock returns (again dividends plus price appreciation) during the 30-year period 1936–1966.

But to make such a determination, because of the well-understood principle that riskier companies were fully expected to provide higher rates of return for their shareholders, you first had to control for differences in the risk of the companies themselves. So, after dividing all the companies into 25 portfolios with progressively higher levels of risk, Black and Scholes began by confirming that, as expected, the higher-risk portfolios earned higher total returns over the 30-year period. But when looking at companies *within the same portfolios and risk groupings*, the study reported finding, just as M&M would have predicted, *no detectable relationship* between either the companies' dividend payout ratios (the portion of earnings paid out as dividends) or their dividend yields (dividends divided by current stock price) and the total returns of their stocks.

In sum, once you control for differences in risk, a company's total return turns out to be unaffected by the portion of the return that ends up taking the form of dividends rather than capital gains. And so a dollar paid out in dividends today should be viewed as a dollar less of capital gains in the future.

*　　* 　*

But all that said, it's hard to see dividend irrelevance as more than the occasion or pretext for this second most cited of Franco and Mert's collaborations. And on rereading the paper (almost 50 years later), I was struck by the possibility that its underlying core subject and aim were both more fundamental and more ambitious than rehashing the question of dividends and corporate market values. The real impetus here seems to have been the urge (mostly Miller's, whose name appears first on this article's byline) to clear up once and for all another of the most fundamental questions in corporate finance—what the paper begins by invoking as "the longstanding debate over what investors really 'capitalize' when they buy shares."

SO, WHAT *DOES* THE MARKET "REALLY" CAPITALIZE?

The second, and longest, section of the M&M dividend irrelevance paper is devoted to answering just this question: What is the critical variable—the measure of quarterly or annual corporate operating performance—to which the world's most sophisticated stock market analysts and investors apply their market- or industry-wide valuation multiples when arriving at their price targets or estimates of intrinsic value? Is it the standard earnings, or earnings per share, dutifully reported by public companies in accordance with Generally Accepted Accounting Principles? Or is it some other measure more focused on corporate efficiency in using capital than the EPS held up by practitioners of old-fashioned corporate finance?

M&M's basic insight turns on their distinction between corporate "expansion"—the tendency of relatively mature companies to pour large amounts of investor capital into projects with expected returns just equal to (or even below) their cost of capital—and the "profitable growth" of what M&M referred to as "growth or glamor" companies. The glamor companies could be recognized by the abundance of their "opportunities to invest significant quantities [of investor capital] at higher-than-normal rates of return."

The M&M valuation formula eventually gets boiled down to a fairly simple equation with two main factors that looks like this:

$$V = X/c + [I \times (R - c) / c],$$

where X is current annual profit, c is the cost of capital, I is the amount of new corporate investment, and R is the expected corporate return on that investment. The first of the two terms, X/c, which can be thought of as the company's *current operations value*, is its recurring or "normalized" after-tax operating profit discounted at the appropriate (risk-adjusted) cost of capital. It's what the company would be worth if it invested only in maintaining its existing operations with little or no effort to expand their scale or scope.

M&M's innovation was to propose that, in addition to this *current operations value* (or COV, as it's come to be called), all companies should be thought of as having a *future growth value*, or FGV. In this equation M&M offer a way to quantify that FGV—namely, as the discounted present value of all their *opportunities*, many of them as yet unforeseeable, to use their capabilities and resources to earn returns in *excess of the cost of capital*.

What M&M have provided here is both a working definition of and practical method for estimating what many corporate executives (and legions of consultants and advisers) have since then taken to calling *corporate value added*. Stated as briefly as possible, it's the value created by companies over and above the capital supplied by all their investors, debt as well as equity, and including the earnings that have been retained and accumulated or reinvested over time (instead of being paid out to shareholders).

And the implicit message—again, one of the most important in this book—is that *not all* economic growth is value-increasing (or socially "productive"). As M&M themselves point out, one implication of their valuation formula is that public companies that reinvest capital with below-market returns for the best of motives—say, to preserve jobs and so protect local communities from economic hardship—are likely to end up reducing or destroying economic value, *even while reporting increases in earnings per share*.

EARNINGS OR CASH FLOW?

One question M&M did not raise in their dividend paper was the reliability of reported earnings itself as an indicator of a company's underlying earnings power. As any accountant can tell you, GAAP conventions afford corporate managers all kinds of opportunities to boost reported EPS in ways capable of misleading investors about the long-run profitability of their enterprises.

The Case of LIFO vs. FIFO. As just one example, during periods when prices are rising sharply, companies can increase their earnings simply by changing their inventory costing from "LIFO" (last-in first-out) to "FIFO" (first-in first-out), both of which are consistent with GAAP and permitted by the Financial Accounting Standards Board (FASB). This accounting "magic" works by expensing first the older, lower-cost inventory still on the books, which has the effect of reducing the cost of even recent goods sold.

According to the principles of old-fashioned corporate finance, such an increase in earnings—indeed, almost *any* increase in earnings, achieved by whatever means consistent with GAAP—is assumed to be a good thing, one that should help maintain if not actually increase the stock price. Proponents of modern corporate finance view such accounting legerdemain as not just innocuous—fooling none of the sophisticated investors whose buying and selling effectively determine the level of stock prices—but as potentially value-reducing. In this case, by switching to FIFO and increasing reported net income, management would actually be volunteering to *increase* the company's income tax bill, thereby reducing what matters to investors: the company's long-run, *after-tax* operating cash flow.

In other words, even well-intentioned and otherwise effective corporate execs who tolerate if not actually encourage such accounting practices are effectively viewing the increase in income tax payments as a kind of necessary evil, a "cost of doing business." But why do they do it? *Given* their view of the world—an investment community made up of world of largely ill-informed investors who respond passively to whatever corporate managements report to them—finding ways to increase reported earnings is assumed to be pretty much the only reliable way of keeping their outside investors informed about their companies' earnings power.

*   *   *

What evidence do we have that investors collectively are *not* taken in by this accounting sleight of hand—and that in cases when accounting profits diverge from operating cash flow, the market is smart and sophisticated enough to identify and focus on the cash?

One of Miller's young colleagues at the University of Chicago, an assistant professor named Shyam Sunder, published a study in 1976 in the *Journal of Accounting Research* (also housed at the University of Chicago) that examined the stock market reaction to companies that made the *opposite* choice: By switching from FIFO to LIFO inventory accounting during a time of rising prices, they made clear their willingness to *reduce* their EPS while increasing their after-tax operating cash flow. Sunder reported finding that U.S. companies switching to LIFO experienced a 5 percent *increase* in their stock prices, on average, and *on the day they announced the accounting change*, suggesting that investors value cash over reported earnings.[12] And a follow-on study by others found that the size of the market reaction was directly proportional to the estimated amount of tax savings expected from the switch.

What the market can be seen as doing in such cases is making adjustments for what is generally understood, and often referred to, as the "quality of earnings," assigning higher P/E multiples investors to companies perceived to have "higher-quality" earnings. We mentioned this habit of markets in the Prologue when describing the "magic" of finance capitalism, and we'll return to it in the

Epilogue, where the focus is corporate sustainability and today's struggling "ESG" (short for environmental, social, and governance) movement.

But for now, let's take a look at one other case where the market can clearly be seen discriminating between companies with higher- and lower-quality earnings.

The Case of Purchase vs. Pooling. Before the accounting method known as "dirty pooling" was effectively banned by the FASB in 2001, it was used to boost the earnings of many U.S. public companies that relied heavily on acquisitions to achieve their growth targets. The attraction of "pooling of interests" for acquisitive companies was as follows: When one company acquires another healthy going concern, it generally has to pay a significant "premium" over the book value of the assets to persuade the sellers to sell. Under the standard "purchase" accounting, GAAP requires the acquiring company to record that premium on its balance sheet as "goodwill," and then write it down, or "amortize" it, in annual installments. The effect of such amortization can be significant reductions in the reported earnings of those acquirers forced to use the purchase method— generally any acquisition involving significant amounts of cash (as opposed to the acquirer's stock) as the form of payment.

But for the many acquirers who qualified for pooling of interests (before the option was eliminated in 2001), the appeal of pooling was the higher earnings stream it enabled them to report. And adding to pooling's attractions, the fact that goodwill amortization was a non-cash and non-tax-deductible expense meant that, unlike the LIFO-FIFO dilemma, no tax savings were being passed up by choosing to report higher net income.

For practitioners of old-fashioned finance, pooling thus appeared a godsend as well as an irresistible temptation. What CEOs or CFOs could say no to higher earnings with no additional taxes? But for the growing number of practitioners of modern corporate finance, these benefits were almost certain to prove a chimera at best.

* * *

What verdict on this question have the studies provided? The first, by Hai Hong, Robert Kaplan, and Gershon Mandelker at Carnegie-Mellon back in the late 1970s (when it was relatively easy to qualify for poolings), found that the accounting differences had essentially *no effect* on stock market pricing. Despite the differences in accounting, the post-acquisition stock returns of purchasers and poolers in the three to five years following the closings of the deals were largely indistinguishable from each other. And so although there was little sign of harm from the use of dirty pooling, there was also no evidence of benefits.[13]

But more suggestive were the findings of a study of purchase versus pooling deals we published in the *Journal of Applied Corporate Finance* in 1999, a year or so before pooling was banned. In that study, Eric Lindenberg, then head of Salomon Brothers' research group, and his colleague Michael Ross began by looking at the stock market's initial reactions to announcements during the 1990s of some 1,442 proposed acquisitions of U.S. companies, 387 of them structured to qualify as poolings, and the remaining 1,055 as purchases.[14]

Casting doubt on the perceived benefits of pooling-of-interest accounting, the market response to the announcements of the nearly 400 poolings was to *reduce* the acquirers' stock price by almost 4 percent, on average. In pointed contrast, investors' response to the much larger group of announced purchases was a significantly positive 3 percent, on average, suggesting that investors were not the least discouraged by the prospect of the acquirers' being forced to amortize goodwill. Among the most plausible explanations of this (almost shockingly) negative response to poolings is the encouragement this accounting method provided acquiring company execs to overpay just to ensure their deals would close.[15]

But in some ways even more revealing were the findings of the second part of the Salomon study, which looked at the market pricing of purchasers and poolers in the years *after* the deals closed. Completely consistent with, and reinforcing the soundness of, investors' initial positive assessments of the purchases, Lindenberg and Ross reported that although the purchasing companies continued to report lower earnings while amortizing goodwill in the ensuing years, the market appeared to make continuous upward adjustments of the purchasers' P/E multiples (relative to the poolers') to reflect their higher earnings quality.

And this, of course, is what we would expect to find in a stock market where the world's most sophisticated investors can be counted on to see through temporary, often management-fabricated fluctuations in reported earnings to the companies' underlying earnings power.

THE DISTINCTION BETWEEN "P/E-BASED" AND CASH-FLOW-BASED INDUSTRIES (AND WHAT IT COULD BE TELLING US)

Yet another insight of the Salomon Brothers' study of purchase vs. poolings comes from its closer look at the well-known practice of Wall Street analysts of classifying some industries as "P/E" or "earnings-based" and other industries as "cash flow-based." "Earnings-based" industries are those in which reported earnings are generally understood to do a reasonably good job of capturing the underlying cash operating flow, to the point where there is remarkably little variation in P/E ratios among industry competitors. "Cash-flow industries" are those where earnings are much less informative, and where analysts tend to rely instead on cash measures like EBITDA (earnings before interest, taxes, depreciation, and amortization), and where total enterprise- or firm value-to-EBITDA ratios are seen as hovering around industry-wide averages.

After examining the effects of goodwill and its amortization on both the P/E ratios in earnings-based industries and the firm-value-to EBITDA ratios in cash-flow industries, Lindenberg and Ross found that in those industries where earnings and operating cash flow diverge, investors capitalize a cash-flow based measure that looks at the earnings power of the total enterprise—much as M&M thought they would.

THE REAL PERIL OF EARNINGS-BASED MANAGEMENT (OR HOW OLD-FASHIONED CORPORATE FINANCE THREATENED TO HAMSTRING CORPORATE AMERICA)

The problems with earnings per share and earnings-based management go well beyond misleading (mainly unsophisticated) investors, not to mention a surprisingly large number of investment bankers I've gotten to know. The deep threat of old-fashioned corporate finance is that, by tempting managers to limit their focus to producing a steadily growing stream of reported EPS, it distracts and discourages them from what ought to be their goal—finding the profitable growth opportunities that M&M identified as the distinguishing feature of "growth or glamor" companies. You don't create the next Amazon.com by agonizing over next quarter's EPS. What you look for are opportunities to put investor capital to work with projected rates of return that exceed the cost of capital, and as many such opportunities as you can find.

This is an apt description of the "playbook" at Amazon.com, where CEO Jeff Bezos appears to have spent few moments fretting about shareholders who care first and foremost about reported earnings.

THE AMAZON CREDO AND MISSION STATEMENT (EXCERPTS FROM THE COMPANY'S 1997 LETTER TO SHAREHOLDERS)

We believe that a fundamental measure of our success will be the shareholder value we create over the long term. . . . Because of our emphasis on the long term, we may make decisions and weigh tradeoffs differently than some companies.

- We will continue to make investment decisions in light of long-term market leadership considerations rather than short-term profitability considerations or short-term Wall Street reactions.
- We will continue to measure our programs and the effectiveness of our investments analytically, to jettison those that do not provide acceptable returns, and to step up our investment in those that work best.
- When forced to choose between optimizing the appearance of our GAAP accounting and maximizing the present value of future cash flows, we'll take the cash flows.
- We will share our strategic thought processes with you when we make bold choices (to the extent competitive pressures allow), so that you may evaluate for yourselves whether we are making rational long-term leadership investments.
- We will continue to focus on hiring and retaining versatile and talented employees, and continue to weight their compensation to stock options rather than cash.

We aren't so bold as to claim that the above is the "right" investment philosophy, but it's ours, and we would be remiss if we weren't clear about the approach we have taken and will continue to take.

To make the novelty and audacity of Amazon's approach as a public company even clearer, it helps to set Bezos's thinking about and approach to financial management against what might be described as its *antithesis*: Jack Welch's much celebrated reign as CEO of General Electric from 1981 to 2001, which, as mentioned earlier, might be thought of as the embodiment (and high-water mark) of old-fashioned corporate finance.

Welch, to be fair, got right many of the things known to economists as "real" or "operating" (as opposed to financial) decisions, otherwise how explain GE's enormous increase in shareholder value during his nearly two decades at the helm.[16] But as many of his own direct reports and "disciples" have attested, Welch's mantra—the principle to which he devoted much of his executive energies—could well be summed up in these words: Show yourself willing to do most anything before you miss an EPS target—which, apparently, he never did!

But what Welch left behind—and to this writer Welch's legacy as a corporate *financial* manager—was an unwieldy, heavily finance-based conglomerate that no one else proved able to run. Which in turn means that finance scholars may have to face up to what to at least hard-core Chicago-school efficient-markets types tend to find unthinkable: the possibility that a generally astute stock market, in assigning P/E multiples of well over 40 to GE's carefully managed earnings stream when Welch retired in 2001, was in fact *fooled*—taken in—by his carefully orchestrated financial maneuverings. Is it too farfetched to suggest, in the spirit of the old quip that "you can fool some of the people most of the time," that GE during Welch's tenure may have succeeded in attracting—like GameStop in recent years—the equivalent of EPS-obsessed "groupies" (finance scholars call them "clienteles") who could be counted on to buoy GE's stock as long as its miraculous-seeming EPS growth could be sustained?[17]

At any rate, and what now seems clear, Welch's earning machine was not sustainable. And possibly sensing this himself, Welch appears to have gotten out while the getting was still good. For after several failed attempts by Welch's successors to reorganize this strategic mess (with McKinsey & Co. apparently deserving much of the credit for GE's ill-fated forays, first into long-term care insurance and, later (when Welch was long gone), commercial real estate), only Larry Culp, GE's current CEO, appears to have succeeded almost completely in restoring GE's profitability—and (as of this writing) a remarkably large percentage of its almost certainly overinflated former value under Welch.

How has Culp accomplished this? By dismantling Welch's earnings machine, selling off most of the finance and commercial real estate businesses, capping the potentially enterprise-threatening liability associated with its long-term care insurance business, and restoring GE's pre-Welch focus on what are now three separate publicly traded businesses: aerospace, power, and healthcare, each of which appear to be performing remarkably well as standalone companies.

＊ ＊ ＊

But getting back to the case of Amazon, what could possibly have given Jeff Bezos the confidence, as early as 1997, to buck the conventional wisdom about earnings just as Jack Welch appeared in full stride toward realizing his dream of being recognized as America's greatest financial executive, and GE as among the world's most valuable companies? Why would a public company, of which Bezos himself was by far the majority owner, be so direct in telling the market that Amazon was not first and foremost in the business of producing GAAP earnings?

The cynic's answer, of course, is that Bezos had no other choice. He knew there was no way Amazon, in its early years, could have reported earnings of any consequence. And he also knew that the effort to produce a lot of earnings early on was the surest way of limiting the company's growth potential.

Though he never went to business school himself (he graduated summa cum laude from Princeton in 1986 with degrees in electrical engineering and computer science), Bezos worked at hedge fund DE Shaw for four years until starting Amazon (as a bookseller) in 1994. And during those years he would also likely have made at least casual contact with some of the scholarly evidence about how financial markets really work that could be used to buttress Amazon's far-sighted thinking and approach. If he needed further assurance, he could also point to the example of Warren Buffett, who though he never claimed to understand high-growth, high-tech businesses, routinely dismissed GAAP accounting as a useful guide to decision-making, all the while reaffirming his intent and commitment to "never pay a dividend."

But with that, let's take a brief look at some of the research that would have long been available to Bezos when composing his credo, his remarkable letter to Amazon shareholders in 1997.

THOUGH CORPORATE MANAGERS MAY BE MYOPIC, MARKETS ARE NOT

In the opening pages of chapter 2, we saw Merton Miller, still in the afterglow of his 1990 Nobel Prize, telling his audience of Japanese executives at the Keidanren that, yes, many U.S. corporate managers have made, and will no doubt continue to make, shortsighted decisions, sacrificing long-run value to meet next quarter's earnings. But that's not really the story of the U.S. stock market, which has repeatedly shown itself more than willing and able to capture the value of promising long-term investment in current stock prices.

But how did Mert know that? What evidence did he have to back his claim, apart from the handful of studies of the market reactions to LIFO vs FIFO, and purchase vs pooling, that we've already mentioned.

Among the most interesting, and suggestive, is a study published in the *Journal of Financial Economics* in 1985 by John McConnell, longtime chair of the finance department of Purdue's Krannert School of Business, and his Ph.D. student Chris Muscarella. The McConnell-Muscarella study looked at the stock market reactions to some 547 announcements of large capital spending projects by 285 different publicly traded U.S. companies during the period 1975–1981. What they found is that, even during this period of corporate turmoil, announcements of *increases* in corporate spending were greeted with positive (and statistically significant) stock-price changes, while decreases in spending were viewed as bad news.[18]

But equally important and telling, the market applause for such corporate spending programs was far from indiscriminate. For example, when Federal Express unveiled its plan in early 1984 to invest heavily in Zapmail, an express service designed to compete with fax machines, the company lost nearly a quarter of its market cap in a matter of days, falling by nearly $10 from the mid-$40s. And on the day several years later when the project's cancellation was made public, the company's market price recovered most of its lost ground, jumping by $8.

It was much the same story for the large oil companies that continued to announce large drilling and exploration projects, even as oil prices were plummeting and the industry was awash in excess capacity. Each new announcement by "the majors" of new drilling plans was met with further stock price drops—until the intervention of corporate raiders like Boone Pickens put an end to such value-destroying investment.

But what about corporate R&D spending, and other forms of corporate investment, like outlays on advertising and brand building? GAAP accounting requires that *these kinds* of capital spending, like most of Amazon's "capital investment," be expensed immediately against earnings, as opposed to being capitalized and held as assets on corporate balance sheets. How has the market responded to increases in this kind of spending?

For starters, McConnell and Muscarella's sample included 87 announcements of changes in R&D, and with the same outcome: increases were rewarded with higher stock prices, and reductions led to lower prices. By contrast, in the case of 111 capital projects announced by 72 public utilities, there was no market reaction. The explanation: it's the job of the state commissions who regulate utilities to ensure that they earn no more than "normal" rates of return on their investment. And as the M&M valuation model tells us, the value added by investments that just equal the cost of capital is zero.

But perhaps the most convincing evidence of the stock market's ability to recognize the value of promising corporate R&D, and to distinguish it from the less promising (and likely value-reducing) kind, was provided by an article published in the *Journal of Financial Economics* in 1990 by finance profs Su Chan, John Martin, and John Kensinger. The article begins by reporting a positive (two-day) stock market response of 1.4 percent to 95 announcements of increases in R&D by 64 different companies between 1979 and 1985. But when the same sample was further culled and broken down into 55 such announcements by *high-tech* companies—notably, drug and electronics and semiconductor companies—and 24 by *low-tech* enterprises such as chemicals and natural resource and paper products producers, the market's willingness and ability to discriminate between profitable and unprofitable growth comes more clearly into focus. Whereas the market responded positively to over 70 percent of the R&D increases announced by the high techs—and the average response was over 2 percent—only 20 percent of the low-tech announcements got positive reactions—and the average response was a negative 0.9 percent.[19]

THE PROSPECT OF THE END OF ACCOUNTING— AND THE GOOD NEWS FOR FAR-SIGHTED COMPANIES AND THEIR INVESTORS

Back in the 1970s, during the heyday of what we have been calling "old-fashioned corporate finance," the statistical correlation between year-to-year changes in

U.S. companies' GAAP-based reported earnings and their annual (market-adjusted) stock returns used to run as high as 50 percent. But in the four or five decades since then, that same correlation has been shown to be steadily falling, to the point where accounting scholars like New York University's Baruch Lev now see the "relevance of earnings" as virtually indetectable.[20]

But what does this all mean, and why has it been happening? As we have just seen, the billions now spent year in and year out by companies like Amazon in developing new commercial uses and markets for their capabilities do not show up anywhere on corporate balance sheets—and the payoffs from such investments may not show up on their P&Ls and in higher earnings for years, in fact not until the company shows the first signs of "maturing." Especially in the case of companies like Amazon in its early supercharged growth phase, the insistence of the FASB that almost all corporate investment spending on intangibles be expensed immediately on the P&L virtually guarantees that reported GAAP earnings provide *little if any indication* of the underlying earnings power and long-run value of the business.

But just how representative today are companies like Amazon, which have never paid a dividend and continue to reinvest 100 percent (or more) of their operating cash flow in new businesses or markets? As finance profs Dave Denis and Steve McKeon pointed out in a 2023 *JACF* article, the economy-wide rise in corporate investment in intangible assets (as opposed to plant and equipment) starting in the 1970s has been associated with a corresponding rise in the proportion of public companies with not only *negative* "free cash flow"—that is, after-tax operating profits *after* subtracting capital expenditures. But what Dave and Steve (and I too!) find truly extraordinary is the dramatic increase in the percentage of *public* companies with persistently negative *operating* cash flow—that is, operating earnings calculated *before* subtracting capital investment. In other words, these companies at least *appear* to be losing more money with each additional dollar of revenue! And what makes this so striking, as Dave and Steve point out, is that

> Before 1980, the percentage of companies reporting negative OCF almost never exceeded 10 percent in any given year. Since 1980, the percentage has steadily grown such that, by 2018, the final year of our sample, fully *one-third* [emphasis mine] of the companies publicly listed in the U.S. had negative OCF.[21]

The conundrum this poses for financial accountants—and the challenge for the people who run and invest in such companies—arises from the fact that so many of these perennially money-losing companies have been and continue to be accorded not only positive, but in many cases *very large*, market valuations that seem to grow *only larger* along with their increasing operating losses. Whereas companies with negative OCF in the 1970s were generally viewed as suspect (if not actually distressed) companies, with market-to-book ratios typically well below 1.0, the prospects held out by today's (seemingly) profitless companies had risen so dramatically that, by the 2010s, the median market-to-book ratio of negative-OCF companies was roughly 1.6. In other words, companies with negative cash flow these days tend to be viewed not as "zombies," as they continue to be portrayed in the popular press, but as blessed with abundant growth opportunities.

But if operating cash flows and earnings no longer provide reliable indicators of long-run value for at least a third of our public companies, then what does?

Financial economists and statisticians looking to "explain" the remarkably high corporate stock returns of U.S. companies during the past 30 years could do far worse than narrowing their focus to increases in just two variables: (1) corporate selling, general, and administrative expenses, or SG&A, and (2) R&D spending. As Dave Denis reported in an earlier *JACF* article, total SG&A for U.S. public companies somehow had jumped from 25 percent of total assets in 1970 to an astonishing 55 percent by 2017.[22] How do we make sense of what looks like a mind-blowing "discontinuity"?

While some portion of it represents normal operating expenses, this remarkable growth in SG&A is being driven by significant increases in categories such as marketing and promotion, and all variety of "investments" in human, brand, and reputational capital—in other words, by a massive corporate investment in *intangible* assets.

For anyone concerned about the outlook for U.S. corporate competitiveness, the good news from Denis's (and others') analysis is that U.S. corporate R&D spending during the past 50 years has been rising even more sharply than SG&A, from about 1 percent of total assets in 1970 to as high as 20 percent in recent years. And when one adds the sharply rising R&D and SG&A to the (more gradually falling) traditional capital expenditures of all U.S. publicly traded companies during that period, the rate of *total* U.S. corporate investment can be seen as *more than doubling*, from an average of just 33 percent of total assets in 1970 to nearly 80 percent in 2017.

In sum, whatever you may have read in the popular business press, there is no sign of a U.S. private-sector underinvestment problem. But apart from the high stock returns of U.S. public companies generally since around 1980 (a period when S&P 500 stocks have provided their shareholders with average annual returns of 12 percent), what evidence do we have of the payoffs from such intangibles-heavy investment?

Perhaps most telling, Denis's analysis shows this economy-wide increase in U.S. corporate R&D and SG&A "investment" to have had a remarkably strong positive correlation with corporate market values, to the point where it seems to mirror the long-term upswing in stock prices. Finance theorists and scholars can, of course, be counted to debate whether this correlation reflects a *causal* relationship—to question the extent to which it reflects simply the natural tendency of more inherently profitable or promising businesses to spend of their operating cash flow on future opportunities than their less profitable counterparts. But what also seems quite clear, the stock market appears to be pricing companies with very high levels of R&D and SG&A as if they indeed have substantial growth opportunities. And U.S. companies have responded to such market pricing by continuously increasing their investment in intangibles—and being rewarded for such investment. A virtuous cycle indeed!

* * *

In sum, the U.S. stock market now appears to be working pretty much the way M&M proposed that it would back in 1961. What matters is not today's earnings or its projected growth rate, as practitioners of old-fashioned finance persist in believing. What really matters to the world's most sophisticated investors—and to the private equity firms and shareholder activists that we bring into focus later in this book—is a company's earnings power and, more specifically, its ability to produce returns on investor capital that exceed the cost of capital.

TWO PIECES OF UNFINISHED BUSINESS IN CLOSING

Before we move on to chapter 4 and the market for corporate control, I want to warn, and try to disabuse, readers of a common misunderstanding about the "doctrine" of stock market efficiency, a concept long and quite properly associated with the University of Chicago. The efficient markets hypothesis, or EMH for short, was formulated by Mert's long-time Chicago colleague Eugene Fama, who co-wrote a book with Miller in 1972 called *The Theory of Finance* (which quickly became known in academic finance circles as "the white bible") before receiving his own Nobel Prize in 2013.

Contrary to the popular misconception, EMH does not say that capital markets are infallible, and that corporate managers should always view current stock prices as the "right" prices. A better interpretation is that anyone without privileged information, or exceptional fundamental analytical abilities or insights about a specific company, should view its current stock price as an "unbiased" predictor—neither too high nor too low, on average—of its future value. Taking this view, corporate managers should be comfortable using stock prices as guides to their investment decisions, as Miller suggested, but without feeling bound by them.

Nor should efficient market theory be taken to say that fundamentals-based investors "cannot beat the market." The theory of stock market efficiency, as the University of Chicago's Ray Ball argued in a 1996 *JACF* article, is best interpreted as a statement about the expected returns to investors from providing valuable information in a competitive market.[23] Consistent with Ball's view, studies over the past three decades have shown that *active investors*—a group that includes top-tier private equity and fundamentals-based activist hedge funds—end up earning "above-normal" returns that justify their efforts to discover the underlying, or potential, value of the companies they follow. At the same time, a considerable body of research (much of it done at the University of Chicago) also suggests that if you bring no special skill or insights to investing, you can expect to earn zero market-adjusted returns—and so you should probably entrust most of your savings to Vanguard or other index funds. Otherwise, you're likely to wind up failing to match the S&P 500, a fate that year after year seems to befall as much as 80 percent of all U.S. professional money managers.

HOW BANK TRADING ROOMS REALLY MAKE MONEY

In what is my own favorite demonstration of market efficiency, a study conducted in the early 1990s by consulting firm Oliver Wyman of the Chase Manhattan Bank's highly profitable currency trading operations over a five-year period in the late '80s began by classifying all of Chase's currency trades into one of two categories: "market-making" (those designed to earn just the bid-ask spread while minimizing the bank's principal positions) and "position-taking" (those designed to profit from its traders' superior insight and forecasting ability).

What the study concluded was that the consistently large annual profits from Chase's currency trading operations could be attributed *entirely* to its *market-making* franchise and capabilities—that is, from acting as an intermediary between buyers and sellers while seeking to minimize the bank's principal positions. By contrast, the bank's five-year profit from its currency position-taking was estimated to be *zero*—just what one would expect to find in an intensely competitive and highly efficient market.[24]

*   *   *

The second piece of unfinished business is the question that naturally arises, and invariably gets asked, about the practical import of the M&M irrelevance propositions: If corporate financing decisions "do not matter," why bother reading (or writing) this book?

The short answer to this question was provided by Miller himself when looking back at the M&M propositions after 30 years. "The view that capital structure is literally irrelevant or that 'nothing matters' in corporate finance is," as Mert put it,

far from what we actually said about the real-world applications of our propositions. Looking back now, perhaps we should have put more emphasis on the other, upbeat side of the "nothing matters" coin: showing what doesn't matter can also show, by implication, what does.[25]

The remaining chapters of this book are devoted to showing how and why corporate finance might in fact "matter"—and matter a lot.

CHAPTER 4

MICHAEL JENSEN, WILLIAM MECKLING, AND THE ROCHESTER SCHOOL OF CORPORATE CONTROL

I n 1993, the same year Merton Miller presented his defense of the U.S. corporate governance system to his Japanese audience at the Keidanren, Harvard Business School's Michael Jensen provided a considerably less optimistic outlook when delivering his President's address to the American Finance Association. At this point in his career, Jensen had spent nearly a decade at Harvard after over 20 years on the finance faculty at the University of Rochester's Simon School of Business.

The title of his speech was, even by Mike Jensen's standards, a portentous mouthful: "The Modern Industrial Revolution, Exit, and the Failure of Internal Control Systems." And as the title suggests, while first at Rochester and then at Harvard, he had continued to expand the scope of his research well beyond the questions of stock market efficiency and the design of "event studies" that were the focus of his Ph.D. and early work at the University of Chicago.

Jensen began his 1993 speech by invoking the spirit of the great Austrian economist Joseph Schumpeter and the process of "creative destruction" he saw at the core of capitalist economic progress. Like Schumpeter, Jensen was troubled by a side effect of the technological advances that drive down consumer prices and raise our standard of living—namely, the obsolescence and massive overcapacity in the industries being displaced that ends up putting a lot of people out of work. What troubled Mike, however, was not so much the displacements themselves—which he believed a vigorous economy like the U.S. was well positioned to deal with— but the vulnerability of public companies' managements to political and social pressure to continue "overinvesting" with the aim of preserving jobs and market share. Jensen's fear of such pressure was so great that, in his darkest moments, he envisioned corporate managers as being overwhelmed by the demand for "exit" he foresaw being set off by the recent end of the Cold War and the flooding of two to three billion new low-wage workers into global labor markets.

But after evoking this nightmare scenario, Jensen took his analysis well beyond Schumpeter's in pointing out the solution to this looming problem: the critical social function of stock market pricing and capital market transactions like mergers and takeovers in bringing about a reasonably orderly and efficient "exit" of resources—capital and people—from fading industries. Set in this context, the wave of highly leveraged takeovers and LBOs during the 1980s was seen as producing enormous economic value just by limiting the huge waste of corporate capital and resources that takes place in the mostly futile attempts to prop up sunset industries our political systems insist on. And in some ways most controversial, Jensen argued that, in carrying out this function, the allegedly short-sighted financial "predators" pilloried by our media and politicians should instead be *praised* for preserving the capital required to fund the next wave of growth opportunities.

Viewed in this light, the remarkable successes of the U.S. venture capital market could be linked directly to the supercharged stock returns from the leveraged restructuring of U.S. public companies during the 1980s. In the world according to Mike Jensen, the outsized returns of U.S.-style, VC-backed companies were the mirror image of the outperformance of U.S. LBOs, the predictable outcome of using the same governance model of intensely concentrated ownership and control.

Jensen's argument could also be seen as providing a rationale for the eventual combination of high-growth, business-building VC and highly leveraged, often business-*shrinking* LBOs under the single roof of "private equity." Such an outcome provided explicit confirmation of Jensen-Schumpeter's recognition of the necessary connection between corporate exit and future growth, the paradox of the need to demolish (or at least continuously prune) commercial enterprises to rebuild (or grow) them.

And Jensen's argument did not, of course, apply just to the U.S. By law and custom, Japanese companies, as we saw in chapter 2, continue to be much more susceptible to political pressure to maintain employment and investment than U.S. companies. All of which led Mike, as early as the mid-1980s, to predict that "the Japanese corporate governance system" was on the verge of failing.

In the pages that follow, I follow Jensen in suggesting that the U.S. capital market activity that critics of finance capitalism routinely deplore as a major cause of widespread economic insecurity may well be the most reliable longer-run solution to the challenge of providing opportunities for an expanding, and increasingly global, workforce. And let me cite one piece of supporting evidence that Americans tend to view with skepticism if not indifference: According to a fairly recent IMF report, the global percentage of people deemed to be living "in extreme poverty" had fallen from 36 percent in 1990 to under 10 percent in 2015.[1] And more recent estimates of Americans living in poverty, after making adjustments for transfer payments and systematic overstatements of inflation largely ignored by reported government statistics, show the percentage dropping from roughly 15 percent in 1967 to as low as 1.1 percent in 2017.[2] This is the kind of economic and social progress that most financial economists—including the people whose research and writings are featured in this book—seem more than willing to attribute to technological advances working not in spite of, but *in concert with*, our capital markets.

THE CASE FOR CONTROLLED CAPITALISM: A FAILED EXPERIMENT

But Jensen was by no means the first to recognize the potential for corporate managers to fail to serve their shareholders. Decades earlier, in the midst of the Great Depression, Columbia Law professor Adolph Berle, Jr. was the co-author with Harvard economist Gardiner Means of a book called *The Modern Corporate and Private Property*. "Berle and Means," as the book became known to legions of U.S. law and finance scholars, warned of the consequences of the growing separation of ownership from control in large U.S. public companies. The book's basic message was that America's largest corporations, with their thousands of shareholders with relatively small holdings, were now under the effective control of professional managers owning few shares and beholden to no one but themselves.

But if the authors at first professed to be troubled by this discovery, Berle himself later welcomed the powerlessness and passivity of U.S. shareholders as providing a vacuum to be filled by like-minded policymakers while carrying out their vision of "controlled capitalism." By some accounts the most influential member of FDR's Brain Trust,[3] Berle is widely credited with having crafted and enacted the three most important *financial* components of the New Deal: Glass-Steagall's separation of commercial from investment banking; the establishment of the

SEC and its corporate disclosure requirements; and federal deposit insurance guarantees for U.S. banks. And throughout the 1950s and '60s, Berle was widely viewed as the chief architect of American economic prosperity. It was a social planners' paradise made possible by well-trained professional managers and sustained by the scale economies of large public corporations. Another key element of Berle's program was regulatory protection of such companies against would-be domestic as well as foreign competitors. But of critical importance to Berle himself was that this kind of large-scale business enterprise was all happening under tight regulatory control and the oversight of the governing political elite.

*   *   *

Then the "golden" years of the 1950 and 1960s came to an end, first and most visibly with the political and social turbulence surrounding the Vietnam War and civil rights protests. But inflicting far greater economic pain and dislocation—which Berle himself neither foresaw nor lived to see—was the "stagflation" of the 1970s, when the combination of wage and price controls, and the War on Poverty and other massive government programs led to an unprecedented mix of high unemployment and runaway inflation. And the market value of U.S. S&P 500 companies, at its low point in October of 1974, dropped by almost 50 percent from its peak roughly two years earlier.

The main contributors to the bear market of the '70s, as we saw in the Prologue, were rising inflation and the general collapse of U.S. corporate profitability. Protected from domestic as well as foreign competitors, U.S. public corporations had become bloated conglomerates like the General Mills "All-Weather Growth Company." Like so many other conglomerates of that period, General Mills pursued growth and diversification with little regard for cost—mainly by buying other companies in businesses its management knew little or nothing about.

And it was at this point, nearing the end of the '70s, that Jensen and his Rochester colleague William Meckling[4] were sufficiently disheartened by the state of U.S. corporate governance that they wrote their polemic (also cited earlier) called "Can the Corporation Survive?" In this article that appeared in 1978, and might be viewed as the sequel to their best-known piece of writing, the two men voiced their concern that U.S. shareholders had become "the *only* corporate constituency with no serious representation in corporate boardrooms."

But with the new decade, all this was about to change.

THE RISE OF THE MARKET FOR CORPORATE CONTROL

The most compelling explanation of what went wrong with Berle's controlled capitalism had been provided by Jensen and Meckling just two years earlier. Until publication in 1976 of "Theory of the Firm: Managerial Behavior, Agency Costs, and Ownership Structure," the theory of corporate finance—which aims to explain things like how investors value companies, how corporate managers evaluate and finance their investment projects, and how companies measure and reward the performance of their managers—this entire collective inquiry rested on the assumption that the managers of publicly traded companies are reasonably effective "agents" for their shareholders, committed to serving their interests by aiming to maximize long-run "firm value." The main advantage of the public corporation was seen as its ability to spread risk among a large, well-diversified pool of outside investors, thereby providing a low-cost source of equity capital to fund corporate investment. The availability of such capital in turn allowed "professional" managers to specialize in the day-to-day running of operations.

But for all its benefits, Jensen and Meckling pointed out that this separation of ownership and control, risk-bearing and management, also gives rise to "agency costs," conflicts of interest and incentives between managers and shareholders that effectively reduce the value of all *public* companies. The most obvious of these conflicts is the temptation faced by corporate managers to use corporate resources for "private benefit," including perk consumption in all its many forms. But much more subtle, and potentially far more costly, is the natural tendency of corporate managers to place a higher value than their shareholders on corporate growth, size, and diversification.

Investors, as finance scholars long before Jensen and Meckling had pointed out, can and generally do diversify their portfolios. And mainly for that reason, public company shareholders have greater tolerance than corporate managers for corporate risk-taking, *provided the anticipated returns on capital are high enough to justify the risks.* But when the expected returns fall below investors' (risk-adjusted) required rate of return—or what we have been calling the *cost of capital*—investors want the excess capital to be paid out as dividends or stock repurchases. Risk-averse managers, on the other hand, typically prefer to keep the cash inside the firm, unless and until pushed by active investors to "disgorge" it.

• • •

Corporate America's dismal operating and stock-market performance during the 1970s was the clearest sign that shareholders were becoming restless, and that Jensen and Meckling could be onto something important. But another hint of the shareholder activism in the 1980s was provided by the article's closing admission of its failure to explain the continuing predominance in the U.S. of "the very large corporation whose managers own little or no equity." And toward the end of the '80s, Jensen became a forceful advocate of much larger equity stakes for corporate executives—so forceful that a 2002 article in the *New Yorker* by its finance columnist John Cassidy attributed much of the rise in U.S. CEO pay during the '90s to Mike's writings and influence.[5]

Another glimpse of what lay ahead was contained in Jensen and Meckling's observation that debt financing could play a major role in increasing corporate efficiency and values. And as if to confirm they were on the right track, then came the leverage revolution of the 1980s—the emergence of the junk bond market, hostile takeovers by unaffiliated "raiders," and the wave of leveraged buyouts, or LBOs.

In 1986, and now ensconced at Harvard Business School, Jensen published an article in the *American Economic Review* that identified a somewhat new—or at least more precisely diagnosed—corporate agency problem. Called "The Agency Costs of Free Cash Flow: Corporate Finance and Takeovers," the article noted the tendency of managers in mature industries to hoard capital, and then reinvest it in low-return businesses or diversifying acquisitions, instead of returning it to shareholders. The LBOs and other leveraged recaps or "control" transactions of the '80s were seen as creating significant value just by forcing capital out of industries with massive excess capacity—everything from oil and gas and car, tires, and steel manufacturing to broadcasting and finance. The role of the heavy debt loads in such transactions was effectively to convert what were once smaller and "discretionary" dividend payments into much larger, contractual payments of interest and principal. And for the corporate managers now subjected to this new capital market discipline, the cost of capital had become "explicit and contractually binding."[6]

As the pre-eminent champion of the market for corporate control, Jensen had also become, by the end of the '80s, the foremost academic spokesman for LBOs. In 1989, he published his most famous *Harvard Business Review* article, "Eclipse of the Public Corporation"[7]—and he continues to be widely recognized as the intellectual father of what would later become known as "private equity." When LBOs and other highly leveraged transactions came under attack by Congress and the media, Mike responded in public House and Senate hearings by defending what he called "LBO associations" as the most promising solution—at least for mature companies that didn't need outside equity capital to grow—to the agency cost problem that he and Bill Meckling had pointed out 15 years earlier.

As Jensen argued in his *Harvard Business Review* piece, and later in his Congressional testimony, the concentrated equity ownership made possible in part by high leverage, the large equity stakes provided operating managers, and the active oversight and participation by major investors were coming together to create what he saw as "an important innovation in organizational form." In Mike's view—and as foreshadowed in Jensen and Meckling—the LBO promised not only to dominate the mature or declining sectors of the global economy, but to provide important lessons for increasing the long-run efficiency and value of public companies.

At the same time, Jensen continued to sound his warning that the Japanese corporate governance system was failing to serve its shareholders and, in so doing, undermining the economic future of Japan.

THE ONGOING CHALLENGE OF THE THIRD INDUSTRIAL REVOLUTION

As things have turned out since 1989, Jensen's expectations for LBOs and private equity have been not only realized but outrun. During the past 30 years, as we discuss later in chapter 7, the returns to the limited partners in private equity-led buyout funds, even after netting out the princely fees extracted by the GP firms (which continue to average as much as 200 basis points), have continued to outperform the S&P 500 and its European counterparts by some 300–500 basis points. And such returns have continued to attract ever larger allocations of capital from pension funds, university endowments, and other large institutional investors. As just one example, the entire University of Texas system endowment, known as "UTIMCO," now allocates fully 25 percent of its assets to PE funds.

As for the "breakdown of Japanese control systems" that Mike was warning about at the end of the '80s, the Japanese economy has since experienced three decades of stagnation—a period during which the Nikkei 225, after falling by as much as 60 percent in the 1990s, has only recently returned to its 1989 peak.

Nevertheless, when Jensen sat down in the early 1990s to write his President's address to the American Finance Association, he couldn't have known that his predictions about private equity (and the Japanese stock market and economy) would pan out so completely. Having just watched the U.S. regulatory curbs on high leverage and corporate control transactions prove highly effective in shutting down economic activity and intensifying the recession of the early 1990s, he became deeply pessimistic about the future. At one point, he claims to have "sold every piece of paper [he] owned."[8]

●   ●   ●

Jensen started his AFA address by citing the astonishing wave of technological innovations in the 19th century—everything from the railroads and telegraph and sewing machine to the McCormick reaper and the Bessemer steel process. These innovations, which historians have collectively dubbed "the Second Industrial Revolution," ended up displacing so many industries and producing so much overcapacity that, by 1904, the number of large U.S. industrial companies had fallen from roughly 1,800 a decade earlier in 1895 to under 160 ten years later. The part of this massive consolidation not brought about by failure or bankruptcy was accomplished through acquisitions, reflecting an earlier version of the workings of the U.S. market for corporate control.

Having set the stage with this historical precedent, Mike went on to propose that, since the early 1970s (he chooses "1973" as the date of the first big oil price spike), the U.S. economy has been undergoing what amounts to "a Third Industrial Revolution." The massive restructuring of the American business community that began in the '70s—and that was in full swing in the '90s and arguably continues to this day—was being driven by not only changes in technology, but a number of relatively new forces. In addition to advances in physical and management technology (including the LBO form itself), he pointed to the widespread deregulation of U.S. industry and the sharp rise in global product market competition. But perhaps the most important—and, in Mike's eyes, the gravest threat to American prosperity—was the ongoing conversion of once closed, centrally planned socialist economies to capitalism, which was expected to release billions of new relatively unskilled workers into the global labor supply.

After outlining the challenge that such forces were expected to pose for corporate managements, Mike then pointed to evidence of the effectiveness of U.S. capital markets in working off excess capacity during the '80s. One indicator was the doubling of manufacturing labor productivity growth from 1980 through 1989, as compared to the three previous decades 1950–1980. Even more telling for Jensen was the reversal during the '80s of a 30-year *decline* in *capital* productivity—a shift from productivity that had been falling by 1 percent a year, on average, from 1950–1981 to annual increases of 2 percent from 1981–1990.

Reflecting these productivity gains, the market capitalization of U.S. public companies more than doubled during the '80s, from roughly $1.4 to $3 trillion. And Mike's research showed the market for corporate control playing a major role in this reversal. During the period 1976–1990, some $1.8 trillion of control transactions—that is, mergers, takeovers, divestitures, and LBOs—were seen as producing over $750 billion in above-market "premiums" for the "selling" investors alone, to say nothing of the presumably large gains to the "buyers" in such deals.

Contrary to the widely reported criticism that such gains came in large part from cutting corporate R&D budgets, Mike pointed out that real U.S. R&D expenditures set record levels every year from 1975 to 1990, growing at an average annual rate close to 6 percent. And even with all the control market disruption and displacements, the total number of workers in manufacturing stayed pretty much the same, although the extraordinary growth in wages from 1950–1980 came to an end.

And so, despite all the change involved in the '80s restructurings, Jensen found himself hard-pressed to find clear "losers" from such transactions. But where he saw clear problems ahead was in the combination of the "massive rereg-ulation of financial markets"—specifically, the curbs on leveraged transactions and banks—and the influx of billions of very low-wage workers from places like China and Eastern Europe into the free-world economy caused by the collapse of communism. As Mike predicted, this mass of new low-wage workers would create a wave of competition for workers in developed economies that would make their lives much tougher.

And this in turn would generate more counterproductive political and media focus on the market for corporate control as the culprit. With the market for cor-porate control now put out of commission by U.S. policymakers and regulators, Mike's fears about corporate America once again got the upper hand.

THE RESTORATION OF THE U.S. CORPORATE CONTROL MARKET

But, again, as things turned out, Jensen's reports of the death of the U.S. corporate control market, and his fears about the future of U.S. corporate governance, proved greatly exaggerated. The governance vacuum left by the regulatory shutdown of the leveraged corporate control market was filled quickly and decisively by large U.S. institutional investors, who took a page out of Mike's (and private equity's) playbook by insisting that U.S. companies strengthen the equity incentives of their top managements. And in the ensuing (now nearly three) decades, the U.S. private equity markets, both in their lower-growth LBO and high-growth VC manifestations, have continued to outperform their public counterparts through at least two major cycles, including the Global Financial Crisis.

During the same period, moreover, our largest (S&P 500) U.S. public companies, though outdone by their U.S. PE-controlled counterparts, have continued to earn much higher shareholder returns than their European and Asian counterparts—a feat they have accomplished pretty much since "Jensen and Meckling" came out in 1976.[9]

In sum, something about U.S. corporate governance appears to be working. And the U.S. market for corporate control, rather than the fundamental *cause* of rising economic insecurity identified by critics of unbridled, "rough-and-tumble" finance capitalism, should instead be viewed as an ongoing part of the solution. The Third Industrial Revolution identified by Jensen is still very much underway; and even during the COVID pandemic, the U.S. control market could still be seen at work, making use of the collective wisdom of markets to sort out what might be described as an overcapacity problem in some parts of the global economy, but a supply problem in others.[10] As of this writing (April 2024), the performance of both the U.S. labor *and* stock markets since the onset of COVID has been nothing short of extraordinary. And it's instructive to keep in mind that such performance has been achieved despite the bout of inflation and interest rate hikes that business economists have long been telling us was bound to send us back to the misery of the '70s.

TRANSACTION MAN: FACT AND FICTION

None of this is to deny that there have been, and will continue to be, "losers" in this capital market-orchestrated process of creative destruction, when jobs are eliminated and companies displaced. Such finance-implicated hardship and misery take center stage in a book by Nicholas Lemann, the former dean of Columbia Journalism School, that was published with considerable fanfare in 2019 by Farrar, Straus, and Giroux. Bearing the provocative title *Transaction Man: The Rise of the Deal and the Decline of the American Dream*, the book provides indisputably moving accounts of lives disrupted and institutions displaced by the workings of the U.S. market for corporate control.

But Lemann doesn't content himself with this by now pretty much standard and expected attack on finance and hostile takeovers. The aim of this book is nothing less than the identification of a *single finance professor*, a mere academic, as the "transaction man"—the embodiment of a national type who is somehow made to assume responsibility for this collective misery. The prof in question is the main subject of this chapter, Mike Jensen, a man whose ideas and influence, if unchecked, are seen as a threat to American prosperity.

While sharing Lemann's view of Jensen's preeminence in the world of academic finance and the history of its ideas, I find the book a serious misreading of Jensen's body of work. And for all the book's considerable virtues, the most notable of its failures is to recognize—or show any awareness of—the social benefits of a well-functioning corporate control market. As suggested at the top of this chapter, the capital market activity Lemann deplores as a major cause of widespread economic insecurity is likely to be the most effective longer-run solution to the challenge of providing opportunities for an increasingly global workforce. And Jensen's message, here again, is that finance capitalism, far from discouraging technological advance, works hand in hand with—and in fact is essential to—its commercialization and the resulting spread of its social benefits.

UNDERSTANDING THE UNFORTUNATE CASE OF GM

Interwoven throughout Lemann's book is an account of the tribulations of Nick D'Andreas, decades-long owner of a General Motors dealership in Chicago's South Lawn that is shut down by the mother company during the Global Financial Crisis. The main effect of the story is to dramatize the plight of the small business owners and blue-collar workers whom Lemann views as the collateral damage, if not outright victims, of U.S. financial market activity.

But what Lemann fails to mention is that General Motors, far from operating as a single-minded value maximizer, may well have destroyed more shareholder value since the 1970s than any other U.S. public company during the 40 years leading up to its rescue in a 2009 Fed-orchestrated chapter 11 (bankruptcy) restructuring. Also ignored is the fact that GM has proved to be the only company to fail to repay the U.S. Treasury for its bailout, leaving U.S. taxpayers on the hook for some $11.2 billion.[11] GM thus offers the perfect illustration of the failure of internal control systems that kept Jensen up at night.

And he foresaw big problems at GM *specifically* as far back as the early 1980s, when the company's top management proposed a guarantee to all its full-time workers of lifetime employment (with 96 percent pay at retirement). Jensen publicly declared that proposal to be both unsustainable and socially irresponsible.

And, once again, he turned out to be right. At the time of its Fed bailout in 2009, GM's workforce was discovered by ex-investment banker Steve Rattner and his government restructuring team to have ballooned to roughly *1.5 times* the level its sales would support *under normal conditions*. With the aim of giving the enterprise a viable future, the bankruptcy reorganization plan approved by Judge Robert Gerber, and fully backed by the Obama administration, ended up cutting GM's U.S. manufacturing workforce from 113,000 in 2006 to just 38,000 by 2011.[12]

By contrast, *all* the banks and financial institutions (even the government-backed mortgage lenders Fannie Mae and Freddie Mac) that Lemann flogs for taking bailout funds from the U.S. Treasury ended up repaying in full a total of $267 billion, a sum that included over $21 billion of interest and gains on the loans of $245 billion they received during the crisis.

Was the $11 billion cost to taxpayers for the GM bailout—and this one was truly a bailout—worth it? My guess is that if we all knew we were going to have to pony up that amount of money to rescue our largest companies, we would have never let the companies raise public capital in the first place. (My personal hero Alexander Hamilton would be rolling in his grave at the prospect.[13])

One of the great ironies of Lemann's story, then, is that the real problems at GM came not from the operation of the market for corporate control, but from its *failure* or *absence*. GM was so large and politically entrenched (as the outcome of the GM dealer story makes clear) that it was essentially immune to takeover or shareholder activism of any kind until faced with ruin. And it was this absence of market discipline that encouraged and enabled the extreme mismanagement that Jensen foresaw would lead to the company's elephantine condition.

Another of the clear lessons is the social folly of allowing states to regulate companies' contracts with their suppliers. *Requiring* automakers to maintain *all* their dealerships under virtually all circumstances is a clear prescription for too many dealers—and for fraying GM-dealer relationships.

THE GLOBAL FINANCIAL CRISIS

This brings me to what I find Lemann's most glaring omission, which is the book's near-complete failure to recognize or acknowledge the large role played by public policy and regulation in the social ills that he chronicles. This failure becomes most visible in his depiction of the Global Financial Crisis, which he views as "the direct consequence of deregulation." Indeed, Lemann manages to suggest that the market for corporate control and shareholder activism were at the root of the near collapse of global markets in 2008.

Now there's some support for Lemann's story, in the following limited sense: It's true that our commercial and investment banks were seriously overleveraged, in part because of a failure of regulators like the U.S. Federal Reserve Bank to insist on higher capital requirements. And it's also true that, fueled in part by equity incentives, the top managements at financial firms (including Morgan Stanley, where I worked from 2004–2013) invested way too heavily in what turned out to be excessively risky mortgage-backed securities.

But what Lemann fails to mention—and what ongoing investigations are continuing to unearth—is how little U.S. bankers and their regulators actually *knew* about the amount and quality of the underlying mortgages *at the time of the crisis*. As Charles Calomiris, Columbia University's distinguished banking and finance scholar (and former chief economist of the Office of the Comptroller of the Currency) points out in his magisterial history of global banking crises, *Fragile By Design: The Origins of Banking Crises and Scarce Credit*, the banking crises experienced with almost predictable regularity by developed as well as developing economies tend to reflect what the authors call "the game of political bank bargains."[14] The U.S., for example, has experienced 12 major banking crises since Hamilton set up and began running our banking system in 1789, thanks in significant part to restrictions on interstate banking enacted and preserved by state politicians—the same pols who protected U.S. car dealers from the 1930s until well into the 21st century.[15] In the meantime, as remarkably few Americans seem aware, our northern neighbor Canada, which adopted and (unlike the U.S.) stuck with Hamilton's banking system by insisting on (instead of prohibiting) cross-provincial banking, has *never* experienced a major banking crisis, and didn't lose a single bank during the Global Financial Crisis.

In explaining what he takes to be the origins of that crisis, Calomiris summarized the underlying U.S. bank bargain as follows: low (or no) down-payment mortgages (in many cases, for less creditworthy borrowers; in effect, off-budget mortgage housing subsidies) in return for very low capital requirements (on the order of 3–5 percent of total assets) for the banks. Through a set of housing policies initiated by President Bill Clinton in the 1990s, and continued by the Bush administration in the 2000s, the until then largely ineffectual Community Reinvestment Act was reinvigorated and combined with new quotas for subprime (and later alt-A) mortgages for government-sponsored Fannie Mae and Freddie Mac.

The effect, if not the intent, of all this was a dramatic relaxation of mortgage underwriting standards. (Who could object to mortgages and home ownership for all?) And this relaxing of lending standards, when combined with low bank capital requirements and kept in place over some 25 years, had at least two major unintended and unwanted consequences. The first was unprecedented house price appreciation and vast numbers of people, many of them Lemann's South Lawn denizens, who could not afford (or flat out refused) to repay their mortgages (because they were underwater). Second, and completely ignored by Lemann, was the $4.6 trillion of "toxic" (subprime and alt-A) mortgages that, as we are only now coming to fully understand (but didn't at the time of the crisis), had been originated and were floating around in the world's financial circulatory system. These $4.6 trillion of mortgages ended up producing the financial equivalent of a heart attack.[16]

To see how something like this could happen, it helps to know that residential mortgages have long been understood by bankers throughout the world to be low-risk securities, with historical losses averaging well below 1 percent. That's why the Basel risk standards had long continued, even just before the crisis, to require only 1 percent capital (as a percentage of asset values) as backing for mortgages, while insisting on 4 percent for conventional corporate loans.

But, again, the U.S. government played a huge role in not just encouraging, but effectively *requiring*, the relaxation of mortgage underwriting standards. It was that policy choice, embraced by Republicans and Democratic legislators alike, that American Enterprise Institute scholar Peter Wallison has identified as the *sine qua non* ("without which nothing") of the Global Financial Crisis. And with considerable help from U.S. and European banks, once the Basel risk committee and the U.S. Fed gave them the "all-clear" by assigning minimal capital requirements for mortgages, it was that U.S. public policy choice that succeeded in turning an asset class widely expected to produce less than 1 percent losses into one with losses—as we are only now coming to learn—of 10 percent or more.[17] As most bankers will tell you, backing large asset pools with expected losses of 10 percent with capital ratios of 3–5 percent is not a winning proposition. And though it's true that bank capital has since been significantly strengthened by provisions of Dodd-Frank, the United States, as Calomiris pointed out recently when stepping down as Chief Economist of the OCC, continues to be the only nation on earth where 3 percent-down payment mortgages are still viewed as consistent with safe and sound banking practice.

NETWORK MAN—A SOLUTION FOR (NONE BUT) GROWTH COMPANIES

Near the end of his book, having considered and found wanting both Berle's controlled capitalism and Jensen's market for corporate control, Lemann seems to hold up a possible successor to Jensen's "Transaction Man" that he calls "Network Man." The prototype for Network Man is provided by Reid Hoffman, the founding CEO of LinkedIn, Netflix, and a number of other successful high-tech companies. At the core of Hoffman's proposed solution is the issuance of two or more classes of stock, with the non-voting kind fobbed off on the pesky outside shareholders, and with Hoffman and his team largely entrenched.

Lemann, to be fair, expresses his own doubts about both the sustainability of multiple-class issues and the new gig (or temporary-worker) economy such issues are sometimes associated with. And we should not be surprised to learn that Hoffman's solution has not turned out to be the "new form of capitalism" he envisioned. When the market pummeled LinkedIn's stock price after several down quarters, Hoffman, instead of than trying, say, a series of roadshows to win over his largest institutional investors, instead sold (out?) his company to Microsoft in one of those deplorable corporate control transactions—a transaction that, if the truth be told, ended up serving the interests of all concerned. (The sole identifiable victims were perhaps Hoffman's ego and the credibility of his views on capitalism and corporate governance.)

In sum, Hoffman, like most critics of the market for corporate control, appears to have given little thought to the role of efficient exit in the functioning of the world's greatest economy. Having presided over only high-growth enterprises with remarkably small workforces, he appears never to have considered where the resources for growth companies come from. The short answer—which he might have gotten from consulting Jensen—is from managing mature operations with discipline.

Growth opportunities like those presented by LinkedIn are scarce enough that IPO investors may well line up to buy the shares even when they don't come with voting rights. But once the growth trajectory begins to fade, the company's market value will likely fall enough to prompt investors to clamor for large-scale returns of capital (through dividends or stock buybacks) as well as a one-share one-vote regime—or sale to another company, like Microsoft, with one-share one-vote.

So, the lesson in all this is that dual class shares may not be sustainable—that is, tolerated indefinitely by minority investors. We could all do worse than to hark back to one of Jensen's favorite sayings: "You can't make the public a *minority* shareholder." On the other hand, the surge of dual-class-share IPOs over the last decade or so may suggest that Mike was wrong, and that what he should have said was something like this: "You might be able to start by making the public a minority stockholder. But at some point, your company's growth is going to slow; and when that happens, your stock price is going to fall, and investors are going to demand higher payouts and, eventually, more control."

That's pretty much what happened at Google a few years ago when they hired Morgan Stanley's then CFO Ruth Porat to bring a new financial order and discipline. Just the announcement of Porat's appointment as the new Google CFO seemed to have the effect of reassuring investors by restating management's commitment to long-run profitability *as well as* growth. And Google, of course, though it now has a different corporate name, has done pretty well since then.

GOOD OLD-FASHIONED "PLURALISM": BACK TO THE '70S?

Lemann's book ends with an Epilogue that holds up as a possible alternative to Jensen's finance-driven capitalism the "pluralistic" vision of an obscure and idiosyncratic political economist named Arthur Bentley. After a brief teaching stint at the University of Chicago, Bentley spent much of the rest of his life on a farm in Indiana composing a very long book formulating his doctrine of how government and corporations *really* work, and how they can be reformed to better serve the public interest.

Bentley's pluralism begins with the recognition that politics consists of the search for effective compromise among warring interest groups that aims to make us all better off. But rather than seeking "a public interest" that can be identified and served, Bentley abandons the search as futile and calls for "an equitable sharing" of benefits and costs by *all* groups who manage to get themselves represented at the table.

Now, as an account of what happens in the U.S. federal (or any) political process, Bentley's "pluralism" seems, though hardly new, pretty much on the mark. And it may well be the best solution *when operating in the political sphere.*

But in the economic or corporate sphere, pluralism is almost certain to become stakeholder "balancing." It was Jensen and Meckling who first defined the corporation itself as "a nexus of contracts" among different interest groups, with the implication that all parties' claims must be met before the shareholders get anything. And nobody does a better job than Mike Jensen in explaining what happens to companies that become "confused about their mission." Think once more about General Mills and its plan to become the "All-Weather Growth Company."

It was also Jensen who, around the year 2000, formulated and published his concept of "enlightened value maximization." As defined by Jensen, it means "taking care"—to the point of inspiring the commitment and even the emotional allegiance—of *all* corporate stakeholders capable of affecting a company's long-run efficiency and value.[18] And for this writer at least, enlightened value maximization seems to hold out the most promising solution to today's social and economic problems—and it's one that we return to in the final chapter of this book. As discussed there at length, the precepts of enlightened value maximization can be seen clearly at work in some (although not all) parts of today's still viable, if somewhat battered ESG (short for Environmental, Social, and Governance) and sustainability movements.

But it means devoting the *right* amount of investment and resources to each interest group—not too little, but not too much. Mike's key insight here is that our stock price and labor markets are likely to do a far better job of determining those amounts than political bureaucrats subjected to media and social pressure of every imaginable kind.

* * *

In providing the most *efficient* solution to such problems, our financial markets are also likely to end up providing the most *humane* solution. As Hamilton recognized well over 200 years ago when setting up the first Bank of the United States, you have to create the wealth before you can start redistributing it. And when you begin to redistribute, you want to make sure you're not shutting down the engine of growth.

So, yes, we need to find a way to care for everybody we can, but without breaking the Bank (and the banks and the companies they fund) on which so much of our economic and social progress depend.

CHAPTER 5

STEWART MYERS AND THE MIT SCHOOL OF REAL OPTIONS AND CAPITAL STRUCTURE

S tewart Myers, now in his 57th year on the finance faculty at MIT's Sloan School of Management—and by many accounts the world's most accomplished *corporate* finance scholar since the death of Merton Miller in 2000—once thought that finance was "boring." At least that's what he told Alex Robichek, the Stanford finance prof demanding to know why Stew had stopped showing up for his MBA class in the early 1960s. And he expressed much the same discontent with the diet of case studies that Stanford MBA students, like their East-coast counterparts at Harvard, were force-fed in those days. In Stew's words,

> It was just one Harvard Business School case after another. No doubt the cases taught useful practical lessons, but the next case never built on the last one. There was not much there intellectually.[1]

Robichek's response was to hand Stew a bunch of research articles on corporate finance and then, two years later, become the director of Stew's Ph.D. dissertation and his co-author of a book called *Optimal Financing Decisions*, as well as what turned out to be three path-breaking studies of corporate capital structure and capital budgeting.

ACT I: VETTING THE M&M PROPOSITIONS

In a retrospective account that appeared in MIT's *Annual Review of Financial Economics* in 2015, Stew described his work as a corporate finance scholar as "a life in three Acts."[2] The first task he was assigned as "Alex's research assistant" was to assess both the theoretical soundness and the practical import of Modigliani and Miller's irrelevance Proposition 1. M&M's Prop 1, as we saw in chapter 3, is the idea that whether a company chooses to finance its operations mainly with debt or with equity capital has no predictable effect on its market value. The basic insight is that such *financing* decisions amount to little more than different ways of dividing up a company's expected stream of future operating earnings and "repackaging" them for investors. It is these operating earnings or cash flows— the ones that get counted *before* subtracting interest charges or corporate income taxes (which come into the picture later)—and their associated predictability or risk that are the main engine of value.

But when M&M Prop 1 first appeared in 1958, neither professors nor practitioners had an easy time signing on to the argument. For one thing, why would corporate CFOs get paid such handsome sums to make decisions that, in the most often heard phrase of Chicago financial economists, "do not matter"?[3]

Both theorists and practitioners in the mid-1960s faced a number of obstacles when trying to understand the state of thinking in corporate finance. Among the most important, neither professors nor practitioners always distinguished clearly between the corporate goal of maximizing the market value of the company and maximizing the personal well-being or utility of its top executives. It would take another ten years before Jensen and Meckling used their famous paper on agency costs to demonstrate how CEOs' *private* or personal risk preferences—however often expressed as evidence of their *social* concerns—led them to shun debt financing, even in cases where shareholders viewed it as the low-cost source of capital.[4] But, as Stew and Alex argued in a pair of 1966 papers, Miller and Modigliani were right to suggest that the level of financial risk-taking by the corporation should reflect the viewpoint and preferences not of management (or other corporate stakeholders such as employees), but of the investors supplying the company's equity capital.[5]

Professors and practitioners back in the '60s also had a tendency to view financial risk as reflecting only the extreme possibilities of default and bankruptcy. M&M's Proposition 2, as we saw earlier, says that a company's financial risk is reflected in the market pricing of its common stock in the sense that its expected or required rate of return—and thus its "cost" of equity capital— increases in pretty much "linear" fashion with increases in corporate leverage. In general, the more highly leveraged a company, and holding all other things equal, the lower the P/E multiple that investors are willing to put on its earnings when pricing its shares.

But that wasn't how most CFOs, and a good many finance scholars back then, saw the world. As long as debt ratios were moderate and the prospect of default remote, a company's required rate of return or cost of capital was assumed to fall with increased levels of debt to reflect some combination of the riskless leveraging of EPS and the corporate tax savings from larger interest tax shields. And by failing even to mention the subject of default risk and the costs associated with financial distress, M&M left their skeptics with the impression that they had "simply skirted over," in Stew's words, "a serious objection to their proofs."[6]

Other critics of Prop 1 focused on the arbitrage arguments M&M used to support it—the idea that investors seeking heavily debt-financed investments could manufacture "homemade leverage" simply by, say, buying stocks on margin. To the extent that investors' borrowings were a perfect substitute for corporate debt, there seemed to be no compelling reason for investors to prefer *any* degree of corporate leverage over another and so pay more for companies that operated with more—or less—debt.

An MIT statistician named David Durand, who became M&M's most vocal and tenacious critic, claimed to be so vexed by this arbitrage argument used to buttress Prop 1 that he rushed out to the local Stop & Shop to confirm his sense of people's willingness to pay more for separate containers of skim milk and cream than for the same volume of whole milk. Why, Durand asked, couldn't companies increase the size of the "corporate pie" just by adjusting the number and size of the slices to meet the quirks and shifts of investor demand?

But as Stew responded to this charge, there are two necessary conditions for the sum of the pieces to sell for more than the whole. First, the customers—in this case, the company's investors—must be willing to pay extra for the separated products, the slices of debt and equity versus the entire pie. And an equally important condition: would-be competitors must somehow be deterred. For unless there are high costs of supplying the sliced or separated products, competition should drive the price of the separated products back to the M&M equilibrium.

The operation of such supply-demand conditions in financial (as in all) markets was central to how M&M thought about and presented their argument. There is investor demand for different kinds of corporate securities—for example, debt and leveraged equity instead of the stock of debt-free all-equity companies. But for public companies operating in reasonably well-functioning financial markets, the marginal cost of supplying the debt and equity separately has to be at most a very small fraction of total firm value. And so if public companies could increase their own values just by changing their mix of debt and equity, the supply of the combination most favored by investors would increase rapidly until the value premium disappeared.

REPACKAGING CASH FLOWS FOR INVESTORS: THE CASE OF MORTGAGE-BACKED SECURITIES

As Stew points out in his retrospective, the history of mortgage-backed securities (MBS) provides a dramatic example of experimentation with investor demand for different kinds of securities. Commercial banks could choose to sell the cash flows from pools of mortgages as simple pass-through securities or as collateralized mortgage obligations (CMOs). CMOs allocate the cash flows to different tranches, with AAA-rated tranches backed by tranches with progressively lower ratings and a final residual claim to what's left over.

Because the tranches amount to several different classes of debt and equity, the ability to make money issuing CMOs instead of simple pass-through MBSs would appear to violate MM's proposition that capital structure is irrelevant to value.

But as things worked out, the supply response turned out to be massive, and appears to have "overshot the MM equilibrium," providing what some economists now view as the main impetus for the Global Financial Crisis. And for long after the GFC, there was no functioning *private* MBS market, with the MBS market consisting entirely of securities backed by the government-sponsored entities Fannie Mae, Freddie Mac, and the FHLB.

Stew and Alex went on to show that M&M Prop 1 holds for not only "risk-free" or safe" debt, but for "risky" debt as well—those corporate notes or bonds that were *expected* to experience losses under (generally only the worst) outcomes. Prop I was also shown to apply to any *mix* of debt maturities, from 30-day notes to 30-year (or longer) bonds.

And after satisfying themselves that the M&M logic was sound, *given its underlying assumptions*, Stew and Alex then set about relaxing some of those assumptions to see if the answers changed and the relevance of corporate finance became clearer.

THE TRADE-OFF THEORY OF CAPITAL STRUCTURE

Most critics of M&M Prop 1 when it first came out directed their attacks on the so-called "perfect markets" assumptions—no taxes or transactions costs, costless reorganizations of financially troubled companies, and the availability of reliable information about corporate plans and future profits. But possibly inviting greatest skepticism was M&M's assumption that corporate managers would continue to be perfect agents for their shareholders, taking on all positive-NPV projects while rejecting all others, regardless of how their companies were financed.

Though we didn't mention this in chapter 3, M&M themselves were the first to relax the no-taxes assumption and recognize the value of interest tax shields as an essential benefit of debt financing. (In fact, as we take up in more detail below, M&M's first foray into this "debt-and-taxes" question (in 1963) led them to suggest that each dollar of debt financing added as much as 40 cents (reflecting a corporate income tax rate of 40 percent) to a company's current market value.) But by going on to suggest—or at least emboldening others to think—that such a benefit was significant enough to lead risk-seeking companies to operate with capital structures leveraged as high as 99 to 1, M&M failed to identify or recognize any *costs* associated with debt that would cause corporate managers to limit their use of it.

And in this sense, M&M's initial conclusions about debt and corporate values defied everyday experience. Anyone who cared could see that public companies did not then—nor do they now—operate with 99 percent debt. (But that said, many U.S. companies acquired in the first wave of leveraged buyouts during the 1980s did in fact end up with debt ratios remarkably close to those levels, as we will see in chapter 7.)

In launching their challenge of M&M Prop 1, Stew and Alex ended up focusing on two other underlying assumptions: The first was that the costs associated with reorganizing financially troubled companies, whether in or outside chapter 11, were at most a small fraction of firm value. The second was that corporate investment decisions were unlikely to be affected by financing choices—so that, for example, corporate managers were unlikely to be distracted by heavy debt loads from taking on value-increasing projects.

After proposing and exploring several ways in which these two assumptions were likely to fail to hold up in the real world, Stew and Alex came up with a

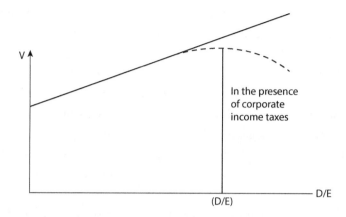

In the presence
of corporate
income taxes

"trade-off theory" of corporate capital structure that continues largely intact to this day. The basic theory proposes that corporate managers have *targeted* leverage ratios—ratios of debt to equity that, even if not strictly adhered to, managers aim to converge on over time. And in the process of formulating such targets, corporate CFOs and treasurers are seen as weighing the tax benefits of more debt against the higher expected future costs of financial distress. Chief among such costs are those expected to arise from the so-called "underinvestment problem," the distortion of normal management incentives, discussed in more detail below, to fund all investments that promise to increase (or preserve) the value of the franchise.

Though Stew did not give the trade-off theory its name until his President's address to the American Finance Association in 1984,[7] most finance textbooks that have appeared since the publication of Alex and Stew's articles in 1966 have continued to illustrate the theory by reproducing some version of their exhibit reproduced here in the figure above.

CLARIFYING SOME UNRESOLVED QUESTIONS ABOUT DCF: WHEN IT'S SUPPOSED TO WORK AND HOW TO USE IT

Besides providing the rudiments of the theory of capital structure that continues to provide at least the point of departure for academics as well as practitioners,

Stew and Alex used their three papers in the late '60s to clear up some of the difficulties companies encounter when using the DCF method to value investment opportunities.

In the typical DCF approach, the projected future cash flows are discounted at a constant risk-adjusted discount rate. In this sense, DCF gives each cash flow what Stew likes to call "a haircut for risk." And without getting too technical, the size of the haircut for a given cash flow—say, the operating profit expected one year from now—is the ratio of its *certainty equivalent* to its expected value. For example, if the expected cash flow one year from now is $100, and the risk haircut reduces that estimate by 10 percent, the certainty equivalent is $100 × .9, or $90. A cash flow two years out gets two haircuts, so the certainty equivalent today is $100 × .9 × .9, or $81—and so on for more distant cash flows.

Since the certainty equivalents themselves are fully discounted for risk, those cash flows can then be discounted at the risk-free rate (like the U.S. Treasury rate) as if they were certain. So, let's suppose the Treasury rate for the relevant maturity (let's call its five years) is 4 percent. In that case, we could do this valuation in a single step in one of two different ways: We could discount all the expected cash flows at a single rate—in which case the rate would turn out to be 15.6 percent. Or we could instead discount the series of certainty equivalents—which, incidentally, is what legendary investor Warren Buffett likes to do[8]—at the risk-free rate of 4 percent. Either way we get the same answer.

But as Stew and Alex wanted to make clear, we would be justified in using these two methods *only when the risk haircut is expected to be the same for every future period*—that is, only in cases where *risk* is assumed to be *increasing at a constant rate* as one looks farther out in time. And using this simple logic, Stew and Alex clarified several questions regularly encountered or raised by practitioners and other would-be users.

First, it corrected the popular, but mistaken intuition that longer-dated cash-flow streams must be riskier and discounted at a higher rate than short-lived streams. What Stew and Alex showed is that the standard DCF set-up *automatically* gives more distant cash flows larger haircuts for risk.

Second, it discouraged practitioners from the widespread practice of using "fudge factors" in the form of "risk premiums" added on to the already risk-adjusted discount rates, with the aim, say, of offsetting the effects of excessive managerial optimism. Such a practice effectively involves a "double" discounting or punishment for risk by ignoring the implied risk haircuts on distant cash flows.

Third, it gave practitioners a way of handling the many cases in which the certainty-equivalent haircut did not increase at a constant rate. Take the case of oil prices, with their well-documented tendency to fluctuate and then revert toward average levels. To the extent that current oil prices appear depressed or unusually low, the use of risk-adjusted discount rates based on current spot price movements is likely to understate the present value of an oil field with an expected productive life of, say, 20 years. In cases where such mean reversion is expected, Stew and Alex argued that lower discount rates should be used to reflect the reality that cumulative risk is *not* increasing at a constant rate as one looks farther out into the future.

CAPTURING RISK WHEN USING DCF—AND EXPOSING THE FALLACY OF CORPORATE DIVERSIFICATION

Another important matter that Stew himself took up in a 1968 article (in an MIT publication called *Industrial Management Review*) was to show how differences in company risk affect the equilibrium values of corporate stocks and bonds, and how such analysis should be used by companies when evaluating their own capital investments. For companies intent on maximizing their own market value, management was instructed to view the company's investment opportunities using the same criteria used by individual investors when valuing corporate stocks, but *with one important exception: no value* should be assigned to corporate efforts to diversify their portfolio of businesses. In evaluating possible mergers, for example, the company values should simply add up, with no gain or loss of value arising from the expected degree of correlation of their earnings. However obvious this point might seem now, Stew's concept (which he called "additivity") was presented during the heyday of the conglomerates, whose popularity reflected in significant part the assumed benefits of *corporate* diversification.

In fact, today's readers might also be surprised to learn that corporate capital budgeting was viewed in the 1960s largely as a matter of choosing, much like individual investors, so-called "mean-variance efficient" portfolios of *businesses* that would perform well in all stages of the business cycle. One well-known Harvard Business School finance professor went so far as to argue that "the problem of determining the best capital budget . . . is formally identical to the solution of a security portfolio analysis."[9]

Stew was the first to demonstrate why this view was wrong and, in so doing, provide the theoretical basis for the insight—now part of the conventional wisdom—that corporate diversification is at best redundant, given investors' ability and incentives to diversify their own portfolios. And as we saw in the previous chapter, Jensen and Meckling were then about to come up with good reasons why such corporate portfolios would turn out to be worth significantly *less* than the sum of their parts.

Thanks in part to Stew, then, today's corporate managers value most projects (including acquisitions) on a standalone basis, generally using the DCF method, while dismissing the old temptation to use diversification to justify empire-building projects as worth more than the sum of individual project values.

THE CAPITAL ASSET PRICING MODEL, OR QUANTIFYING CORPORATE RISK

One critical step in valuing potential corporate investments was to find an objective way to quantify risk that could be incorporated into the discount rates used by practitioners. The answer was provided by the Capital Asset Pricing Model, or CAPM. Although John Lintner and Bill Sharpe are generally credited with—and Sharpe received a Nobel Prize for—formulating the CAPM, Stew and Alex were actually the first to provide a workable statement of the CAPM formula.[10]

The CAPM formula instructed practitioners to estimate the expected rate of return on a company's stock as the sum of two main variables:

(1) the risk-free rate of interest—as estimated by the current yield to maturity promised by, say, five-year U.S. Treasury bonds; and

(2) a company-specific risk premium estimated by multiplying the company's "beta" by a market-wide risk "premium."

A company's beta is a measure of the extent to which the stock price moves with the broad market, with 1.0 indicating a stock of average risk whose price movements tend to mirror the market's. The market-wide risk premium is typically estimated by subtracting the risk-free rate from the expected market-wide return, with estimates of the latter ranging from as low as 3–4 percent to as high as 8 percent. So, for a company of average risk, and assuming a risk-free, five-year

U.S. Treasury rate of 3 percent and a (mid-range) estimate of the market risk premium of 6 percent, the cost of equity capital would be estimated using the CAPM as follows: 3% + (1.0 × 6%) = 9%.

PUTTING THE WACC TO WORK

In a study published in the *Journal of Finance* in 1974, Stew introduced a valuation approach or "framework" that would enable analysts to value companies and their investment opportunities while using what came to be called the "weighted average cost of capital," or WACC, as the rate for discounting the expected cash flows.[11] To illustrate with a simple example, for a company of average risk (that is, with a beta of 1.0) with a target debt ratio of one third debt (with a borrowing rate of 5 percent) and two thirds equity (with a cost of equity of 9 percent from above), the WACC (using the old corporate income tax rate of 35 percent) would be estimated as follows:

$$.33 \times (5\% \times (1-.35)) + (.67 \times 9\%) = 7.1\%.$$

Today's corporate analysts, thanks in large part to the efforts of Stew and colleagues, routinely use such a WACC as the discount rate when using the DCF method to value contemplated acquisitions or other investment projects.

APV AND VALUING THE TAX ADVANTAGE OF DEBT

Stew's 1974 paper also addressed another practical challenge that had been finessed by M&M. Although they recognized the value of corporate interest tax shields even when formulating Prop I in 1958,[12] M&M took five more years to decide how the tax shields should be valued. At first, they discounted the tax shields at the same rate used to value after-tax operating cash flows. But in their 1963 "correction," M&M decided that the tax shields should be assumed to be fixed, certain, and thus discounted at the lower debt rate (instead of, say, the WACC). They also assumed a fixed, permanent amount of debt in the company's capital structure. With those assumptions, the "corrected" present value of interest tax shields is simply the tax rate, t, multiplied by the amount of debt, D, or tD.

But what if a company's financing policy aims to hold fixed not the *amount* of debt it operates with over time, but instead its leverage *ratio*—that is, debt as a percentage of its total (debt plus equity) firm value? For companies whose professed intent is to maintain a relatively fixed debt *ratio*, the M&M approach effectively assumed that future *levels* of debt—even when expressed, as they generally are, as percentages of the *book* (as opposed to the *market)* value of equity or total assets—would be forced to adjust up or down as the company or its project did well or poorly. For companies with explicit debt targets (or even just targeted *ranges)*, adhering to such targets would likely mean raising more debt in good years, when the *need* to raise more capital is likely smallest, while retiring debt in lean years, when it would be most costly and disruptive to do so.

So, although M&M's assumption of a fixed, permanent *level* of debt—rather than a constant ratio—simplified exposition of their theory, it sowed confusion in practice, where WACC tends to be used as a discount rate for projects with finite lives and different patterns of cash flows. And this meant that the implicit assumption underlying the use of WACC was a continuous rebalancing of capital structure that few if any companies were likely to even contemplate.[13]

In search of a practical solution to this challenge in implementing WACC, Stew used his 1974 paper to pose the question: what happens when we relax this assumption of fixed, permanent debt? What he concluded was that once we allow the corporate leverage ratio to change over time, discounting at WACC doesn't work. In large mature companies with long-range leverage targets—even those from which they expect to depart regularly—managements might still feel comfortable continuing to discount their expected cash flow streams at the WACC. But in dealing with smaller companies and projects where future adjustments of corporate leverage were expected to be significant—in some instances even scheduled and thus part of the financing strategy from the start—Stew came up with a practical alternative he called "Adjusted Present Value, or APV, and that was expressed by the following simple formula:

APV = Operating NPV (assuming all-equity financing, and so discounted at the
opportunity cost of total assets, or the cost of unlevered equity)
+ PV of interest tax shields.

The great advantage of the APV over the WACC-based approach is that it allows companies to separate the real or operating value of contemplated investments from any financing benefits. As Stew also took pains to make clear, the use of WACC, when done properly, effectively yields the same answer as the APV—and in a single step. But where APV was likely to be especially useful, and maybe essential, was in cases like project financings and leveraged buyouts, where initially heavy debt loads were expected to be paid down according to a predetermined schedule. The APV approach could also be used to incorporate the benefits of special financing arrangements, such as those associated with leasing (instead of acquiring) a new fleet of trucks.

ACT II: A WORLD AWASH IN REAL OPTIONS—AND ANOTHER LOOK AT THE DETERMINANTS OF CORPORATE BORROWING

The formulation of the trade-off theory, and the challenge of incorporating it into WACC and discount rates, were far from the end of Stew's thinking about corporate capital structure and capital budgeting. Looking around in the early 1970s, he was struck by the fact that so many large and consistently profitable companies chose to operate with very low debt ratios. In many cases, the size of their cash holdings meant they had *negative* debt ratios! If the M&M argument about the tax benefits of debt were right, these companies could have increased their own market values significantly just by issuing bonds and buying back their stock. In so doing, they would be boosting their interest tax shields, thereby cutting corporate income taxes and increasing their after-tax earnings and cash flows—the key variables at the core of the M&M valuation model. And as Jensen and Meckling showed in the previous chapter, the requirement to service interest and principal could function as a valuable control mechanism, an early-warning signal of cash flow and overinvestment problems that could alert outsiders to potential problems and so help hold management's feet to the fire.

So, taxes and control benefits were two good reasons to issue debt and avoid outside equity. But what factors or considerations were working to *limit* the use of debt? Again, the obvious answer was the increased threat of default and bankruptcy. But apart from management's losing its job—not necessarily a bad thing, in most economists' eyes—what were the costs *to investors and the economy* associated with financial trouble and reorganization?

One study that had attempted to answer this question—a 1976 article by the University of Rochester's Jerry Warner—found that the actual *direct* costs of bankruptcy—mainly the filing and legal fees associated with chapter 11—were surprisingly small, less than 1 percent of the market value of the companies at the time of filing. And for companies choosing to reorganize "privately," or outside of chapter 11, those costs turned out to be appreciably smaller than that.

Then in 1977, in what might be described as the nearest approach to a solution to this puzzle of the costs of high leverage, Stew published an article in the *Journal of Financial Economics* called "Determinants of Corporate Borrowing." Appearing in the same journal a year after Jensen and Meckling's classic, Stew's article began with a simple demonstration of how just the *prospect* of default can limit a highly leveraged company's ability—while undermining its managers' normal incentives—to raise capital to fund not only value-increasing investments, but even just value-preserving measures like ordinary maintenance.

Companies with a large *debt overhang* face investor resistance when trying to raise new, and especially equity, capital. That resistance, as Stew's example showed, stems from the "new money's" unwillingness to bail out the old creditors, whose debt at this point is likely to be trading well below 100 cents on the dollar.

The crux of the problem is that the investors committing the new equity capital are effectively being asked to share the gains from their investment with the creditors, which are thus getting at least a partial bailout. Or to put it a little differently, the new investment effectively enables the creditors to capture part of the value if and when the company invests enough to recover and even grow. And, again, just the prospect of this transfer of wealth to creditors is likely to deter would-be new equity investors.

As Stew recognized, the outcome of this conflict over future gain-sharing was likely to be a financing impasse—one capable of producing a corporate *underinvestment problem* and serious loss of value. But as he also recognized, some companies were far more vulnerable to this problem than others. Where high leverage and the debt overhang impasse were likely to prove especially destructive, and thus to be avoided if at all possible, was in *growth* companies—companies whose current value derived less from their current earnings and more from what Stew recognized and described as "growth options." (M&M referred to them as "growth or glamor" companies.)

Such growth companies were notably different from the value companies at the other end of the corporate maturity spectrum, which were described as consisting mainly of "assets in place." Whereas value companies could be recognized by their low P/E ratios and market-to-book ratios (near or even well below 1.0), growth companies often traded at multiples of their book values, and at levels that appeared well above the capitalized value of their current earnings—if they had any earnings at all!

Stew's critical insight was that companies perceived to have abundant growth opportunities should be viewed as possessing valuable *real options*. Examples of such options are the right—but, critically important, not the obligation—of bio-tech or pharma companies to commercialize drugs in their R&D pipeline, or of high-tech firms to find new products or markets for promising technologies they have patented and invested in developing.

OPTION PRICING THEORY AND THE THEORY OF REAL OPTIONS

In the early 1970s, three other financial economists then working with Stew at MIT—Fischer Black, Myron Scholes, and Robert Merton—were developing what would become the Black-Scholes option pricing model. This model and variations thereof were quickly put to work by options traders and other practitioners to value not only puts and calls on widely traded stocks, but warrants, convertible bonds, and other securities with built-in or embedded options.

The beauty of the model, for practitioners and theorists alike, was its ability to express the value of calls, puts, and all variety of call- or option-like securities using just five or six variables—all but one of which you used to be able to find reported in the business sections of many newspapers:

(1) the value of the underlying assets (say, the stock price on which the call is written);

(2) the exercise or strike price of the option;

(3) the maturity or time to expiration of the option;

(4) the risk-free interest rate;

(5) the dividend yield (if the asset pays a dividend) on the underlying asset; and

(6) the variance of (reflecting the degree of uncertainty about) the value of the underlying asset.

(continued on next page)

(*continued from previous page*)

Of these six variables, only the last, the variance of the underlying asset, could not be directly observed. But the variance was a critically important variable in the paradoxical sense that the greater the uncertainty about the value of the underlying asset, the larger the value of the option. And so whereas uncertainty generally discourages investors and reduces value, in the case of options it becomes a fundamental source of value.

Within months of publication of the Black-Scholes model in 1973, professional options traders could be seen walking the trading floors armed with commercial versions of the model programmed into their TI hand-held calculators.

●   ●   ●

For Stew, option pricing theory represented a different opportunity, one that would have an important bearing on both the theory and, like so much of Stew's work, the practice of corporate finance. And there's no better example than a short article he published in 1984 called "Finance Theory and Financial Strategy."[14] Its goal was nothing less than unifying the often rivalrous disciplines of corporate strategy and finance.

Corporate strategists, as we saw in chapter 2, have long been fond of castigating the shortsightedness of their finance colleagues. And in the spirit of Merton Miller in Tokyo, Stew begins his article by offering a general defense of the discounted cash flow valuation method and the underlying principles at the core of modern finance.

But having defended DCF against its imagined shortcomings, Stew went on to identify one real and serious limitation of DCF: its inability to "link today's investments to tomorrow's opportunities," a function that might be described as the essence of corporate strategy. What's more, it's important to recognize that such options include not only real *call* or growth options to develop promising opportunities, but also real *put* or abandonment options to cut back or shut down investments or businesses that were failing to pan out. And as most strategists (though not most capital budgeters) readily understand, one of the critical sources of the value of real options, whether puts or calls, is that they are *one-sided* arrangements that enable corporate managements to "truncate the distribution of outcomes," to eliminate the bad or failing projects or possibilities while keeping alive only the most promising ones.

That said, when making his case for the importance and pervasiveness of corporate real options, Stew focused mainly on growth or expansion options by presenting the value of Apple (again back in 1984) as the sum of two components: (1) the capitalized present value of its "normalized" current earnings; and (2) the net present value of its future growth opportunities. And after proposing that we think about those opportunities as a "portfolio of options—the firm's options to invest in second-stage, third-stage, or even later projects"—Stew then went on to identify option pricing methods as the most promising way of trying to quantify the value of such strategic possibilities. And Stew's suggestions helped spawn a new valuation approach that quickly attracted an impressive body of disciples and promising potential applications (but whose technical complexities put it beyond the scope of this book).

The Import of Real Options for Capital Structure. As Stew also recognized, the near ubiquitous presence of both expansion and abandonment options had profound implications for not only corporate valuation and strategy, but also for corporate financing and capital structure. For companies like Apple in the early '80s, when the lion's share of its market cap could be attributed to growth options and not current earnings or cash flow, the company's nearly exclusive reliance on equity financing with minimal debt was viewed by Stew as adding value just by working to ensure the preservation of financing flexibility—flexibility that management would need to "exercise" its real investment options if and when they materialized, or came "into the money." Putting a heavy debt load on a company like Apple at that early stage of its development could easily have led to the "debt overhang" and financing impasse described earlier, forcing management to pass up promising growth opportunities.

The preservation of financing flexibility to fund such growth options continues to be viewed—by finance scholars, corporate strategists, and a great many practicing CFOs—as the main reason for companies to limit their use of leverage and payouts. And as we show in our next chapter, whose main focus is corporate risk management, the preservation of financing flexibility also plays a big role in corporate decisions to hedge significant financial exposures.[15]

ACT III: USING INFORMATION COSTS TO HELP SOLVE THE CAPITAL STRUCTURE PUZZLE

Besides providing George Orwell with a title for his most famous, dystopian novel (though by no means his best book), 1984 was a big year for Stew. In what was widely acknowledged to be a long overdue honor, he was elected President of the American Finance Association. It was also the year he published, with MIT colleague Nicholas Majluf, the path-breaking paper titled, "Corporate Financing and Investment Decisions When Firms Have Information That Investors Do Not Have."[16] Now known simply as "Myers and Majluf," and having amassed citations numbering in the thousands, it was the first paper to investigate the implications for corporate finance of this "information asymmetry" between corporate insiders and their investors.

Stew gives full credit to Majluf, then an MIT doctoral student in corporate strategy, for their basic idea that financial "slack"—by which they meant both cash and unused debt capacity—could be valuable to companies and their investors just by enabling them to fund strategic investments *without recourse to equity markets*. When Stew asked his co-author, "What's wrong with equity financing? What market imperfection do you have in mind?," the response he got was, "Corporate managers really don't want to issue undervalued stock."

Stew says that, up to that point, he had never thought seriously about the possibility of significant under- or overvaluation of their stock affecting managers' decisions. But he suddenly realized that there might be "an equilibrium" in which managers were so optimistic about the firm's prospects (relative to its current value) that they would pass up a clearly positive-NPV investment rather than issue undervalued new shares to fund it.

Myers and Majluf starts off pretty much from the same place as Stew's 1977 classic, "Determinant of Corporate Borrowing." The set-up of the example and the model are the same: a company with both assets in place and a real option that requires a decision about whether and when to exercise. As in the 1977 paper, corporate managers are assumed to act in shareholders' interest.

What is new about the 1984 article is that managers have information that investors don't about *two* important variables: the value of assets in place and the NPV of the real option—which is the value of that option *if and when exercised at the best time*. In this story, the company is assumed to have enough financial slack to continue funding its assets in place or ongoing operations, but not enough to finance the investment should the option-like opportunity materialize. The firm is also assumed to raise new equity from shareholders.

But in what is the critical departure from the 1977 article, Myers and Majluf describe an equilibrium in which the company's shareholders respond to the announcement of a new equity offering by adjusting downward the value of the shares both to reflect and, in effect, to compensate themselves for their own informational disadvantage relative to managers. And as if to confirm the plausibility of this part of their "story," a wave of recent event studies of seasoned equity offerings by U.S. companies had reported a negative market reaction (of some 2–3 percent) to the announcements of such offerings.[17]

Faced with this dilemma of sorts, the managers whose now lower share prices fail to reflect their companies' prospects may well decide to sacrifice a promising (positive-NPV) investment rather than issue undervalued shares. And thus the key prescriptive insight of Myers and Majluf is that companies with valuable real options should (and do in fact) preserve more financial slack to avoid the need for new equity issues.

THE CAPITAL STRUCTURE PUZZLE AND THE PECKING ORDER

Building on the foundation provided by Myers-Majluf, Stew used his 1984 President's address to the American Finance Association to introduce what amounted to a new—or at least significantly modified—theory of capital structure. Called "The Capital Structure Puzzle," Stew's speech fleshed out a *pecking order theory* of corporate financing that, for most finance scholars, represents the only serious challenge to the trade-off model that Stew and Alex proposed almost two decades earlier.

The core insight, and main prediction, of the theory is that debt issuance is likely to be considerably less expensive than equity when corporate managers have inside information about the value of both their companies' growth options and their assets in place. Recognizing their own information disadvantage, investors respond through their willingness to pay "up"—or at least par value—for safe securities while reducing the value of companies that announce new public equity offerings. And to the extent that companies that issue equity are undervalued as a consequence, there is a transfer of wealth from the old shareholders to the new. The upshot is that companies seeking funding for their (positive-NPV) investments turn first to internal financing—cash on hand. Then, if they need outside capital, they issue debt until their debt capacity is exhausted. Equity finance is used as little as possible, and only as a last resort.

One clear piece of evidence in support of the pecking order theory is the scarcity of seasoned equity offerings by large, mature public companies. But there is another relatively straightforward way of seeing—and testing—the pecking order at work: focusing on the extent to which changes in corporate capital structures simply mirror the changes over time in their operating profitability and cumulative requirements for external finance. For example, when looking at companies within the same industry, studies show a clear tendency for less profitable companies to have higher debt ratios. And the main reason more profitable companies have lower debt ratios is pretty straightforward: their larger retained earnings give them less need for external financing to fund their investment opportunities.

One limitation of the pecking-order theory is that it deliberately, in the interest of simplicity of exposition, ignores the effects of taxes and costs of financial distress, the main elements of the trade-off theory. But as Stew wrote over 30 years later (in 2015) when explaining these omissions,

> I agree that these elements can be important, but I left them out in the pecking order derivation in order to present a simple theory that is easily testable. I wanted to present a simple competitor to complex trade-off theories. [As I said in my 1984 speech,] "People [felt] comfortable with the static trade-off story because it sounds plausible and . . . rationalizes 'moderate' debt ratios. Well, the story may be moderate and plausible, but that does not make it right."

And as he went on to say, "I doubted whether the theory had really been tested." According to Stew, a simple, testable version of the trade-off theory would predict that mature companies—those with relatively few valuable growth options—would stay close to their target debt ratios, which implies prompt adjustment of actual debt ratios toward targets. The theory would also try to identity, and be as specific as possible, about the business characteristics that determine the targets.

Today, we have what Stew refers to as a "relaxed version" of the trade-off theory, one that incorporates the transactions and information costs of issuing securities, and other costs of adjusting capital structure as well as risk-averse managers, to explain low debt ratios. This relaxed version says that companies are willing to stray far from their leverage targets, if indeed they have them at all. But Stew's biggest quarrel with the trade-off theory is its failure to make predictions that are specific enough to be rejected by data. In Stew's words,

> It is a coat rack for researchers, who can hang up whatever empirical results they can find and rationalize. No one seems concerned if the coats on the rack clash. This coat rack version of the trade-off theory was clearly emerging in 1984. There was no point adding information asymmetry to the coat rack and giving the relaxed trade-off theory one more dimension of flexibility.

And as he sums up his dissatisfaction with the current state of the theory, "The capital structure puzzle arises when we try to find a compact theory to explain the regularities and predict new ones."

So, in Stew's eyes, the capital structure puzzle is still very much with us. But as we try to persuade you in our next chapter, some recent work on corporate stock offerings by the University of Rochester's Cliff Smith appears to have worked information costs and the pecking order onto the trade-off "coat rack" in a way we think sheds an instructive light on actual corporate decision-making.

THE REMARKABLE RUN OF BREALEY AND MYERS

Among his many accomplishments, Stew became a co-author, with London Business School's Richard Brealey, of the all-time bestselling corporate finance textbook, *Principles of Corporate Finance*, first published in 1981 by McGraw-Hill, and whose 15th edition is set to come out in 2024.

Stew and Dick met in the early 1960s when Dick was working as a quant for Keystone in Boston and regularly attending MIT finance seminars. Dick later joined and helped develop the fledgling London Business School, where Stew spent six months in 1975. By that time, Dick had completed several chapters of a corporate finance text. When he asked Stew to join his project, they embarked on what surely must be one of the longest and most productive collaborations in publishing history. And as Stew has described the collaboration,

(*continued on next page*)

(*continued from previous page*)

The drill never changes: We agree that Dick will work on chapters x and y and I will work on i and j. Dick is back with nice drafts of x and y before I have organized my thoughts for i and j. I have spent 35 years playing the tortoise to Dick's hare.

Dick and Stew's book is premised on the idea that "good theory makes common sense and simplifies practice," and that the field of modern corporate finance has much to offer practitioners. As Stew has summed up "modern finance theory," it encompasses the following:

the objective of maximizing market value, portfolio theory, the CAPM, the efficient-market hypothesis, and the principles of option pricing. [It also includes] MM's leverage and dividend-policy proofs as starting points for capital structure and payout policy. At a more applied level, it includes DCF and APV valuation methods and the use of WACC as a discount rate.

Sensing the tendency of popular finance texts to "shy away from the theory" for fear of making finance "more difficult and less practical," Dick and Stew saw the opportunity to provide "the first corporate-finance text to apply modern finance theory in a consistent and practical way."

Brealey and Myers's *Principles* is routinely and justly praised by its legions of undergraduate as well as graduate readers as "clear," "engaging," and even "entertaining." Stew himself modestly acknowledges that "the blend of Dick's and my writing styles . . . has hybrid vigor." And as he notes with some amusement,

The first reviews of the manuscript were mixed. One reviewer offered faint praise for several chapters but went out of the way to warn that American professors and students would be put off by Dick's "English humor." All the jokes cited by the reviewer were mine.

As in many if not most marriages, ascertaining the individual contributions of partners in a publishing collaboration is a tricky business. But in this merger of the energy and talents of two of the world's most dedicated and accomplished finance scholars, the value of the whole has turned out to be vastly greater than the sum of the parts.

EPILOGUE: THE IDEA OF RISK CAPITAL—AND THE GLOBAL FINANCIAL CRISIS

Much of Stew's work from the start focused on the corporate capital structure choice—on how a company's capital should be divided between debt and equity, and whether there is a value-maximizing corporate leverage ratio. Later in his career, Stew turned to a somewhat different question: What is the value-maximizing *amount* of capital. Investor capital, after all, is not free, and sometimes not even accessible. And companies that operate with too little, or too much, are effectively reducing their own value.

In an article published in the *Journal of Financial Economics* in 2015, Myers and Jamie Read, a partner at a consulting firm called The Brattle Group, teamed up with Isil Erel, an Ohio State risk-management specialist, in fleshing out a theory of *risk capital* that Stew and Jamie had outlined almost 20 years earlier. Broadly speaking, risk capital is the amount of cash or equity investment needed to ensure a management team's ability to meet its obligations to all its liability holders, including creditors, customers, and contract counterparties, under most foreseeable future conditions, while also preserving its normal incentives to invest in all positive-NPV opportunities.

Stew and Jamie first defined, and demonstrated how to estimate, this amount of risk capital for an entire company, and then they provided a method for allocating the costs of such capital to a company's different business lines. Although designed with banks and other financial firms in mind, the approach and methods were seen as potentially useful for estimating the amounts of risk capital for industrial companies as well.

Stew and Jamie's work in this area had begun with the insurance industry—a logical choice since insurance, like banking, is a business in which both the amounts and kinds of capital maintained are important enough to both the companies' solvency and profitability that they are actually set and monitored by state or federal regulators. In 2001, Stew and Jamie won the annual best-paper award from the *Journal of Risk and Insurance* for their paper addressing the insurance industry's challenge of allocating capital (the industry term is "surplus") to their different lines of business, such as life and property and casualty.

But it's important to start by recognizing that insurance companies then as now do not finance their different lines of business separately; if and when they default on one line, they default on them all. And in deciding how much capital or surplus is required to support all the lines under one roof, the aim of the company's capital allocations, and overall risk management program, is to reduce the probability (and associated costs) of financial distress to an acceptably low level. The company's financial planners therefore need to understand which lines of business impose the most risk on the firm and hence soak up the most surplus, and which lines consume relatively little.

To solve this problem, Stew and Jamie came up with the concept of *marginal default values*, which are calculated using option-pricing methods. To get a sense how this concept gets applied, consider a company holding a portfolio of different business lines, some volatile and others safe, and some whose profits are more highly correlated than others with the profits of the entire firm. Marginal default values are measures of the contributions of each business line to the firm's probability of default. And such measures can be used to develop a capital allocation scheme that ensures that the entire firm and each of its business units has sufficient capital support and protection.[18] The resulting capital allocations are also designed to help ensure that their managers make the right investment decisions.

The Case of the Global Financial Crisis. To see why this kind of approach to capital planning could be important, consider the run-up to the Global Financial Crisis in 2008. There may well be no better example of how capital requirements that are clearly too low can stimulate investment that ends up undermining both private companies and society at large. With federal relaxation of mortgage underwriting standards—mortgages that once required 20 percent down payments could suddenly be had for 3 percent down or less—along with low bank capital requirements and the full blessing of the U.S. Federal Reserve Bank, the world's largest banks almost without exception gave in to the temptation to originate or take massive positions in subprime or other kinds of nontraditional U.S.-originated mortgages. And we know how that ended.

But just as banks holding too little capital were clearly prone to the excessive risk-taking at the core of the crisis, banks forced to hold too much capital could limit economic growth by precipitating a credit crunch—a charge that was ultimately leveled against banks *after* the GFC by many of the same politicians who had condemned their excessive risk-taking! Clearly, we need good answers to two questions: what are the costs and benefits to value-maximizing entities from raising—and operating with—more versus less capital? And along with those private costs and benefits, what are their *social* benefits and costs (to taxpayers and potential borrowers as opposed to the banks themselves)? In developing the concepts of marginal default values and risk capital, Stew and Jamie may well have provided a new and better way of addressing a question of critical social as well as private import: how much capital should commercial enterprises have to protect, support, and maximize the value of their activities?

* * *

As Stew and Jamie's work also made clear, ensuring that companies have large enough "cushions" of equity or residual capital to absorb losses and ensure continuity during downturns is important for capital planners and risk managers. And figuring out the optimal, or value-maximizing, amounts and kinds of capital—whether debt, equity, or some hybrid thereof—is likely to play an important role in providing "signals" to and incentives for business managers about which investments to expand and which to cut back on.

In this sense, Stew's work can be seen as ending where it began. Perhaps the most important goal in designing a company's financial and capital structure, as virtually all of his work during the past nearly 60 years has tried to show, is to ensure that corporate managers are making the best *investment* and *operating* decisions. Which brings us back full circle to the first principle of modern corporate finance. For, as we saw earlier when discussing M&M, a company's investment decisions are the primary source of long-run corporate efficiency and value. And to restate the main proposition of this book, it is that efficiency and value that in turn that are the fundamental sources of the wealth of nations and provide the most reliable basis for social prosperity.

CHAPTER 6

CLIFFORD SMITH, RENÉ STULZ, AND THE THEORY AND PRACTICE OF *CORPORATE* RISK MANAGEMENT

A**t the end of the last chapter, we saw Stewart Myers expressing his dissatisfaction with collective academic efforts to clear up "The Capital Structure Puzzle" that he had laid out in 1984. It is this unsettled state of affairs—which Stew likened to an overburdened "coat rack"— that Clifford Smith of the University of Rochester's Simon Business School, and his former Rochester Ph.D. student Fangjian Fu, have been trying to tidy up in their decade-long research project on seasoned equity offerings (or SEOs) by U.S. public companies.

There is perhaps no one better qualified to undertake this research than Cliff Smith. Now officially retired, he has received 37 Superior Teacher awards during a Simon School tenure that has spanned nearly 50 years. Both his deep-register Georgia drawl and ingenuity in extending the length of the spoken sentence are matters of local legend. This chapter will give readers a sense of both the scope and practical relevance of Cliff's research and writings, on subjects ranging from capital structure and SEOs to the often-overlooked case for rights offerings, before moving on to the main focus of this chapter: *corporate* risk management. Along the way, and after bringing into the picture Smith's erstwhile Rochester colleague René Stulz (long since moved on to his current home, Ohio State), we touch on organizational design and even, at the very end, questions of business ethics and corporate culture.

WHAT SEOs COULD BE TELLING US ABOUT OPTIMAL CAPITAL STRUCTURE

The conventional wisdom about SEOs, mostly consistent with Stew Myers's pecking order story described in the previous chapter, is that companies will do almost anything to avoid issuing new stock. Why? Because the resulting increase in the number of shares outstanding will "dilute" (that is, reduce) their reported earnings per share and cause their stock prices to fall, even upon the merest hint that such an offering is being contemplated by management.

As we saw in the last chapter, stock prices do indeed fall—by 2–3 percent on average—upon SEO announcements, as Stew predicted they would. But the question is, *why* do they fall? Stew's explanation, as we saw, focuses on the information disadvantage of outside investors vis-à-vis managers or other insiders about matters likely to affect the value of the firm. This information disadvantage is said to cause outside investors to reduce, more or less reflexively, their assessments of the issuing company's value in response to announcements of new stock offerings, and for two main reasons:

- The plan to raise *any* capital—debt or equity—increases the possibility, and investors' suspicions, that the company is seeking new capital mainly just to make up for an unexpected shortfall in earnings or cash flows, and *not* to fund necessary or promising investment.
- Investors view managements as seeking to raise equity *opportunistically*— that is, when they think the company's shares are overvalued—and to avoid issuing new shares when the company is *under*valued, since this would effectively transfer value from the old shareholders to any new shareholders who take up the offering.

And investors' concerns about companies' incentives to issue overvalued shares appear to be justified. Past studies of U.S. public companies issuing new shares have shown that such companies' shareholders, after experiencing the typical 2–3 percent losses upon announcement, end up with longer-run (two- or three-year) risk-adjusted share returns that are roughly equal to those of the broad market. Viewed in this light, the SEO market has turned out to be a *fair game* in the following sense: Investors recognize, and are effectively compensated for, their informational disadvantage by marking down the value of the shares in response to the announcements—and then eventually end up earning a fair return on that marked-down value.

So far, so good. But shouldn't it matter to the market what the SEO issuers plan to *do* with the equity capital they are raising? If you're the manager of one of those fortunate growth companies with extraordinarily abundant and promising uses of capital, does it make sense for your company to be penalized in an "equilibrium" in which, just by announcing a new equity offering, your market cap is almost certain to be given the standard 2–3 percent haircut? Should this enforced 2–3 percent discount be viewed as simply another cost of doing business, or are there deeper questions of valuation and corporate financing involved? More fundamentally, with so many factors working against SEOs, how do we explain their sheer number—over 7,000 by U.S. industrial issuers, and another 1,500 by regulated utilities, between 1970 and 2017?

These are the kinds of questions that Cliff and Fangjian (and we'll call them "C & F" to save space) set out to answer.

THE SURPRISING PREPONDERANCE OF GROWTH SEOs

First of all, in what appears to contradict the original version of Stew's trade-off theory of corporate capital structure, C & F find that the vast majority, or roughly 80 percent, of the industrial issuers were already *under*leveraged at the time of their SEOs (based on a comparison of their capital structures with those of otherwise similar companies not doing SEOs). By raising amounts of equity that averaged roughly 20 percent of their existing market cap, corporate issuers have accordingly moved *away from*, not toward, their target leverage ratios. And at odds with Stew's pecking order story, in which equity offerings are supposed to be a desperate last resort, most SEO issuers have turned out to be financially robust companies with considerable unused debt capacity.

Having revealed some limitations of the original versions of both the trade-off and pecking order explanations, C & F go on to cast doubt on a relative newcomer known as the "market-timing" theory, which views the issuance of *over*valued shares as the dominant motive for SEOs. Consistent with the claims of market-timing proponents, C & F find significant stock price run-ups—on the order of 25–30 percent, on average—during the six to 12 months leading up to the SEOs. But they also report that most SEOs appear to be driven *primarily* by the sharp increases in capital spending that take place soon after—much of them *in the same quarter* as—the SEOs themselves.

In other words, for the vast majority of industrial SEOs, new equity is being raised to fund large investment projects and growth opportunities whose expected value is presumably reflected in the large stock price run-ups. In this version of the SEO story, favorable market conditions and possibly overvalued stock prices are at most secondary considerations, not the dominant motive.

A BRIEF LOOK AT THE IMPORTANT DIFFERENCES BETWEEN VALUE AND GROWTH SEOs

To what extent can these observations be explained by intrinsic differences among SEO issuers? For example, what about value versus growth issuers?

Using Stew Myers's distinction between assets in place and growth options in the last chapter, C & F distinguish value from growth SEO issuers by their low market-to-book valuations, with their implied limited growth prospects. In contrast to the 5,689 growth SEO issuers (in their total sample of 7,122 industrial (non-utility) issuers), which have an average market-to-book ratio of 2.32 one year before the transaction, the 1,433 value issuers have an average market-to-book ratio of just 1.01. And whereas the typical growth issuer is significantly *under*leveraged, and becomes progressively more so in the run-up to (and in part thanks to) its SEO, the typical value issuer is significantly *over*leveraged before its SEO.

So, where the primary motive for SEOs by growth issuers appears to be to ensure funding for large capital expenditures and strategic investment, an important—if not indeed the main—motive for value issuers appears to be *rebalancing* the capital structure, presumably to enable the company to fund both future investment as well as normal operations. In support of this conjecture, C & F report finding that while growth SEO issuers are underleveraged three years before the SEO, the typical value issuer begins in an overleveraged position, uses the new equity to move toward (if not past) its leverage target, and *never returns* to that initially overleveraged level during the five years following the SEO. At the same time, and also furnishing support for what might be described as a "longer-run" version of the trade-off theory, C & F find that the growth SEO issuers that predominate in their sample tend to follow their stock offerings with one or more debt offerings that *raise* their leverage back toward their targets.

TOWARD A UNIFYING, MULTI-PERIOD TRADE-OFF THEORY

Which brings us to the main thrust of C & F's argument: in contrast to today's leading theories of capital structure, which are all "single-period models" that suggest some degree of shortsightedness and opportunism by corporate managers, C & F's findings present a picture of *longer-range* value-maximizing *strategic* financial management—a story in which corporate capital planning and financing decisions take account of the company's leverage in relation to its *longer-run* target, investment opportunities, and capital requirements. In such a process, CFOs consider the costs and benefits associated with not just *single transactions* viewed in isolation, but entire *sequences* of transactions in which companies continuously return to and seek capital from more or less the same community of investors. Such capital-raisings are what economists like to identify as *repeat transactions* between reasonably well-informed and consenting parties, with all the same implied commitments and reciprocity. In this story, the kind of opportunism implied by the market timing theory is not likely to work out well in the longer run for those companies that practice it, nor will it continue to be tolerated by investors who find themselves again and again on the short end of the deal.

Viewed in this light, the outline of Stew Myers's original trade-off model might be seen as coming back into favor, perhaps ready for a dusting off. But whatever the relative merits of the different versions of the model, the basic economic function of capital structure and financial planning should be seen as much the same for Stew Myers and Cliff Smith. In their thinking and work, the corporate financing decision is shown as adding value not as a profit center unto itself—in the way that, say. trading operations often function within energy and finance companies. Corporate finance is instead seen as contributing value through its effectiveness in complementing and helping carry out the corporate investment decision and business strategy. Much like Stew's general view of equity financing, C & F view growth SEOs as first and foremost a means of ensuring corporate readiness to fund—*when the opportunities materialize*—the investments that drive much of today's corporate long-run corporate efficiency and value.

THE ORIGINS OF MODERN CORPORATE RISK MANAGEMENT

Most of Cliff Smith's first years at Rochester were spent coming to grips—as Stew Myers did before him—with the import of the M&M propositions while keeping up with the latest twists in the thinking, and growing pile of empirical studies, on corporate investment and financial policy. But a series of late afternoon meetings in the mid-'70s with another finance professor, David Mayers, then visiting Rochester from UCLA, rekindled Cliff's longstanding interest in insurance. That interest had first been instilled in him by his father, who was the president of the largest bank in Cliff's hometown of Greensboro, Georgia, where he was also the owner of the town's best-known insurance agency.

The aim of Dave Mayers's work at the time was to find some way of working individuals' "human capital" considerations into a broader portfolio context, like the framework provided by the Capital Asset Pricing Model. Given Cliff's exposure to the insurance industry, the discussion turned naturally to the standard uses of insurance contracts—those involving the shifting of financial risks from individuals with limited wealth and information about such risks to insurance companies with the actuarial knowledge, operating expertise, and financial resources to bear the risks. But the focus of those discussions gradually shifted toward the uses of insurance by *large public companies*, and how and why they were likely to be different from their typical uses by individual homeowners and investors.

THE CORPORATE DEMAND FOR INSURANCE

What came out of these deliberations was a paper published by Dave and Cliff in 1982 in the University of Chicago's prestigious *Journal of Business* called "On the Corporate Demand for Insurance"—a paper that might be viewed as laying the foundation for the modern theory of corporate risk management. The theory begins by recognizing how the public corporate form functions as a powerful risk management tool in and of itself. By selling shares of stock—that is, equity claims on their future operating cash flows—into the marketplace, public companies allow their securities to be priced by individual investors who tend to hold well-diversified portfolios of stocks and bonds. And as we have seen in previous chapters, the stockholders of public companies effectively replicate—and so make redundant—diversification of the "corporate portfolio" of businesses.

Thanks to this diversification by investors, the public corporate form itself is seen as managing a variety of *insurable* corporate risks—the subset of what finance academics call "diversifiable" risks that includes everything from property and casualty losses to product liability suits and toxic torts. And in this sense, corporate deliberations over whether to purchase insurance are fundamentally different from the decisions by the likes of you and me to buy homeowners' and life insurance.

MORE ON THE IMPORTANT DIFFERENCE BETWEEN INDIVIDUAL AND CORPORATE INSURANCE

As Dave and Cliff start by noting in their paper, the basic function of insurance for individuals is to allow them to reduce uncertainty about their own net worth and standard of living by transferring financial risks to insurance companies better able to bear them. In return for accepting the risk of losses, insurers charge a premium that contains, along with a charge for its operating costs and expected losses on the policy (determined by actuarial tables and calculations), a so-called premium "loading" that includes the profit for the insurer.

The insurance company's comparative advantage over the policyholder in bearing the risks in question comes from three features of insurers: (1) their ability to limit their risks by pooling large portfolios of similar risks; (2) their risk monitoring and claims-processing expertise; and (3) their greater access to capital markets. Given most individuals' limited ability to cover their own potential losses, they tend to be quite willing—and in the case of homeowners' insurance, their mortgage lender typically requires them—to pay premiums year after year to protect against the possibility of losses that most of them will never experience (with the notable exception, of course, of the risk insured by life insurance).

As Dave and Cliff point out, corporations that are private or closely held purchase insurance for much the same reasons as individuals—that is, their limited ability to bear certain risks relative to the risk-bearing capacity of insurance companies. The owners of such companies, whether out of a desire to maintain control or some other motive, tend to have much of their wealth tied up in the firm. Both logic and experience tell us that these owners will self-insure—that is, choose to bear their own risk of losses—only for those risks where they have specialized expertise and hence a kind of comparative advantage.

In the case of large, widely held public corporations, however, there are some important differences that standard insurance textbooks have only recently begun to acknowledge. The conventional wisdom when Dave and Cliff were writing their paper was that because the "owners" of public corporations—their stockholders and, if things go far enough south, their bondholders—are themselves risk-averse individuals, corporate managers should attempt to minimize *their investors'* exposure to large, insurable risks. But this explanation, as already suggested, fails to recognize the incentives and tendencies of corporate stockholders and bondholders to diversify their own holdings—and that, by so doing, the investors themselves effectively limit the effects of most corporate risks that could be managed by buying insurance.

Corporate Insurance and the Cost of Capital. As we saw in the last two chapters, the stock market effectively assesses companies a risk premium of sorts when setting their cost of capital. The greater a company's perceived risk, the higher its cost of capital or the rate of return it must earn on average and over time to satisfy its shareholders. But the critical insight underlying Dave and Cliff's analysis—and Stew Myers's critique of corporate diversification as well—is that because a company's cost of capital depends on its so-called systematic or "non-diversifiable" risk, as reflected in the tendency of its stock price to move together with the broad market, the capital markets do not "reward" companies for insurance purchases by reducing their cost of capital. Why? As we saw earlier, most insurable risks are effectively "diversified away" by market investors when making their portfolio decisions.

In other words, the stock market does not reward the expected earnings streams of companies that choose to insure their diversifiable risks with a higher P/E multiple for so doing. As a result, corporate insurance purchases—at least when viewed as vehicles for transferring risk—are viewed as largely redundant and a waste of investor capital.

But how, then, do we explain those corporate insurance purchases that appear to have long been standard practice for generations of large public companies—short of perpetuation of the status quo as well as the ingenuity of insurance company salespeople in peddling their products to unsuspecting corporates?

A big part of the answer has to do with insurers' expertise, and their resulting comparative advantage, in helping companies evaluate and monitor their ongoing risks and processing their claims efficiently when losses materialize.

RETHINKING CORPORATE INSURANCE STRATEGY: THE CASE OF BRITISH PETROLEUM

In the early 1990s, and thus roughly a decade after the publication of Mayers and Smith's paper in the *Journal of Business*, British Petroleum, then the largest public company in the UK, made a major policy change that turned the conventional insurance industry wisdom on its head. Until the BP decision, the traditional practice of large public companies was to buy insurance against large potential losses (those ranging from $10 million to the then rarely exceeded maximum obtainable coverage of $500 million) from things like product liability suits and property and casualty losses, while mostly self-insuring against smaller losses. The logic behind this strategy was as follows: For corporations of any size, the small losses associated with events such as localized fires, employee injuries, and vehicle crashes occur with such regularity that their total cost and aggregate losses are fairly predictable. Insuring against such losses amounts simply to "trading dollars"—exchanging *known* dollars of premium for roughly equivalent and relatively certain losses, with no actual risk transfer. Larger losses, by contrast, are rare and much less predictable. And because such losses are borne by the company's owners—first and foremost by the stockholders but also, if the losses are large enough, by its bondholders—the conventional wisdom and practice, reinforced by the reigning risk and insurance literature of the day, was that such exposures should be and were managed with corporate purchases of insurance.

In the early 1990s, however, BP's top management came to a very different— indeed the opposite—conclusion. After undertaking a comprehensive review (with the help of Cliff and Neil Doherty at the Wharton School) of all its major risks and risk management solutions, BP instituted a new policy of insuring against most smaller losses while self-insuring the company's *largest* exposures.

The company's decision to abandon its longstanding policy of insuring only its largest exposures came down to factors affecting the market *supply* as well as the corporate *demand* for insurance. On the demand side, and drawing on Cliff and Dave's analysis, BP's management concluded that the primary source of demand for insurance by large public companies like their own—namely, to transfer risk—stemmed from the common fallacy of confusing large corporate with much more limited individual risk-bearing capacity. The massive capital backing supplied by the company's already well-diversified stockholders and bondholders suggested that BP's effective cost of capital—and hence its P/E ratio—was largely unaffected by insurance purchases.

At the same time, however, BP's management concluded that allowing its operating managers to insure smaller losses (less than $10 million) on a decentralized basis was justified by insurers' comparative advantage in providing risk assessment, risk-monitoring, and other mitigation measures, and loss-settlement and claims-processing services—services that were expected to save BP money. Some of the smaller policies even took the form of "claims only" contracts, which meant that there was *no* effective transfer of risk; in such cases, BP chose to bear 100 percent of its insurable losses while benefiting from its insurers' other efficiencies. By contrast, BP's analysis of its larger policies showed it having shelled out $1.15 billion in total premiums over the ten-year period ending in 1989, in exchange for loss settlements that amounted to just $250 million—suggesting that the insurers' premium loadings were far exceeding the amount of risk transfer.

But the real eye-opener in this comprehensive risk analysis came on the supply side, where BP's management ultimately recognized that the capacity of insurance (and reinsurance) companies and markets to underwrite very large or highly specialized exposures was actually quite limited. And that risk-bearing capacity was likely to remain limited, especially when *compared to the industry expertise and financial resources of companies like BP.* As noted, the largest insurable loss in those days was generally about $500 million. Given BP's size and potential exposure, any expected losses large enough to be of concern would exceed the capacity of the insurance industry. And thanks to the widespread practice in the insurance industry of charging "experience-rated" premiums—which amounts to rolling prior-years' losses into the following years' premiums—BP concluded that there was very little effective transfer of risk going on. The company was simply "forward-funding" its expected losses, and hence there was no expected gain to BP from insuring its largest losses.

* * *

Now as things turned out, BP would end up facing massive litigation and multi-billion dollar losses for its culpability in the Gulf of Mexico oil spill in 2010. But as any decision scientist worth her salt will tell you, the soundness of longer-range financial decision-making can and should be assessed only on an *ex ante*, or expected value, basis. Even reasonable decisions—and this is one of the trickiest parts of risk management—often fail to "pay off."

As for the Gulf of Mexico disaster, even if BP had been able to insure a significant fraction of the losses it ended up incurring, the company would almost certainly have found itself on the hook for "experience-rated" losses. Why? Again, BP had a significant comparative advantage, both in its information and specialized industry expertise—and even in its access to capital—over Lloyds or publicly traded insurers that could have stepped up to insure it.

In sum, the basic conclusion of BP's analysis was a simple one: this large public company was seen as having a comparative advantage, both in terms of industry expertise and access to capital—relative to the *entire insurance* industry—in bearing its own largest losses. Hence its decision to self-insure.

And as we will see when extending this analysis to the corporate uses of derivatives in managing *financial price* risks, this principle of comparative advantage will be found at the core of the theory and practice of corporate risk management. The general rule is that for companies with significant exposures, there are usually significant gains from transferring those risks to investors or other companies with a comparative advantage in bearing them—but not otherwise.

OTHER REASONS TO INSURE (OR MANAGE) LARGE RISKS

Another potentially important outcome of BP's comprehensive risk review was a resolution to consider hedging a significant portion, as much as a third, of BP's oil price exposure. Oil price fluctuations accounted for much of the volatility in BP's earnings and cash flows, which was said to be of concern to at least some of its equity investors. Hedging this exposure could be accomplished using a variety of derivatives such as oil futures and swaps.

But if shareholders effectively manage price risks on their own, why might BP's management consider efforts to limit such volatility—and why did it end up choosing not to?

Let's take the second question first. There is one matter about which large oil company executives never express the slightest doubt or hesitation: oil companies' shareholders buy the shares mainly to make bets on oil prices! To which economists invariably reply: "Well, if you want to bet on oil prices, wouldn't it be more efficient just to buy oil futures or options? Why mess around with oil company shares if your only interest is the price of the commodity?"

In response to the first of the two questions, Dave and Cliff devoted most of their *Journal of Business* paper to exploring several other possible corporate motives for insurance purchases—motives that *do not involve transferring risk from shareholders and other investors*. In addition to the insurers' efficiencies in monitoring risks and processing claims we noted earlier, Dave and Cliff also pointed to possible, though not particularly large, reductions in BP's expected corporate income taxes from the "smoothing" of earnings accomplished by most hedging strategies.[1]

But more compelling than possible tax savings are the potential benefits of limiting the risk exposures of a company's other, non-investor stakeholders. Corporate managers, employees, and suppliers all tend to be at a significant disadvantage in risk-bearing relative to diversified investors. And these groups are thus likely to require extra compensation to bear any risk not assumed by the owners or transferred to an insurance company.

Employees, for example, will demand higher wages or reduce their loyalty or work effort at companies where the probability of layoffs is significantly higher because of unmanaged financial exposures. Managers with alternative opportunities are likely to demand higher salaries, or maybe significant equity stakes, to run companies where the risks of insolvency or financial embarrassment are significant. And suppliers will be more reluctant to enter into long-term contracts—and trade creditors will charge more and be less flexible—with companies whose prospects are more uncertain.

Such stakeholder risk exposures are likely to be a major concern, as Dave and Cliff pointed out, for companies in service industries, many of which are thinly capitalized. Because the claims—and hence the risks—of managers and employees are likely to be disproportionately large in such cases compared to the risks of investors, there could be major benefits from transferring risk to an insurance company.

But such thinking, again, does *not* apply to large, well-capitalized companies like BP. Nevertheless, there was another major area that insurance, and possibly other kinds of corporate risk management, could help with—one aimed at strengthening, and reassuring outsiders about, BP's management's commitment to invest in the company's future. And this is where the corporate underinvestment problem (described by Stew Myers in the previous chapter) again comes into play.

INSURANCE (AND RISK MANAGEMENT GENERALLY) AS PROTECTION AGAINST THE CORPORATE UNDERINVESTMENT PROBLEM

As Dave and Cliff pointed out, well-diversified shareholders and bondholders are unlikely to be troubled by uninsured losses *per se*—although they will become concerned if such losses raise doubt about the company's solvency. But why is insolvency so unsettling? After all, even in workouts and bankruptcies, the claims eventually get reorganized, and most companies of any size emerge and continue as going concerns.

A big part of the answer is the potential for the mere prospect of financial trouble to cause significant reductions in companies' expected long-run operating cash flows and enterprise values. In the extreme case, companies that actually wind up in chapter 11 face considerable interference from the bankruptcy court with their investment and operating decisions, not to mention the direct costs of administration and reorganization. But even for companies well short of bankruptcy, financial difficulty can impose significant indirect costs, especially for companies with large growth opportunities that could require funding.

For cash cow-type or "value" companies with limited growth opportunities, a stay in chapter 11 may cause little or no reduction in their operating or franchise value. In fact, a reorganization may even *increase* that value just by forcing a change in owners. Merton Miller liked to point out that every one of the grand hotels on Chicago's Michigan Avenue had, at some point in its existence, gone through chapter 11 or the equivalent—without disturbing either the elegance of their façades or the sturdiness of the brickwork behind them.

But for companies with growth opportunities, the story is very different. For them, the most important source of such costs is the potential underinvestment problem stemming from the possible conflicts of interest between shareholders and bondholders, and the financing impasse that results from "debt overhang." As we saw earlier, the major challenge in such cases is raising new capital in ways that both shareholders and bondholders find acceptable.

To see how insurance could help manage this "debt overhang" problem, Dave and Cliff use the simple example of a company with a large amount of debt outstanding that chooses *not* to buy fire insurance for its plants. When its most valuable profitable plant is destroyed by fire, the company is then faced with a possibly difficult reinvestment decision: if and when to rebuild the plant. In these circumstances, the large casualty loss cuts further into the company's already deflated equity cushion, effectively ruling out new funding from capital markets.

If the company's debt burden is heavy enough, a management acting on its owners' or shareholders' behalf might have an incentive to pass up even a clearly positive-NPV investment like *rebuilding its most profitable plant*. As Stew Myers showed in his 1977 paper, this would be a *rational* decision—not just the result of managerial shortsightedness—if enough of the value from rebuilding the plant went to shoring up the bondholders' position and making them whole, resulting in a large wealth transfer from stockholders to bondholders. Even long-run value-maximizing managers would thus choose either not to rebuild or to defer rebuilding, thereby sacrificing overall long-run firm value to avoid ceding to creditors the lion's share of the value added by the new investment.

Dave and Cliff then go back and assume that management chooses instead to buy fire insurance on the plant. After pointing out that debt covenants typically *require* companies to purchase such insurance, they show how the loss settlement ends up proving especially valuable as a "leverage-neutral" source of financing that allows the company to avoid the costs of a hurried and underpriced new issue. The insurance settlement in such cases also helps ensure that management won't have to face the dilemma over whether to reinvest, thus serving in part to control the underinvestment problem.

＊　＊　＊

To sum up, then, the fundamental insight emerging from Dave Mayers and Cliff Smith's delvings into corporate insurance is that neither insurance purchases nor most of the other vast array of activities that go under the rubric of corporate risk management are likely to add value *simply by transferring risk* from the company's shareholders to other companies or investors. The corporate form of organization itself has had, and can be expected to continue to have, a highly beneficial effect on the value of individual companies and the allocation of risk across our economy. In short, the public corporate form has proven to be a remarkably efficient way of spreading the risks associated with funding corporate growth.

THE EMERGENCE OF "DERIVATIVES" AND THEIR USES IN CORPORATE RISK MANAGEMENT

Having discussed Dave and Cliff's foray into corporate insurance, we now backtrack to another of Cliff's major interests: stock options and other financial "derivatives." Derivatives get their name from the fact that the primary source and determinant of their value *derive from* another asset, which finance professionals refer to as "the underlying asset," or just "the underlying." The underlying can be a stock price, or it can take the form of any number of financial measures, including exchange rates, commodity prices, and the interest rates (or yields) on all kinds of corporate and government debt securities.

Cliff became interested in identifying the *proper* uses of derivatives as elements of a long-run, value-adding corporate risk management strategy. But as had already become clear, this was quite different from the ways many corporate managements were (and still are) tempted to use derivatives—namely, as high-probability, but nonetheless speculative, bets to pad their operating profits. (And as we'll also see, this was a temptation that even the largest U.S. bank, JP Morgan Chase, whose CEO Jamie Dimon has long been viewed as among Wall Street's savviest risk managers, proved unable to resist.)

When asked to identify the main impetus spurring him to explore the newfangled world of derivatives, Cliff points to a pair of phone calls from J. Richard Zecher, a macroeconomist with a Ph.D. from Ohio State. The first call came in 1976, when Dick Zecher was Chief Economist of the U.S. SEC. The burgeoning trading of stock options on the then-recently established Chicago Mercantile Exchange had come under attack by representatives of the major U.S. stock exchanges. The main charge leveled at the flourishing new options exchange was that the supercharged trading of options was somehow increasing the volatility of and otherwise distorting stock prices on the New York Stock Exchange. Zecher, in his role as defender and preserver of the integrity of the SEC, was feeling pressure from his colleagues in Washington to respond to such charges.

Zecher's first call was to well-known Swiss-born economist Karl Brunner, who directed Zecher's Ph.D. at Ohio State (and became the economic adviser to Margaret Thatcher in the early '80s). Zecher asked Brunner to recommend an academic expert—a relatively inexpensive one, given his SEC budget—on options. Brunner, who had moved to the University of Rochester in 1971, told Zecher to contact an assistant professor named Cliff Smith, then in his second year at Rochester—and that was the beginning of what proved a long relationship with numerous "repeat dealings."

In their first round of exchanges, Cliff explained to Zecher and his small staff what stock options are—rights, but not obligations, to buy the "underlying" stocks at a specified price for a specific period—and how such rights can be valued and priced, with particular attention to the Black-Scholes(-Merton) model that had recently come out of MIT. Most important for Zecher's purposes, Cliff showed the SEC staffers how the mere existence of such options, and a vibrant market for trading them, was likely to *improve* the reliability of stock prices and the workings of stock markets.

The basic insight of Cliff's analysis was that because options are in effect "leveraged" versions of the underlying asset (with the Black-Scholes model viewing options as continuously changing combinations of debt and the underlying asset), the most sophisticated and aggressive traders with valuable information about a particular stock were almost sure to view options rather than the stock market as their first choice. The "built-in" leverage of an option gives them more "bang for their buck," a higher return on investment. And the existence of active options markets also provided skeptical investors with more cost-efficient ways of betting *against* stocks.

The net result of all this was that what economists refer to as "price discovery" was more likely to occur in options markets than in stock markets. And even though this development was likely to make stock prices *appear* more volatile, investors in general—and the SEC as their guiding shepherd—should feel reassured that such prices were now likely to do a better job of reflecting corporate prospects for earnings and long-run value.

*   *   *

The second call that Cliff received from Dick Zecher came a few years later—around 1981, soon after Zecher had assumed his new role as Chief Economist of the Chase Manhattan Bank. This time the focus was not just on options or other derivatives but on how companies might use such instruments to manage their financial price risks, including the effects of swings in interest rates or currencies or commodity prices. At the time, the business of advising corporations on the effective use of swaps, futures, options, and combinations was dominated mostly by investment banks—and by two outlier commercial banks, Bankers Trust, with Chemical Bank following close behind. Zecher was intent on training Chase's bankers to get in on this action, and Cliff was once again asked to help.

After steeping himself in the arcana and lore surrounding all variety of swaps, Cliff said that he one day had a revelation of sorts: When broken down into their simplest "building blocks," the most convoluted and complex-looking interest rate and currency swaps turned out to be nothing more than a series of forward or option contracts strung together. Viewed and analyzed in this "Lego-like" fashion, complex derivatives became comprehensible, and even reasonably straightforward, in their valuation and pricing. And once they understood how derivatives were valued and priced, corporate managers could now use them to hedge financial exposures in ways designed to increase shareholder value.[2]

ENTER RENÉ STULZ AND THE INTERNATIONAL CAPM

Around the time Cliff was finishing up his consulting assignment with Chase, Fischer Black, the co-architect of the Black-Scholes option pricing model, called from MIT to ask his good friend Mike Jensen if Rochester's Simon Business School might have a faculty spot for his most promising Ph.D. student, René Stulz, who was doing ground-breaking work on international applications of the Capital Asset Pricing Model. And so René, who hails from one of the French-speaking Swiss cantons, left MIT and came to Rochester.

Working under Black's direction, René had used his thesis to explore the possibility that the steadily growing integration of international financial markets since the 1970s was increasing the values of companies in fully developed and developing economies alike, *without having any direct effects on their expected earnings or cash flows*. René's work suggested that, for companies large and visible enough to attract global investors, having an international shareholder base would translate into higher stock prices by *reducing investors' required rates of return and the companies' cost of capital*. As we saw earlier, a lower cost of capital is tantamount to investors' collectively assigning a higher P/E multiple to the same expected cash flow stream, as if they now perceived the company's earnings prospects to be less risky.

René attributed a significant part of this increase in value to an *international portfolio effect*. Thanks to the ongoing globalization of stock holdings, the risks of stock ownership were effectively being shared among more investors with different portfolio exposures and risk appetites. Japanese investors, for example, appeared willing to pay more than U.S. investors for the shares of IBM if only because a position in IBM helped them diversify their portfolios away from what turned out (by the end of the 1980s) to be a wildly overvalued Nikkei 225. And this diversification by Japanese and other overseas investors was viewed as reducing the equity risk premium for *all* U.S. companies large or promising enough to attract a global following. Similarly, investments by U.S. and other investors in the largest, best-known Japanese companies were seen as raising *their* values.

Consistent with Stulz's proposition, and in what proved to be a fascinating "natural" experiment, when the Swiss multinational Nestlé decided to allow U.S. and other foreign investors to buy the company's "registered shares" (which until then had been reserved for Swiss citizens only)—instead of limiting foreign ownership to the "bearer shares" that all investors had long been allowed to buy—the value of the registered shares nearly doubled overnight! And since the accompanying drop in the aggregate value of the bearer shares was much smaller than the total gain in the value of the registered shares, the net effect on Nestlé's total market cap was a significant *increase*—on the order of 10 percent, implying a reduction of Nestlé's cost of equity that René estimated to be roughly 300 basis points!

Along with these benefits of international portfolio diversification, the integration of global capital markets was also seen as increasing the value of companies operating in less developed economies with weaker governance systems and assurances for minority stockholders. When Chinese or Israeli companies list or raise capital on markets like the NYSE or Nasdaq, they not only gain access to lower-cost equity capital, but can also be seen as "importing" elements of the corporate governance systems that prevail in those markets. For such companies, listing on the NYSE provides some assurance to would-be minority investors that other investors, with greater experience in governance matters gained from having long operated within a more shareholder-friendly legal and regulatory environment, will now be participating in the general monitoring of their performance. This governance effect, together with international portfolio diversification in general, is the main reason why the same Chinese or Israeli companies often command significantly higher values when allowed to trade on U.S. exchanges rather than (or as well as) on their local domestic exchanges.

BACK TO A GENERAL THEORY OF CORPORATE RISK MANAGEMENT

For finance academics like Cliff Smith and René Stulz, trained to believe that most if not *all* corporate value comes from investment decisions and the asset side of the balance sheet, there was a paradox in the idea of *corporate* risk management.

The overall objective of corporate risk management programs is often expressed in terms of reducing, or limiting, the variability of corporate earnings or cash flows. But according to corporate finance theory, reductions in the volatility of earnings and cash flow *per se* should not be expected to increase a company's market value. In the case of public companies owned by lots of well-diversified investors, the higher earnings volatility stemming from commodity and currency risks should not cause the company to have a higher required rate of return or cost of capital—and so trade at a lower P/E ratio.

The basic question that Cliff and René found themselves asking each other—and ended up addressing in a much-cited paper published in the *Journal of Financial and Quantitative Analysis* in 1985—was this: Are corporate risk management programs capable in theory of adding value for a company's investors; and if so, how they do it?

As Cliff and Dave Mayers had already shown, the "smoothing effect" of corporate hedging on taxable earnings could reduce the firm's expected tax liability under progressive tax codes (like the one in the U.S.). But such tax savings were likely a second-order benefit of hedging. Of greater importance, especially for highly leveraged or thinly capitalized companies, hedging and risk management generally could provide assurances about a company's solvency and staying power to non-investor stakeholders such as employees and suppliers—and in the case of closely held companies, to the owners themselves.

But what about the case of well-capitalized public companies with broad ownership, which was where Cliff and René placed their primary emphasis? Here the critical role of corporate risk management, much as Cliff and Dave concluded earlier, was to strengthen management's commitment to making good on the company's investment priorities, to help ensure (and reassure outside investors about) management's ability and willingness to fund its growth opportunities and carry out its strategic plan.

This role of risk management begins by recognizing the possibility that sharp downturns in earnings together with the high cost of arranging new funding in such circumstances will pressure managers to cut back on promising investments. Even a very large, well-capitalized company like BP found that its managers tended to cut back *too heavily* on drilling and exploration in response to declines in earnings brought on by oil price drops. Hedging a significant portion—say, one-third—of BP's oil price exposure may well have provided its management with the confidence to maintain higher levels of exploration during hard times.

But for a perhaps more compelling example of how financial risk management can add value, let's look at the case of the large pharmaceutical company Merck, and big pharma generally. In a widely cited interview in the *Harvard Business Review* published in 1994, Judy Lewent, Merck's much admired CFO (and longtime member of its Executive Committee), explained the company's uses of currency options as reinforcing management's commitment to continue investing heavily in its fundamental source of value—its R&D pipeline. Having observed a tendency of management to skimp on R&D spending when the dollar appreciated against several European currencies and threatened to depress reported earnings, Lewent directed her FX department to buy currency "puts" that would generate revenue during periods of dollar strength. The explicit purpose of such currency hedging was to guarantee a minimum level of R&D spending throughout such periods. And this financial risk management strategy has served Merck well, adding to its reputation as one of the world's most far-sighted and civic-minded public companies.

COMPARATIVE ADVANTAGE AND THE CASE FOR BOND-HEAVY DEFINED BENEFIT PENSION FUNDS (AND OTHER FORMS OF LDI)

Readers may be surprised to learn that the same principle of comparative advantage in risk-bearing that informs Merck's decision to shift a significant portion of its foreign currency risk to options markets has also provided the impetus for a more recent development known as LDI, which is short for *Liability-Driven Investing*.

LDI involves the design of corporate-owned asset portfolios whose main function is to pay off (or "defease") a set of liabilities that are either (1) the direct result of the company's main revenue-generating activities, as is generally true of insurance companies, or (2) a byproduct of the company's operations, such as the claims associated with the defined benefit pension funds established by many older public companies (but almost no new ones) to fund their workers' retirements.

In the case of insurance companies, both insurance executives and the regulators who oversee their activities have long understood that the core competence of (and main source of value added by) insurance companies is their underwriting and claims processing capabilities, not their investing acumen. The role of the asset portfolios in well-run insurers is thus first and foremost to ensure their ability to pay their claims when they come due—and not to operate as profit centers in their own right. And with that understanding, insurance regulators have long placed strict limits on the amounts of stock (generally just 5–10 percent) that insurers are allowed to hold in their asset portfolios.

But the case of the defined benefit (DB) pension plans of U.S. public companies has, until fairly recently, been viewed very differently. Especially during the heyday of old-fashioned corporate finance (or what might be called "the Jack Welch era"), the DB plans of the largest, blue-chip companies routinely held 60 to 70 percent of their total fund assets in stocks. What's more, the funds became so large that, by 2000, for the median company with a DB plan, the market value of the total plan had grown to *twice* the market capitalization of the firm itself. And at a number of points during Welch's tenure, the stocks in GE's DB plan were actually generating as much as 20 percent of the company's total reported net income.

But once the LDI movement began to gear up in the early 2000s (predictably when the bursting of the dotcom bubble exposed the enormous risk DB plans were taking), not only did insurance companies begin to think harder about and take steps to "de-risk" their asset portfolios, but public companies began to reduce the equity portions of their DB plans.[3] But other than a knee-jerk response to the drop in stock prices and large hit to corporate earnings, why would U.S. public companies accustomed to using DB pension "profits" to pad their reported earnings take such a step?

With the help and urging of financial advisers like (Nobel laureate) Robert Merton and his Integrated Finance Ltd., companies with large DB plans began to recognize that stock market investors were not giving them much credit, even in the good years, for the portion of their earnings stream coming from their DB stock holdings. As became progressively clearer to sophisticated investors, the value of such DB plan-generated earnings streams was exaggerated by "actuarial" accounting that effectively made a dollar investment in stock appear much more valuable than a dollar in bonds. And where CEOs like Jack Welch viewed the company's DB plan as another opportunity to inflate GE's perceived market value (at least in the eyes of unsophisticated, EPS-enthralled investors), Merton was able to demonstrate that, for most public companies, holding large stock portfolios was neither a core competence nor a contributor to value. For most companies, managing their DB plans as profit centers wound up as a distraction from the main operating business, as well as a major source of unnecessary risk and a drag on value that was generally reflected in lower (not higher) corporate P/E ratios.[4]

And as suggested above, this is more evidence of the principle of comparative advantage that informs effective, value-adding corporate risk management. To repeat the general rule: companies with (non-core) risk exposures can and should expect significant gains from transferring those risks to investors or other companies with a comparative advantage in bearing them. And for most public companies, managing financial assets that trade in reasonably competitive and efficient markets is *not* likely to be a core competence.

DERIVATIVES AND THE GAP (ONCE MORE) BETWEEN PERCEPTION AND REALITY

Nevertheless, as suggested earlier, and we now know all too well, not all corporate managers have used derivatives in ways designed to increase the long-run value of their companies. In several widely publicized cases, especially those involving corporate clients of Bankers Trust, the CFOs of companies like Procter & Gamble and Gibson Greeting Cards—and even municipalities like Orange County, California—were discovered to be using sales of well out-of-the-money interest rate options to turn the corporate treasury into a profit center, with some predictably disastrous outcomes. The strategy seemed to work fine, providing an artificial boost to earnings, until interest rates suddenly started to move in ways that few economic forecasters thought possible.

Only then did the risks become clear, prompting Warren Buffett to issue his famous indictment of derivatives as "financial weapons of mass destruction." And following Buffett's cue (while somehow failing to note that Buffett himself was never one to shy away from using derivatives at Berkshire Hathaway), *Fortune* magazine ran a cover story in 1993 that included a particularly shrill and indignant account of corporate abuses of derivatives that ended with the predictable call for more regulation.

• • •

Early in 1994, Cliff and his Rochester colleague Ludger Hentschel aimed to defuse the general hysteria fueled by media accounts like *Fortune*'s by publishing

an article in the *JACF* called "Risk and Regulation in Derivatives (or Why Derivatives Are a Blessing, Not a Curse)."[5] Presenting itself as a systematic assessment
of the risks to companies, investors, and the entire financial system associated
with the operation of the relatively new derivatives markets, the article provided
the following insights and assurances:

- As long as most companies are using derivatives mainly to limit their
  financial exposures and not to enlarge them in efforts to pad their
  operating profits, reported losses on derivatives should not be a matter
  for concern. Complaining about losses on a swap used to hedge a firm's
  exposure is like objecting to the costs of a fire insurance policy if the
  building doesn't burn down.
- To the extent that companies are using derivatives to hedge—and
  evidence from Wharton School surveys suggests that most do—the
  default risk of derivatives has been greatly exaggerated. An interest rate
  swap used by a B-rated company to hedge a large exposure to interest
  rates will generally have significantly less default risk than an AAA-rated
  corporate bond issue.
- Thanks to the corporate use of derivatives, much of the impact of
  economic shocks, such as spikes in interest rates or oil prices, is being
  transferred away from the hedging companies to investors and other
  companies better able to absorb them. And in this fashion, defaults
  in the economy as a whole, and hence systemic risk, are effectively
  being reduced, not increased, through the operation of the derivatives
  markets.

What's more, as Smith and Hentschel warned in closing, the likely effect of the
new derivatives regulation then being proposed was to restrict access to and
increase the costs to companies of using derivatives markets.

RENÉ'S RETHINKING OF CORPORATE RISK MANAGEMENT

In the meantime, René Stulz decamped from Rochester in 1983 and moved on
to Ohio State's Fisher School of Business, where both he and his wife, Patricia
Regan, also an economist, had offers they couldn't turn down. René's thinking

and research have continued to evolve over the years in ways that have ensured his recognition, by practitioners and academics alike, as the world's preeminent scholar and academic authority on corporate risk management.

One of the milestones en route to this eminence was René's publication in 1996 of an article in the *JACF* called "Rethinking Risk Management."[6] In that article, he began by reinforcing the main argument of the theory he had formulated with Cliff Smith more than a decade earlier. As before, effective corporate risk management was seen to be guided by the principle of comparative advantage in risk-taking—one that instructed companies with significant exposures to try to shift those risks to investors or other companies with a comparative advantage in bearing them.

But in this 1996 article, René extended and sharpened the focus of his earlier argument by proposing that the *primary* function of risk management is not to dampen small swings in corporate cash flows or value, but rather to provide protection against the possibility of very costly "lower-tail outcomes," or extreme situations that would cause financial distress and prevent companies from carrying out their investment strategies and business plans. Besides enabling and encouraging corporate managers to fund the company's strategic investments, risk management works to increase value by persuading outsiders to provide financing for such investments on advantageous terms. The protection against catastrophic outcomes offered by risk management thus has the potential to increase a company's debt capacity and reduce its cost of capital.

This view of corporate risk management as a means of limiting mainly catastrophic risks was quickly and broadly accepted by financial economists. In the corporate world, however, U.S. public companies—especially banks and energy companies with trading operations—have continued to find it hard to resist the temptation to use derivatives and risk management centers to pad and smooth their operating earnings.

Now if making derivatives trading a profit center is generally not a good idea, it's worth noting that, in one of the novel thrusts of "Rethinking Risk Management," René actually provides some justification for this practice by entertaining the possibility that certain kinds of trading operations—say, the copper trading arm of a copper mining company—*could* have an information-based comparative advantage that would enable them to earn consistent abnormal profits. And to the extent that market investors are persuaded that this profit stream is recurring and reliable, they could end up assigning such trading earnings a P/E multiple greater than the 1X that financial economists would otherwise suggest.

* * *

But when revisiting these questions in another *JACF* article almost two decades later called "How Companies Can Use Hedging to Increase Shareholder Value,"[7] René seemed somewhat disappointed by how little traction his views seemed to have gained in the corporate world. The article identified the still-widespread practitioner view of risk management as an earnings-smoothing device as not only misguided, but a major contributor to the considerable losses of value experienced by corporate America both during and after the Global Financial Crisis.

Starting with Bankers Trust's ill-fated efforts to market derivatives to corporations in the early 1990s, Renés retelling of the history of corporate risk management continued to detect a clear tendency for the top managements of mature businesses to ignore its main function of protecting the company's core business. In some of the most egregious cases, like the "Whale" trading fiasco that produced $6 billion of "hedging" losses at JP Morgan Chase—the losses appear to reflect the subverting of the corporate risk management function by turning it into a profit center, another case of a bank's Chief Risk Officer being upstaged by its Chief Investment Officer.

René's general diagnosis and prescription was to clear up and dispel corporate America's "widespread confusion about the proper goals of risk management—and their relation to profitability." While the costs associated with risk management are generally observable and often show up on the bottom line, the benefits in terms of corporate value are much harder to identify. This difficulty in identifying and quantifying the benefits means that, in most large organizations, risk management should at the very least be operated as a cost center and not a profit center.

But even this may not be enough. Even when risk management is officially designated a cost center, the pressure to minimize costs, along with the difficulty of "explaining" losses on even well-constructed hedges, can end up driving risk managers to produce "costless hedges." And as René points out, the insistence on and resort to costless hedges generally means that companies are making some kind of "bet." In many cases, these are bets that involve selling well out-of-the-money (and thus apparently riskless) options, with potentially disastrous consequences.

COSTLESS HEDGES

In the last quarter of 2008, Morgan Stanley CEO John Mack was forced to try to explain to stock analysts how the firm had managed to lose some $8.3 billion on what top management believed to be a well-hedged and largely riskless position in mortgaged-backed securities (MBS). The hedge took the form of a very large bet *against* MBS in the form of credit default swaps that required annual premium payments of some $100 million. But to keep such costs from reducing its reported earnings, Morgan Stanley took out a large *long* position in MBS—assumed to be safe because AAA-rated—which it viewed as "funding its hedge." No one at Morgan Stanley, including the firm's chief risk officer, foresaw the value of the firm's portfolio of AAA-rated positions plummeting to the extent it did, along with the value of its other MBS, and overwhelming the hedge.

Such hedging, in combination with the lethal effect of "fair value," or mark-to-market, regulatory accounting, had the effect of converting assets that turned out to be worth at least 85–90 cents on the dollar into assets temporarily worth as little as 15–20 cents, producing an $8.3 billion loss. And that is one of the perils of so-called costless hedging.

One solution René proposes is that companies that consciously choose to take such bets explicitly recognize them as "speculative operations requiring higher than ordinary returns." Having taken this step and gained the approval of their boards, top management must then set up the appropriate controls and reporting systems for evaluating and rewarding the traders charged with taking those bets. Such a system, had it been in place before the Global Financial Crisis, might have done much to limit the billion-dollar trading losses experienced by the likes of Morgan Stanley and, more recently, JPM Chase—and the shortsighted and self-inflicted corporate value destruction that continues to arise from poorly conceived and poorly executed risk management in general.[8]

IN CLOSING: RISK MANAGEMENT AND
THE MAGIC OF CORPORATE FINANCE

Effective risk management helps corporate managers make better investment decisions, producing a larger stream of long-run expected cash flows. And for this reason alone, a company's reputation for effective risk management can become a major source of value in its own right—and in much the same way as a reputation for integrity and fair dealing with customers and clients, as Cliff Smith himself suggested years ago in a *JACF* article called "The Economics of Ethics," can be among the most valuable of all corporate assets.[9]

To catch a suggestive glimpse of this possibility, consider that Goldman Sachs in 2021 reported after-tax earnings of roughly $21 billion, about 50 percent higher than Morgan Stanley's $14 billion. Nevertheless, at the end of 2021, Goldman's total equity market capitalization was only about $130 billion, as compared to Morgan Stanley's market cap of $170 billion. The difference comes down to the market's willingness to assign a significantly higher valuation multiple to Morgan Stanley's earnings, and for a couple of reasons. One clearly has to do with CEO James Gorman's decision after the Global Financial Crisis to scale back Morgan's volatile trading operations while beefing up its wealth management business, which has created a much more stable revenue stream. But along with this difference in strategy, it's hard to avoid seeing investors put off by Goldman's seemingly endless series of scandals, from the Abacus deal on through the latest Malaysian fund fiasco, as collectively marking down the firm's P/E ratio, which in recent years (until the precipitous drop in Goldman's earnings in 2023) had fluctuated between half and two-thirds of Morgan Stanley's.

This difference in valuation multiples is the market's way of letting corporate managers know a couple important things. First and foremost, ethical behavior pays, certainly in the long run, and probably sooner than people realize—and for the same reason and in much the same way as an effective risk corporate management program: namely, by reassuring investors about a company's long-run staying power and the strength of its ongoing commitment to investing in its competitive capabilities.

＊   ＊   ＊

It's only natural to wonder about both the personal and corporate rewards for sound, farsighted decision-making whose benefits *never materialize*. Think about decisions to hedge exposures that, although they end up reducing near-term profits and cash flows, were the right moves on an *ex ante*, or expected value, basis. Do corporate executives and the companies they serve ever get the credit they deserve for averting potentially disastrous outcomes? If a tree falls in the forest with no one around to see or hear it, does it make a sound?

One of the main contentions of this book is that effective risk management, viewed as a critical component of value-adding financial management in general, can raise a company's value. The sophisticated investors that tend to dominate stock market pricing recognize good management and effective governance by assigning higher P/E multiples to their companies' expected operating cash flows and earnings. And such higher P/E multiples and overall long-run value, which we have been calling the "magic of finance capitalism," are the tangible pay-off to effective corporate risk management.

CHAPTER 7

JENSEN REDUX, STEVE KAPLAN, AND THE REMARKABLE SUCCESS OF U.S. PRIVATE EQUITY

A t the end of the 1980s, hostile takeovers and other highly leveraged transactions, including leveraged buyouts (LBOs), came under fierce attack in the press as well as conventional business circles. Some of the deals at the end of the '80s—notably, Robert Campeau's takeover of Federated Stores (which had the audacity to include Bloomingdales!)—were already beginning to show signs of stress. But the event that concentrated populist rage and set off the first coordinated political response to highly leveraged transactions was the LBO in 1989 of RJR Nabisco, a large, household-name public company, by a then very small and relatively unknown investment firm called Kohlberg Kravis & Roberts.

As we saw in chapter 4, the price paid by KKR to take control of RJR was the eye-catching sum of $25 billion, which made it by far the largest LBO to date. Even more astonishing, that $25 billion price tag was *almost double* RJR's market value at the time, representing an acquisition premium of close to 100 percent for what was then widely believed by most of the investment community to be a profitable and well-run company. That transaction, thanks in part to the bestselling *Barbarians at the Gate*, became the visible embodiment of a general threat posed by activist investors to corporate America—and all the constituencies beholden to and dependent on it.

Such leveraged transfers of corporate control were perceived to be enough of a threat to the public welfare that the U.S. Senate and House saw fit to conduct hearings on "LBOs and Corporate Debt" in early 1989, when the economy was headed into recession. The first to testify at the hearings was then Fed chairman Alan Greenspan. While professing concern about the unprecedented levels of corporate debt, Greenspan viewed the leveraged deals as an extension of corporate America's long history of financial restructuring dating back at least to J.P Morgan's doings at the turn of the 20th century. Leveraged takeovers and buyouts were seen by Greenspan as a mainly positive development whose most notable and important outcome was major productivity gains. Such gains, to be sure, were often accompanied by job losses in the restructured sectors. But as Greenspan suggested in closing, the longer view of U.S. economic history shows that such losses are more than offset, and in relatively short order, by employment gains in other industries.

Next up was Harvard Business School Professor Michael Jensen, with whom we spent considerable time in chapter 4 and whose account of LBOs was consistent with Greenspan's message. "The fact that a firm the size of KKR, with 30 or 40 professionals," Jensen told the lawmakers,

> was willing to bid—and able to raise—$25 billion for the purchase of a company like RJR Nabisco was a revelation to me . . . The sheer waste of value under [CEO Ross] Johnson, and thus the gain from taking the company private, was enormous; it was well in excess of $10 billion . . . The real barbarians were inside the gate.[1]

Jensen viewed the growth of LBOs in the 1980s as part of a general U.S. phenomenon that he identified as "the rebirth of active investors . . . people like J.P. Morgan in the 1920s who held large positions in both the debt and the equity of an organization, often served on the board, and were actively involved in the strategic direction of the firm." The need and impetus for such a rebirth could be traced back to "a series of laws and regulations" that Jensen identified in his testimony as

> dating back to the Depression, including the 1934 SEC Act and the Investment Company Act of 1940, [which] had the effect of driving active investors off corporate boards and pretty much out of the corporate governance arena. And the consequence of these laws and regulations was a corporate America that was largely unmonitored and uncontrolled by outside investors. The result was massive inefficiencies . . . that were both reflected in and made worse by the conglomerate movement of the late '60s and '70s. These inefficiencies in turn provided opportunities for the so-called raiders and restructurings of the '80s, of which LBOs and private equity were an important part.

BACK TO "JENSEN AND MECKLING" AND THE THEORY OF THE FIRM

To understand the challenges and accomplishments of private equity, it helps to revisit the paper for which Jensen is best known among his academic colleagues: "Theory of the Firm: Managerial Behavior, Agency Costs, and Ownership Structure." As discussed in the prologue and chapter 4, that paper, written with colleague Bill Meckling at the University of Rochester in the 1970s, revolutionized the theory of corporate finance by identifying some fundamental conflicts of interests and incentives between the managements and shareholders of large public companies. Unless managed effectively, these conflicts—particularly over a company's optimal size and diversification—were likely to reduce the value of the company. As Jensen and Meckling saw it, the primary responsibility of the boards and internal governance systems of public companies was to manage these conflicts in ways that increase long-run efficiency and value.

Ten years after publication of "Theory of the Firm," Jensen published an article in the *American Economic Review* called "The Agency Costs of Free Cash Flow: Corporate Finance and Takeovers." Here he extended his analysis to the shareholder activism of the '80s by focusing on the tendency of managers of companies in mature industries to reinvest their excess cash in low-return businesses and, in most cases even worse, diversifying acquisitions. In Jensen's view, the highly leveraged acquisitions, LBOs, and other leveraged recaps of the 1980s all represented solutions to this corporate "free cash flow" problem by replacing significant amounts of equity with debt. Such recapitalizations had the effect of converting generally smaller and discretionary dividend payments into much larger, *contractual* payments of interest and principal. And as Jensen pointed out, paying a 40 percent premium for a public company and then leveraging its equity 9 to 1 had the effect of making its cost of capital "both explicit and contractually binding."

Jensen also viewed the heavy use of debt financing as providing what amounts to an automatic internal monitoring-and-control system. If operating problems emerged, top management was forced by the pressure of the debt service to intervene quickly and decisively. By contrast, in a largely equity-financed company, management could allow much of the equity cushion to be eaten away before taking the necessary corrective action.

THE ECLIPSE OF THE PUBLIC CORPORATION—AND THE RISE OF PRIVATE EQUITY

Jensen was so impressed by the first wave of LBOs that, near the end of 1989, he published his much-cited *Harvard Business Review* article with the provocative title, "Eclipse of the Public Corporation." There the rise of LBO partnerships like KKR and Clayton & Dubilier were hailed as a "new organizational form"— one that was competing directly with and even threatening to supplant public conglomerates. With their staffs of fewer than 50 professionals, LBO partnerships were said to do a better job of providing the same coordination-and-monitoring function performed by corporate headquarters staffs numbering, in some cases, in the thousands. As Jensen summed things up, "The LBO succeeded by substituting incentives held out by compensation and ownership plans for the direct monitoring and often centralized decision-making of the typical corporate bureaucracy."[2]

In the average Fortune 1000 company, as Jensen and HBS colleague Kevin Murphy reported in another *HBR* article that came out a year later, CEO compensation changed by as little as $3 for every $1,000 change in shareholder value.[3] By comparison, the average operating CEO of an LBO-owned business in the '80s experienced a change of roughly $64 per $1,000—and the entire operating management team owned about 20 percent of the equity. What's more, the partners of the LBO firm itself—which is the proper equivalent of a conglomerate CEO—owned about 60 percent of the equity, and thus earned close to $600 for each $1,000 change in value.

For corporate operating managers, the LBO thus held out a "new deal": greater decision-making autonomy and ownership incentives in return for meeting more demanding performance targets. Although the profits of LBOs are often attributed to "asset-stripping" and the "gutting" of viable businesses, the ownership structure is designed in part to encourage managers to resist the temptation, which is potentially strong in cases of high leverage, to produce short-term profits at the expense of a company's future. *Precisely because the business must be sold or refinanced* at some point during the next seven to ten years, the operating managers who are also significant owners have clear incentives to devote the value-maximizing level of corporate capital to expenditures with longer-run payoffs, such as advertising and plant maintenance. They know that the amounts and kinds of such investment are bound to be of great interest to the next owners of the business.

So, the key insight here is that regardless of how an LBO eventually "cashes out"—whether by means of an IPO, sale to another firm, or recapitalization involving another private investment group—the greater the level of productive investment undertaken by a PE-owned company's operating managers, the higher the value of their shares when traded in. This is a point that most people—not just business journalists, but even many economists and businesspeople themselves—tend to overlook.

Consider, for example, what Robert Kidder, the CEO of Duracell, had to say about the company's goals and methods a few years after it was purchased from Dart & Kraft by KKR in the late '80s:

> The debt schedule is very effective in forcing management to attend to profitability in the near term. But let me emphasize that another important consideration—in some sense, more important than short-term cash flow—is carrying through on strategic commitments. There is a widespread public misconception that because you're an LBO, you have to do everything possible to generate short-term cash flow, and that LBOs thus simply represent a means of sacrificing future profit for immediate gain. . . .
>
> Now, I don't mean to suggest that we don't do everything possible to reduce waste and cut costs. But when I talk with Henry Kravis at lunch, we don't spend our time talking about cost reductions. We talk about how we're increasing the strategic value of the company—and by that I mean our long-term cash flow capability.[4]

On top of the discipline of debt and stronger management incentives, the boards of companies owned by LBO buyout firms are designed in large part to overcome the information problems that beset the directors as well as the shareholders of public companies. The directors of a typical LBO don't merely *represent* the outside shareholders, they *are* the principal shareholders—and they have become the principal owners only *after* having participated in an intensive "due diligence" process that is intended to reveal the true profit potential of the business.

As James Birle, a general partner of the Blackstone Group during the 1990s, said about the LBO governance process:

> Unlike the boards of public companies, our board members come to the table already knowing a great deal about the operations and expected behavior of

the businesses in various economic and competitive situations . . . So we are able to determine when management has really gotten off the track far more quickly and confidently than most public company directors.

We [also] have a much tighter performance measurement system, by necessity, than most public companies I'm familiar with. The pressure to ensure that goals are being met is just far greater than that which exists in most public companies. At the same time, this sense of urgency does not prevent us from setting and pursuing long-term goals. Our goal at the Blackstone Group is maximizing shareholder value, and you can't command a high price for a business if all you've been doing is liquidating its assets and failing to invest in its future earnings power. And since management are also major equity holders in the company, we are confident that they are constantly attempting to balance short-term and long-term goals in creating value.[5]

And if and when financial trouble or operating problems arise, the board intervenes quickly, often appointing one of its members to step in as CEO. As in the case of *venture capital*—from which, as Jensen points out, the buyout governance model has largely been adapted—the board members in LBOs also typically handle the corporate finance function, including negotiations with lenders and the investment banking community.

⦿   ⦿   ⦿

Much, of course, has changed since Jensen identified the main features of this "new organizational form" with its "better model of corporate governance." The term LBO is rarely heard these days, having been absorbed into the newer, broader class called "private equity," or PE. Today's publicly traded PE firms like Blackstone and Carlyle seem to be casting an ever-wider net, encompassing a relatively new class called "growth equity" along with "private credit" and infrastructure and real estate financing as well as the traditional venture capital and management buyouts.

In clear testimony to the power of Jensen's thinking, the growth and global expansion of private equity during the past 40 years have been nothing short of phenomenal. Back in the late 1980s when Jensen was testifying before Congress, there were at most three or four private equity firms with more than $1 billion in assets under management. Today there are hundreds of "institutional-quality"

PE firms that have collectively raised well over $3 trillion of capital and own or control over 8,000 U.S. companies.

What's more, as the number of PE-backed U.S. companies has exploded, the number of U.S. *public* companies has dropped sharply. The Wilshire 5,000 Index, after reaching a peak of 7,562 public companies in 1998, today has fewer than 4,000—which presents something of a puzzle, one that we revisit at the end of this chapter.

ENTER STEVE KAPLAN

From here we now go on to view the main accomplishments of private equity through the lens of the research and writings of a finance scholar who might be viewed as Jensen's chief disciple, University of Chicago finance professor Steve Kaplan. Steve produced the first major empirical study, while working on his Ph.D. under Jensen's direction at Harvard, of the first wave of LBOs in the early 1980s. And using his body of work as our guide, we discuss both the accomplishments of what has become not only a U.S. but a global PE success story, and the formidable challenges now facing the industry. The good news is that most of these challenges have already been met and weathered by the U.S. PE industry during the three major waves and two complete boom-and-bust cycles that have punctuated its remarkable 40-year run.

In what follows, we now provide answers to questions like the following:

- How have PE buyout companies performed relative to their public counterparts? To the extent there have been improvements in operating performance and productivity gains, how have such gains been achieved? And what role have PE firms played in these gains?
- In light of the large fees—amounting to 3–5 percent of total transaction value, on average—paid by the limited partners (LPs) to the PE firms (or, more precisely, to their general partners (GPs)), and the significant control premiums paid (in the public-to-private deals) to the selling companies, how have the returns to the LPs that provide the bulk of the funding for PE funds compared to the returns earned by the shareholders of otherwise comparable public companies?
- Apart from the princely fees paid GPs, why is private equity so controversial? Beyond its benefits for investors, what are the

employment and other social effects associated with buyouts
and PE?

- What are the prospects for future PE returns to their LPs, especially in light of the enormous volume of capital commitments and high purchase multiples that were being paid, at least until the onset of the COVID pandemic, and in today's higher-interest-rate environment?
- Finally, what are the implications of the accomplishments and limitations of private equity for *public* companies? Should they consider taking a page out of the private equity playbook and, for example, invite some of their largest investors onto their boards?

THE PERFORMANCE OF PE-CONTROLLED COMPANIES

After gathering as much as data as he could about the operating performance of U.S. companies with at least $50 million in sales that were bought by U.S. buyout firms during the period 1981–1986, Steve found that buyouts led to significant increases in operating margins and cash flows, both in absolute terms and relative to public companies operating in similar industries. What's more, for the 76 "round-trip" deals (management buyouts of public companies that went public again through IPOs) in his sample, the operating gains resulted in increases in enterprise values (debt plus equity) of roughly 100 percent, or a doubling of firm value. According to Steve's estimates, the gains from these deals were divided pretty evenly between the selling shareholders and the new investors, with about 5 percent of the total gains taking the form of fees charged by the GPs.

Kaplan's study also found little evidence of a decline in employment levels or average wage rates of blue-collar workers after LBOs. As for the charge that much of their operating gains come from cutbacks in R&D, it turns out that these LBOs were not R&D-intensive to begin with; only about one in ten of his sample companies engaged in enough R&D before the LBO to report it separately in their financial statements.

The study also reported that LBO boards typically have eight or fewer members (public companies tend to have many more), who collectively hold or represent about 60 percent of the equity, on average. In sum, private PE-controlled firms have far fewer board members than public companies, with a far stronger interest in the performance of the firm.

LATER FINDINGS

Many of the findings of Steve's study have been replicated and confirmed by later studies of the 1980s as well as in more recent studies of both U.S. and European deals done in the 1990s and 2000s. In a notable pair of studies—the first published in 2014 and its successor in 2019—the University of Chicago's Steve Davis and a group of five other PE scholars examined the productivity of a large fraction of U.S. buyouts transacted between 1980 and 2011. Perhaps their most interesting finding was the clear tendency of PE-controlled firms to shut down low-productivity plants when first taking control, but then *reinvest* in either building or buying higher-productivity operations. These major resource reallocations were shown to account for roughly 75 percent of the significant increases in total factor productivity reported by these companies.[6]

One clear limitation of PE research to date is its disproportionate emphasis on U.S. deals. Nevertheless, a study of 839 French buyouts during the period 1994–2004 reported that the buyout companies had 12 percent greater revenue increases, and 18 percent greater operating profit increases, than a comparable French control group in the three years following the buyouts.[7]

Another limitation of the research is lack of insight into changes in the sources of value added over time. Following Jensen, many if not most finance scholars continue to attribute much of the success of the buyouts of the '80s to the incentive effects of high leverage and concentrated equity, or to what many in the industry like to call "financial and governance engineering."

But in the late '80s and early '90s, the recession combined with growing competition among PE firms forced them to develop new sources of competitive advantage and value added. When the recession hit at the end of the '80s, the industry experienced its first major correction. And as Steve and Jeremy Stein (later a Federal Reserve governor) reported in their 1993 study titled "The Evolution of Buyout Pricing and Financial Structure of Buyouts in the 1980s,"[8] roughly a third of the deals transacted in the latter half of the '80s defaulted, and the returns to LPs dropped sharply. What's more, in this postmortem of PE's first major boom-and-bust cycle—which might have been subtitled "what went wrong with the first wave of buyouts"—Steve and Jeremy found clear signs of "overheating" in the late '80s buyout market, including progressively higher valuations (as multiples of operating cash flow) and the use of higher leverage in transactions in increasingly risky industries. The study also reported significant reductions in the net equity contributed by LBO sponsors to their own deals—a telling sign that Jensen himself identified as a clear prescription for "too many deals," a phenomenon he later described and analyzed as "LBO overshooting."[9]

The good news in all this, however, is that the industry collectively learned from the experience and responded with at least two important adjustments. The first was the reduction of leverage ratios and other changes designed to increase financial flexibility. Perhaps even more important, however, was the PE industry's growing recognition of the value of "operational engineering," and their efforts to develop or acquire this capability.

The development of an operating capability meant recruiting former senior corporate executives to provide industry operating expertise. Bain Capital, Berkshire Partners, and the old Clayton & Dubilier all established reputations for bringing on managerial talent to help improve the performance of their portfolio companies. KKR went even farther by developing Capstone, an "in-house consulting firm" whose principals bring their operating expertise to transactions in which they participate from their inception and due diligence to the final sale of the firm, and whose compensation is the same as that of the partners on the deal-making side of the business.

The development of this managerial experience and expertise, together with the reduction in leverage and greater financing flexibility, also increased PE firms' ability and inclination to pursue growth opportunities in their portfolio companies as well as performing their traditional cost-cutting function.

As Carl Ferenbach, a cofounder of the PE firm Berkshire Partners and widely regarded as one of the most effective PE operators,[10] summed things up,

> In the deals of the '80s, we viewed most of the change in value as happening on the day you closed the deal; we created value mainly by changing the financial structure and managers' incentives. There wasn't much growth in those companies. It was mainly about improving the existing operations of mature, fundamentally sound businesses that produce a lot of cash flow. But somewhere in the '90s, we and most of the PE industry all started to move toward growth as part of the objective.
>
> Once we started to think about growth instead of just cash flow, we then had to think much more about strategy and management. We now had a business plan—one that included growth as well as efficiency—that we had to deliver on.[11]

The new emphasis on growth opened the door for PE to entire new industries. Take the case of Silver Lake, whose early partners saw themselves as building "a category killer investment firm around technology investing," with an investment model committed to "an unswerving focus on growth." According to partner Mike Bingle,

> Something like half of our investments and more than half of our profits to date have come from unleveraged investments, where the value creation was driven by growth and business transformation and not by financial engineering.[12]

Or consider this statement by Phil Canfield of Chicago-based GTCR, which specializes in buyouts in healthcare and information services and technology:

> We spend a lot of time trying to find really talented leaders, and matching those leaders with companies where we believe there are big opportunities for transformation that can produce higher growth and significant value added.[13]

Statements like these are consistent with and reinforce the findings of a survey of 79 U.S. PE firms that Steve conducted in 2012 with Harvard's Paul Gompers. After getting responses from partners representing a collective $750 billion under management, Steve and Paul reached the following conclusions:

- PE investors target a 22 percent internal rate of return on their investments, on average, with the vast majority of targeted rates of return between 20 percent and 25 percent;
- PE investors expect to provide strong equity incentives to their management teams, and believe those incentives are very important.
- PE investors regularly replace top management, both before and after they invest.
- PE portfolio companies are overseen by smaller boards of directors, with a mix of insiders, PE investors, and outsiders.
- PE investors place a heavy emphasis on adding value to their portfolio companies, both before and after they invest. The sources of that added value, in order of importance, are identified as increasing revenue, improving incentives and governance, facilitating a high-value exit or sale, making additional acquisitions, replacing management, and reducing costs. On average, they commit meaningful resources to add

value, although using a considerable variety of different methods and approaches.[14]

This picture of the private equity model, while consistent with Jensen's "active investors," appears to have expanded in ways that even Mike himself might not have foreseen. The bottom line is that a large and growing number of academic studies have provided clear confirmation of productivity increases in the companies or assets controlled by PE firms. This was true of the U.S. deals in the '80s; it proved to be true of the second great wave of buyouts in the UK and continental Europe; and it has been confirmed for U.S. buyouts in the '90s and 2000s. The lone exception to these general findings of increased productivity involves public-to-private transactions, where a number of studies have reported finding only modest (and statistically insignificant) gains.[15]

HAVE PE'S LIMITED PARTNERS GOTTEN THEIR DUE?

But all this brings us to a different, and still somewhat contentious, question: Have the operating gains in PE portfolio companies translated into high enough returns, *net of fees*, for the limited partners who supply most of the equity capital for the deals? After all, PE firms charge fees, including carried interest, that are estimated to average from 3 percent to 5 percent per year over the life of the fund. The combination of such fees with the control premiums paid to acquire (at least publicly traded) companies could more than offset the value of the operating gains achieved by the firm's new owners, resulting in below-market returns for LPs—less than what they could have earned just by investing in a diversified portfolio of public equities like the S&P 500.

To answer that question, Steve teamed up with Bob Harris and Tim Jenkinson to report, in a 2014 *Journal of Finance* article, the findings of their study of some 1,400 U.S. PE buyout funds raised between 1984 and 2008. Using Burgiss data, which was then a relatively new—and widely viewed as much more reliable—source of information about the actual cash distributions to limited partners, the study reported that the returns to LPs in these funds outperformed the S&P 500 by an average of 300 to 400 basis points per year.[16]

As skeptics pointed out, however, a significant portion of these returns was earned in deals transacted *before* the Global Financial Crisis, when PE was said to be facing a "wall of debt" that raised widespread doubt about its future. Although the industry clearly recovered, the question asked in recent years is this: have the returns to LPs *since* the crisis continued to justify the large capital commitments and massive amounts of committed but uncalled capital (known as "dry powder") the GPs now have at their disposal?

In a widely cited paper published in 2018, three partners of the hedge fund AQR expressed doubt about PE's continuing success, reporting that "private equity does not seem to offer as attractive a net-of-fee return edge over public market counterparts as it did 15–20 years ago from either an historical or forward-looking perspective."[17] The AQR partners also suggested that the continuing and, indeed, steadily rising popularity of private equity among institutional investors reflected little more than reporting cosmetics (along with a suggestion of investor credulity)—which the authors' describe as "investors' preference for the return-smoothing properties of illiquid assets in general."[18]

Using the latest fund cash flow data from Burgiss as of the third quarter of 2018, Steve and Greg Brown of UNC-Chapel Hill responded to such suggestions with an updated study published in 2019. Their calculations showed that, for the 29 PE vintage years from 1986 through 2014 (the most recent year for which they would then have had data for a complete five-year investment cycle), PE funds produced for their LPs an impressive average "direct alpha," or above-market return, of almost 500 basis points (4.8 percent) and an average PME (the "public market equivalent," or the ratio of PE to S&P 500 average returns) of 1.22. After adjusting these results for the different amounts of capital invested in each vintage year, the study reported an annual average *value-weighted* excess return of 3.5 percent, and a PME of 1.15.[19]

This finding is completely consistent with the world we now observe in which allocations to private equity and other "alternatives" by endowments, sovereign wealth funds, and institutional investors of all kinds have long been growing. During the same period, allocations to public equities—along with the number of public companies themselves—have been falling.

DO LP RETURNS NEED ADJUSTING FOR HIGH LEVERAGE AND ILLIQUIDITY?

But with all the capital that has poured into and continues to be raised by PE firms, private equity has no shortage of skeptics. One persistent objection to the

PE record, as already noted, is that the returns to PE are not adjusted for risk or illiquidity. This is the quite reasonable argument that because investor allocations are effectively committed to and tied up in funds for seven to ten years, and are invested in smaller companies with higher financial and operating risk, PE *should* in fact produce significantly higher returns than their public counterparts. But whether 200–300 basis points represent sufficient compensation for such concerns remains an open question—and, in the meantime, the institutional investors that continue to allocate ever larger portions of capital to PE funds don't seem in the least troubled by this.

Along with the institutions' willingness to accept such illiquidity and risk, the problem with this challenge to PE is that the risks associated with PE buyouts have proven very hard to find. For one thing, the outperformance of U.S. PE net buyout returns for at least the past decade has been far larger when set against the (small-firm) Russell 2,000 than against the S&P 500, which suggests that the liquidity premium for the past decade has actually become *negative*—and that something about PE governance has the effect of limiting operating risk.

Consistent with that possibility, new research on the role of leverage and capital structure in PE buyouts' success provides suggestive evidence of PE's comparative advantage in managing "high leverage," both in raising and structuring debt, and in working out of financial trouble.[20] This possibility, along with new secondary markets for PE buyouts that have been opening up, suggest that PE buyouts could end up proving to be *both* less risky, and considerably less illiquid, than PE skeptics have been warning.

A BRIEF GLIMPSE INTO THE WEEDS OF PE RETURN ADJUSTMENTS FOR RISK AND ILLIQUIDITY

The AQR partners mentioned earlier attempt to adjust for the higher risks and illiquidity of PE buyouts by assuming that the market risk inherent in a portfolio of U.S. buyout funds is equivalent to that of a public market fund with a beta of 1.2—which has the effect of reducing the PMEs and "alphas" of the buyouts funds.[21] Steve and Greg Brown responded to the AQR critique by estimating direct alphas and PMEs using a beta of 1.2 for the S&P 500, the Russell 2000, and the Russell 2000 Value indices. What they find when so

(*continued on next page*)

(continued from previous page)

doing is that the performance of buyouts continues to outperform the leveraged indices for the vintages from 1986 to 2014 as well as over the two more recent different sub-periods, as summarized in the exhibit below.

EXHIBIT: DIRECT ALPHAS AND PMEs AGAINST A SIMULATED BETA OF 1.2

	Direct Alpha				KS-PME			
From	1986	2000	2000	2009	1986	2000	2000	2009
To	2014	2014	2008	2014	2014	2014	2008	2014
S&P 500	2.1%	1.9%	2.0%	1.3%	1.09	1.07	1.09	1.04
Russell 2000	0.8%	1.0%	0.6%	2.4%	1.03	1.04	1.03	1.07
Russell 2000 Value	0.9%	1.8%	1.2%	3.9%	1.04	1.07	1.06	1.11

Source: Burgiss Private IQ, as of September 30, 2018. Direct alphas and PMEs are calculated based on capital-weighted, vintage year concurrent cash flows.

Steve and Greg also explored the possibility that U.S. buyouts should be required to earn the small size and value premiums over public equity markets by using the Russell 2000 index (instead of the S&P 500) as their benchmark. When so doing, they found that the excess returns of U.S. buyout funds actually become consistently *larger* when measured against the Russell 2000 index than against the S&P 500 *in all vintage years since 2008*. The buyouts' excess returns have also consistently exceeded the Russell 2000 Value index for vintages as far back as 2004. And the fact that this outperformance of PE buyouts against the Russell 2000 was greatest for the most recent (2009–2014) vintages raises the intriguing possibility that the investment risks attending buyout returns are becoming increasingly unrelated to the risks associated with small-cap public equities, particularly in light of the increasing size of buyout deals and the industry's greater focus on growth in the past 15 years.[22]

DO GPS DESERVE WHAT THEY GET?

But if academic studies suggest that private equity has outperformed public markets on average, it is equally clear that there is lots of *variation* in the performance of PE managers. A 2016 study by David Robinson and Berk Sensoy reported finding that although the average public market equivalent (PME) in their buy-out sample was 1.19, and the top quartile funds produced a PME of about 1.40, the bottom quartile PE funds earned just 0.82, or well below their public-market equivalent or benchmark.[23] This kind of spread in performance, combined with the inherent opacity and illiquidity of the PE asset class and the long periods over which returns are realized, invites the same question we just addressed: are the limited partners getting a good deal by investing in PE?

Critics have argued that the standard private equity contract—in which GPs get a 2 percent fixed management fee and 20 percent of the "carry" or abnormal profits—allows GPs to earn excessive compensation while doing too little to discipline underperforming GPs or provide them with effective incentives to maximize LP returns. Some critics claim that there is too much fixed compensation in the form of management fees versus carry, while others have suggested that the sheer complexity of some management contracts has effectively allowed GPs to charge high fees for low to average performance. Such concerns about fees are especially acute in the case of the largest funds, and particularly during boom fund-raising periods. The fact that PE contractual arrangements and performance are typically shielded from public disclosure not only helps fuel these claims, but also makes them hard to evaluate.

To see whether PE funds that charge higher fees end up providing lower *net* returns to their LPs than do their lower-fee counterparts, a 2015 study by Robinson and Sensoy examined data from a *single large LP* with capital commitments to 837 buyout and VC partnerships during the period 1984–2010.[24] After linking GPs' performance to the fee and carry provisions laid out in the management contracts underlying the funds—and making the assumption, clearly violated in practice, that all LPs actually pay these "headline fees"—the study reported that while fees tended to rise during periods of strong fund-raising, there was in fact *no* discernible relationship between the level of the fees written into the partnership agreements and the funds' net-of-fee performance.

What this tell us is that, on average, partnerships charging higher fees to their LPs tend to deliver better performance (before, though not after, netting out the fees) than lower-fee partnerships—otherwise the authors would have found a *negative* relationship between fees and net returns. In this sense, LPs as a class can be seen as getting what they paid for—no more, but no less. And as this finding also suggests, there is a clear possibility for higher returns for the larger, more influential LPs that are known to have more leverage in negotiating concessions from GPs' "headline" fees.

Does all this mean that the partnership agreement perfectly aligns incentives between LPs and GPs, and that there are no unmanaged conflicts of interest in private equity we need to worry about? Far from it. As funds have become significantly larger, management fees have fallen much less than many predicted, given the greater economies of scale. Many GPs appear positioned to do very well even if they deliver little (or no) abnormal profit to their investors. When combined with the huge spread in performance, these findings confirm and reinforce the importance of careful manager selection. Since high fees are not a *guarantee* of correspondingly high net returns—only an indication of average outcomes—the terms of the contract offer cannot be used to screen funds effectively.[25]

Still, the fact that the returns to the LPs in PE funds—even after paying large fees to GPs and premiums to acquire their portfolio companies—continue to outstrip those of public company shareholders by a significant margin suggests that GPs and LPs have been reasonably effective in managing agency conflicts.

OTHER POSSIBLE SOURCES OF PE'S PR PROBLEMS

For all PE's success in increasing the productivity of companies and providing high enough returns to keep LPs expanding their PE allocations, the industry has long had a bad name in the press. The most common charge is that the high leverage used in many deals puts pressure on the portfolio companies to cut productive investment and forgo even profitable growth. In its relentless quest for efficiency, PE is regularly chastised for "gutting" companies, selling off valuable assets, and cutting jobs and reducing overall employment.

In their 2019 study of U.S. PE-owned companies, Steve Davis and his five colleagues found that employment at the buyout firms' existing plants and operations fell by 4 percent relative to that of other companies in the same industry. But in the new operations of these same portfolio companies, employment actually *increased* (by 2.3 percent) relative to competitors. And so the net effect on employment was a more modest decline.

Perhaps a bigger source of controversy surrounding the PE industry is the amount of money made by the top PE firms and their partners—a controversy reflected in the perennial public debate about U.S. income inequality, and in the long-running call for reform of the taxation of "carried interest," which allows much of GPs' annual income to be taxed at the lower capital gains rates. While most tax authorities seem to believe that the case for taxing carried interest as ordinary income can be argued either way, many also point out that even if the IRS were to change its treatment, ordinary income taxes on carried interest are highly unlikely to ever become a major source of tax revenue for the U.S. Treasury. Why? Because the PE industry will simply find ways to convert most of what is now carried interest into some common stock equivalent that *will* qualify for capital gains treatment. These issues will no doubt remain at the heart of a public discussion that extends well beyond PE.

❋ ❋ ❋

Apart from these questions of jobs and taxes, there are also widespread concerns about and studies of the non-performance related effects of private equity. On the positive side, studies of consumer and worker safety in the past decade have shown that PE-funded restaurants, especially those owned by chains rather than franchisees, actually have *fewer* health violations than their publicly traded counterparts,[26] and that PE-operated companies in general have experienced relative declines in workplace injuries.[27] Studies have also reported that PE-backed companies have increased human capital by improving technical job skills that are valued by subsequent employers.[28] What's more, PE firms have been shown to be more likely than their public competitors to achieve growth by providing new products and in new geographic markets instead of simply raising prices for consumers.[29]

On the negative side of the ledger, however, is growing evidence that PE companies have profited by taking advantage of government regulations in ways that turn out to have significant social costs. For example, one study published in 2018 found that buyouts in the for-profit college education industry were associated with worse outcomes for students, including higher tuition, higher per-student debt, lower graduation rates, and lower per-graduate earnings. One thing that such PE-backed for-profit educators have turned out to be especially good at is securing funding through a generous—and what now appears to have been a very poorly designed—government-subsidized student loan program.[30]

Another much publicized stain on PE's record is its performance in the nursing home industry. A 2014 study of almost 3,000 nursing facilities during the period 2000–2007 reported that PE-owned nursing homes had fewer and, on average, less-skilled registered nurses and worse health outcomes than their non-PE counterparts.[31] Consistent with this finding, a more recent study using facility-level data from 2000 to 2017 found a negative impact of PE buyouts on patient health and compliance with care standards, a finding the authors attribute to fewer front-line nursing staff and higher bed utilization.[32] On the other hand, a more recent study of nursing homes during the COVID epidemic shows that PE-owned homes actually experienced fewer infections and COVID-related deaths.[33]

In sum, PE's social record appears a good deal more complicated than the portrait of ruthless efficiency presented by its legions of detractors. Perhaps the most revealing picture of PE's dual capacity for good and ill is provided by a fairly recent study that aims to document the effect of private equity on the long-run health and career paths of its workers. Examining the career paths of some 55,000 Dutch employees after the PE-led buyouts of 274 Dutch companies between 2007 and 2013, German finance scholar Ernst Maug and two co-authors from Erasmus University reached several conclusions.

First, the companies became more efficient and profitable. Second, after classifying all workers into two categories according to their health records, the study found that healthier-than-average workers experienced gains in wages and ascending career paths, while less healthy workers experienced reduced wages and further declines in health and employment. Finally, providing at least partial mitigation of these outcomes, government transfer payments were estimated to compensate less healthy workers for roughly half of their losses.[34]

In sum, PE-backed companies appear to operate in a profit-maximizing way that, while complying with laws and regulation, is not always what most of us might view as socially optimal. One way to interpret these results is to view private equity as "capitalism in high gear." In other words, PE is a high-powered way to achieve more efficient operations, financing, governance, and, ultimately, higher investor returns—even as it accelerates some of the more destructive elements of the value creation process. And this view carries an important message for policymakers: make sure your policies are not creating loopholes or uneven playing fields, given the propensity for PE firms to find and take advantage of them.

THE FUTURE OF PRIVATE EQUITY—AND THE ECONOMIC CHALLENGES IT NOW FACES

Perhaps the greatest challenge facing the PE industry is the boom-and-bust cycle that appears to have become one of its most recognizable and well-established features. As studies have shown, such cycles are driven by the enormous amounts of capital flooding into the industry when returns are high—generally when interest rates are low relative to stock prices—and the competition for deals that such capital flows unfailingly set off, leading to more deals at higher prices. Toward the end of 2019, for example, the average buyout transaction reached a record high EBITDA multiple paid of almost 13 times.

It's only when the high prices paid in transactions at the peak of a cycle—or the onset of an event like the COVID pandemic in March 2020—lead to expectations of lower returns that LPs start to commit less capital to the industry. The resulting drop in the number of deals and transaction prices allows returns to come up again—and the cycle goes on.

From the late 1970s, when the U.S. PE movement is deemed to have gotten its start, until the present there have been three major waves of private equity deals and thus at least two complete boom-and-bust cycles. The first wave, as mentioned earlier, peaked at the end of the '80s. New capital flowed into the industry, attracted by the high returns earned by firms like KKR and Berkshire Partners. But when the economy turned down at the end of the '80s, roughly a third of the deals transacted in the late '80s, as we saw earlier, ended up defaulting.

The next serious downturn was the collapse of the second great wave of private equity during the Global Financial Crisis in 2008. During this period, the pundits—along with the vast majority of economic forecasters employed by Wall Street banks—were transfixed by the looming "wall of debt" and projected default rates as high as 50 percent. The popular business press responded with story after story about the imminent death of private equity.

Once again, the rumors of PE's demise proved premature. Even though the second wave of PE deals peaked with the large transactions of 2006 and 2007—like TXU (now Energy Future Holdings), which ended up in chapter 11—the overall losses turned out to be quite manageable, and for a number of reasons. First, as mentioned earlier, the deals transacted in the '90s and after were less leveraged than the '80s buyouts, and there was more flexibility built into the capital structures. In addition, the combination of operating capabilities and general financial management expertise, including experience in restructuring distressed debt, proved to be more effective in managing the "wall of debt" than almost anyone seemed to be expecting.

* * *

So that's where private equity has been. What about the future? How will the industry avoid the temptation to put the massive amounts of "dry powder" to work in deals that end up shortchanging their LPs?

Barring significant regulatory developments, the PE industry seems bound to continue to be an important part of the economy going forward, and for at least three main reasons. First, the GPs will continue to bring the core competencies of financial, governance, and operational engineering to their portfolio companies. Not only have they continued to upgrade and improve those operating capabilities, but the massive dislocations associated with the pandemic have, if anything, provided PE with more opportunities to do so. Many companies have been forced to rethink and rework their business models while dealing with unimaginable financial challenges—and have emerged from the process more focused and resilient.

Reinforcing this prediction, Harvard Business School's PE expert Josh Lerner and Stanford's Shai Bernstein studied the performance of PE buyouts in the UK in the aftermath of the Global Financial Crisis. What they found is that while UK public companies were in retreat and cutting investment, PE-controlled British companies were receiving significant infusions of outside capital, enabling them to maintain higher levels of investment and profitability than their public competitors and counterparts.[35] As Jensen has long maintained about highly leveraged companies in general, this is exactly what PE-owned companies and PE firms are *expected* to do: prepare for downturns and crises—and use their stored-up capital to seize the opportunities that are bound to arise from them.

A second important reason for PE's promising future is that private equity continues to be more attractive to public company CEOs and other senior management than in the past. The perennial populist attack on public company CEO pay continues in full fury, even as the CEOs of successful PE-controlled private companies can and do earn significantly more (for superior performance) than their public counterparts. For public company CEOs, the twin burden of regulatory compliance and public scrutiny of communication with investors and other stakeholders shows no sign of going away. As a consequence, the well-documented tendency for private companies to stay private longer—in many cases, permanently[36]—continues. Perhaps the clearest testimony to this trend is the relatively new and rapidly growing phenomenon known as "unicorns"—private companies with billion-dollar or higher market caps.[37]

A third important feature of private equity is that the duration (or average maturity or holding period) of the GPs' investments in portfolio companies roughly matches, by design, the duration of the capital supplied by LPs. PE funds invest in their portfolio companies for five to eight years, and the capital is tied up for that period. This is quite different from, say, hedge funds, where the capital flows in and out, often without regard to the time horizon of the investments. For many if not most hedge funds—and for most investment banks as well—the mismatch between their investments and funding sources caused enormous problems during the Global Financial Crisis. The contracts between GPs and LPs in private equity are designed to prevent such a mismatch. With estimates of their available dry powder now running around $3 trillion, today's PE industry appears to have the capital as well as the managerial capability to deal with the financial and operational challenges that emerged during the pandemic and have continued to crop up since.

ARE THERE LIMITS TO LBOS AND PE OWNERSHIP?

Recent estimates by Steve Kaplan and Paul Gompers of the aggregate franchise value (debt plus equity, assuming 50 percent leverage) of today's over 8,000 PE-owned U.S. companies show PE having attained a total market cap roughly equivalent to 10 percent of the total market cap of U.S. public companies.[38] How much higher is that number likely to go; and if not much, what's keeping PE from increasing its total ownership of U.S. enterprises?

One limiting factor used to be PE's reliance on high leverage. But with today's PE-funded companies now reportedly operating with 50 percent equity or more, high-growth and high-tech companies appear among them with some regularity. So capital structure no longer appears to be a binding constraint on the kinds of companies owned by PE buyout firms and funds.

A second, and likely more binding, limitation on PE-led buyouts stems from one of their principal benefits: concentration of equity ownership. For with such concentration also comes the problem of excessive concentration of risk-bearing. One of the main advantages of the public corporation, as we saw earlier, is its efficiency in spreading risk among well-diversified investors. But

(continued on next page)

(continued from previous page)

this idea alone should suggest that increasing the "firm-specific" risk borne by the board and management team becomes self-defeating. The reality is that, as their risk continues to increase, such owners will require sufficiently higher compensating rewards, in the form of stock or profit sharing (PE owners generally look for returns on equity of 20–25 percent), that there will be less and less left over to attract and reward their minority shareholders (or LPs).

All this means that it's likely to be the heavy concentration of risk and risk-bearing (and the associated desire for "liquidity"), not managerial short-sightedness, that explains why so many LBOs return to public ownership in five years or less. When they enter into an LBO, both the new owners and the operating managers are betting on their ability to increase the value of the organization. But to limit the scope of their bet and minimize their exposure to risks beyond their control, they typically have an exit or cash-out strategy.

In his study of "The Staying Power of Leveraged Buyouts" (cited earlier) and in follow-up work, Steve Kaplan reported that, as of early 1993, roughly half of the LBOs transacted during the 1980s had reverted to public ownership through either IPOs or sales to public companies. And as Steve interprets this finding, there appear to be two distinct kinds of LBOs: (1) a "shock-therapy" variety in which the LBO provides a vehicle for "one-time improvements"; and (2) a relatively permanent "incentive-intensive" type, in which the company's investors and managers become convinced the company is fundamentally more valuable when private. But as Steve also reports, even those LBOs that returned to public ownership through IPOs retain two distinguishing features of the LBO form: (1) higher leverage (though below their buyout levels) than their public competitors'; and (2) significantly more concentrated equity ownership—over 40 percent, on average—by insiders.

LESSONS FOR PUBLIC COMPANIES

What if anything can U.S. public companies learn from the PE success story? The high returns and sheer volume of capital committed to private equity raise questions that many public company managements and boards should be asking themselves:

- Do we have more (or less) capital than we need to operate effectively and safely?
- Is it possible that we would operate more efficiently, and be more valuable, in the hands of a reputable PE firm?
- Even if we're more valuable as a public company, are there elements of the PE governance model we might consider importing?

Thanks in part to the successes of private equity, U.S. corporate governance has improved significantly in recent decades. In an article we ran in the *JACF* in 2003 called "The State of U.S. Corporate Governance," Steve Kaplan joined MIT's Nobel laureate Bengt Holmstrom in making a forceful case that far more had gone right than wrong with U.S. public companies during the 1980s and 1990s.[39] The article was intended as a response to the much-publicized governance failures at companies like Enron and WorldCom that, after the public outcry, provided the catalyst for the governance reforms in the Sarbanes-Oxley Act of 2002. And as such, the article addressed itself to two main questions: was the U.S. corporate governance system really as bad as critics were suggesting? Were the legislative and regulatory changes likely to lead to a more effective system?

Kaplan and Holmstrom began by pointing out that during the two decades stretching back to the early 1980s, the U.S. economy and stock markets had outperformed virtually all others, even in the wake of the corporate scandals in 2001. The most notable changes in U.S. corporate governance in the '80s and '90s—the growth in institutional share ownership of U.S. public companies and the dramatic increase in equity-based executive pay—had worked for the most part (though with regrettable exceptions like Enron) to strengthen the accountability of U.S. managers to their shareholders. As for the effectiveness of Sarbanes Oxley and other reforms, Steve and Bengt concluded that while parts of the U.S. governance system may have failed under the exceptional strain created by the bull market of the 1990s, the corrective market forces built into the overall system—forces that work in tandem with government oversight—had reacted quickly and decisively to address its weaknesses.

And events since the publication of this article in 2003 seem to have borne out their assessment. The shareholder returns to U.S. companies in the most recent two decades, while underperforming the returns to LPs in private equity funds, have largely continued to outpace those of their global competitors. What's more, the incentives faced by today's public company

CEOs, as reflected in their larger equity stakes and somewhat higher pay for performance, along with more vigilant monitoring by corporate boards, as demonstrated by significantly higher rates of CEO turnover, have made the management of public companies a potentially more rewarding, but also a far riskier, job than in the past.

In short, although the U.S. CEO pay system is by no means flawless (as we will see in chapter 9), public company CEOs today are treated much more like the CEOs of PE-owned private companies than in the past. Until the onset of the pandemic in 2020, dividends and stock buybacks were running at near record levels, thanks to greater attention to managing corporate inventories and cash. And since the cessation of the COVID pandemic, and even through the most recent round of Fed interest rate hikes, the resilience and productivity of U.S. public companies have continued to be reflected in stock returns that have defied the projections of most business economists and forecasters.

CLOSING THOUGHTS: THE PROMISE OF SHAREHOLDER ACTIVISM AND THE BLUEPRINT FOR BOARD 3.0

For the steadily shrinking number of U.S. public companies during the last 20 or so years—there are just about half as many of them today as in the late '90s—the poison pills patented, designed, and installed at many of America's largest public companies by Marty Lipton, America's most famous corporate lawyer, have made hostile takeovers a much less visible part of the U.S. corporate control market. What we now call "shareholder activism" has largely taken the place of takeovers, providing evidence of the significant value that continues to be lost through the separation of ownership from control in public companies. Instead of the complete or controlling positions sought by hostile acquirers, today's shareholder activists take large minority equity positions in public companies they believe to be undervalued or underperforming, and then use those positions to propose changes in the companies' operating or financial policies.

The proliferation of such shareholder activists is part of a larger phenomenon that Columbia Law professors Ron Gilson and Jeff Gordon have identified as *agency capitalism*.[40] To the extent that the proxy contests associated with shareholder activism are less disruptive than the hostile takeovers of the '80s, agency capitalism might be viewed as a successor to and dramatic improvement over both Adolf Berle's managerial capitalism and the corporate control transactions hailed by Jensen and the Rochester School.

But as Gilson and Gordon point out, today's shareholder activism would not have been possible without the "reconcentration" of the ownership of U.S. public companies that took place during the past 50 years. Starting from the late '60s and early '70s, legions of individual shareholders have been replaced by the steady growth in the holdings of large institutional investors, such as pension funds, mutual funds, and bank trust departments—to the point where such institutions are now said to own over 70 percent of the stock of the largest 1,000 U.S. public corporations. In many of these companies, as Gilson and Gordon have noted, "as few as two dozen institutional investors"—few enough to "fit around a boardroom table"—control positions large enough "to exert substantial influence, if not effective control."[41]

But this shift to agency capitalism, as Gilson and Gordon also point out, has brought with it a somewhat new and different set of conflicts of interest and their associated costs. Because most institutional investors are "quasi-indexers" with highly diversified portfolios, who compete (and are compensated) on the basis of relative performance, they have little incentive to engage in the vigorous monitoring and investor activism that could correct shortcomings in corporate performance. As a result, these institutional investors—along with the large and growing body of actual indexers like Vanguard and BlackRock—are said to be "rationally apathetic" about corporate governance, at least when it comes to monitoring the performance of individual companies.

The emergence of shareholder activists in the past 15 or 20 years can be seen as the capital market response to the governance vacuum created by this passivity of well-diversified (and indexed) institutional investors. Today's activist hedge funds are now playing a critically important role in supporting this relatively new ownership structure. But rather than taking control positions like the raiders of yore, the activists use their minority stakes to propose major strategic or financial changes that are then decided upon through proxy contests involving *the voting of institutional shareholders.*

Such institutional investors, as characterized by Gilson and Gordon, are not apathetic, but rather rationally "reticent." After the activists do most of the talking, the possibility of a shareholder vote provides what Gilson and Gordon call "the forum for the expression of institutional shareholder voice." And as they add, "It's important to recognize that the institutions are by no means rubber stamps for the activists' proposals; in some cases they vote for the proposals, in many other cases against them."[42] In so doing, the institutions function as the long-term arbiters of whether such proposals should go forward.

The Case for Investor Control Through Shareholder Voting. But all this begs the question: Why should we entrust institutional shareholders with the right to vote on matters of corporate business and financial strategy—matters that the business judgment rule has traditionally made the purview of managements and boards? Are such shareholders really sophisticated and farsighted enough to have veto power over decisions with major long-run consequences?

Without providing a definitive answer to this question, I'm going to close with a few suggestive pieces of evidence from two studies we published recently in the *JACF*. In both cases, we get to see how corporate managers act when faced with the prospect of submitting major financing or strategic decisions to a shareholder vote. And in both cases, they make what at least appear to be significantly better choices for their shareholders than when forced to consult just their own boards.

The first of the two is Boston College finance professor Cliff Holderness's remarkable "meta study" of over 100 studies of the market reaction to announcements of the three main kinds of seasoned stock offerings—public offers, rights offers, and private placements—by public companies in 23 different countries.[43] What Holderness finds is an astonishingly simple, and consistent, empirical regularity: When shareholders are required to approve new stock issues, the average stock returns to announcements of seasoned stock offerings by public companies are *positive*—on the order of 2 percent (and highly statistically significant). But when managers issue stock without shareholder approval, as we have already seen in the case of U.S. public offerings, the returns are significantly negative—-2 percent to –3 percent, on average.

In the second of the two cases, Professors Marco Becht, Andrea Polo, and Stefano Rossi report strikingly consistent positive market responses to announcements of large acquisitions by UK companies that *require* shareholder approval (so-called Class 1 transactions where the target's market cap is at least 25 percent of the acquirer's), in sharp contrast to the zero or negative average announcement returns for the (Class 2) transactions not subject to a shareholder vote.[44] In a follow-up study of U.S. M&A markets—where even the largest deals can easily be (and typically are) structured to avoid shareholder votes—the authors found that the larger U.S. deals provided returns to their shareholders that were significantly negative, on average. Because many of the U.S. deals were so large, they may well have led to very large longer-run (on top of the immediate announcement-related) losses for their shareholders. Think of the massive losses that AOL's purchase of TimeWarner and HP's purchase of Compaq ended up inflicting on their own shareholders! Such deals would never been allowed by UK shareholders.

Providing more direct testimony of the promise of agency capitalism, a study of "The Early Returns to Hedge Fund Activists" by Marco Becht, Julian Franks, Jeremy Grant, and Hannes Wagner looks at the longer-run effects of some 1,740 separate "engagements" of public companies by 330 different hedge funds operating in 23 countries during the period 2000–2010. Like many other studies of activists, this one starts by confirming the market's initial enthusiasm about activists' block purchases and proposals. But the initial positive returns (of around 6–7 percent in almost all countries) are maintained only when the engagements lead to "events" with consequences—outcomes like increases in payouts, board replacements, or restructurings. In such cases, the initial returns end up significantly higher than 6 percent. Also providing support for the idea of agency capitalism, the authors report that the incidence and probability of activist engagements are greatest in companies and countries with large proportions of institutional investors, particularly when the investors happen to be based in the U.S.

To the extent that we expect these findings about shareholder voting to be borne out by future corporate performance, we should join Gilson and Gordon in offering a cautiously optimistic welcome for this new era of agency capitalism. On the basis of this new thinking and evidence, giving "reticent" shareholders more of a say in important corporate decisions seems likely to have far more benefits than costs. On the other hand, the fact that even as progressive an investor as Black-Rock has found itself voting against 75 percent of its ESG-related shareholder proposals suggests that far too many of today's proposals, especially those by investors with minimal holdings, are proving a waste of corporate time and attention.

The Case for Board 3.0. To the extent U.S. public companies can continue to expect gains from replicating PE's financial engineering, perhaps the largest are likely to come from the degree of board-level expertise, incentives, and engagement that characterize companies run by PE investors. Gilson and Gordon have for several years been floating a proposal they call "Board 3.0" that seems well worth considering. In place of today's public company directors, whom they characterize as "thinly informed," "resourced-deprived," and "under-motivated,"

Gilson and Gordon envision directors who are "thickly informed," "well-resourced," and "highly motivated" by equity ownership. Such directors could go a long way toward reducing the costs resulting from the information gaps that can arise between not only management and its outside shareholders, but between management and the directors who are supposed to represent the interest of shareholders.

* * *

Many of the proposals submitted by activist shareholders promise to increase the long-run efficiency and value of public companies, especially proposals made by reputable activists with large ownership positions, operating expertise, and well-established track records. Better-informed and -motivated directors can increase the odds that corporate boards and institutional shareholders choose wisely when responding to the growing number of proposals by shareholder activists.

In particular, managements and boards have to work hard to distinguish value-increasing (or at least value-preserving) ESG initiatives and investments from those that will clearly reduce long-run value, and thus the financial sustainability of the company itself. The kind of Board 3.0 directors envisioned by Gilson and Gordon, as Mike Jensen and Steve Kaplan would agree, are likely to prove more decisive, and long-run cost-effective, in sorting the wheat from the chaff.

CHAPTER 8

THE RISE AND FALL OF STERN STEWART'S EVA FINANCIAL MANAGEMENT SYSTEM

T he information revolution that took off in the 1970s, together with the pace of technological change and the rise of a global economy, led to major changes in the structure and internal control systems of large organizations. Centrally directed economies (notably China's, as we'll see in chapter 11) continue to falter, state-owned enterprises continue to be privatized (almost everywhere except China), and non-profits everywhere continue to experiment with new ways of motivating employees and selling their services.

In corporate America during the 1980s and 1990s, the huge conglomerates built up during the 1960s and '70s—organizations that might be viewed as the epitome of central planning in the private sector—were steadily pulled apart and supplanted by more focused competitors. The spread of powerful computer and telecommunications networks contributed to a worldwide move toward decentralization or, to use the more fashionable term, "empowerment." With the flattening of management hierarchies, corporate decision-making was driven down through the ranks to managers and employees closer to the company's operations and customers.

But as both business leaders and organizational theorists have long understood, there are significant risks and costs associated with decentralizing decision-making. Today's information systems may now be capable of providing top management with real-time monitoring of the revenues and profits of the most far-flung operations. But what software is programmed to report opportunities lost by business unit managers too comfortable with the status quo? And what accounting systems are capable of distinguishing between profitable and unprofitable corporate investment decisions *at the time* the decisions are being made?

The answer, of course, is that this kind of information tends to reside with experienced line managers and employees—those positioned to serve as the nerve-endings of the organization—and it will be used to benefit the firm only insofar as those managers and employees are highly motivated and focused on the right goals. And this means that companies that push decision-making down into lower levels of the organization must also ensure that their internal control systems are up to the challenge. Such companies will often find it necessary to rethink their performance measurement and reward systems to increase the odds that operating managers use their expanded decision-making powers in ways that increase the value of the firm. In this sense, decentralization, performance measurement, and compensation policy can be seen as constituting what some view as a "three-legged stool" of effective corporate governance.[1]

We begin this chapter by showing why, for most large public companies, the top-down, earnings per share-based model of financial management that long dominated corporate America—or what we have been calling "old-fashioned corporate finance"—became obsolete. Among the first serious challengers to the long reign of EPS was Economic Value Added, or EVA, a measure formulated and popularized in the early 1990s by the New York-based consulting firm Stern Stewart & Co. (where, as mentioned, I was one of seven founding partners). Many U.S. companies started using EVA as the basis for evaluating their periodic performance and rewarding not only their CEOs but also the heads of their operating units—and, in companies like Coca Cola, nearly every employee in the company. (Even the U.S. Post Office had a brief fling with the measure—one that ended up producing notable increases in efficiency before politics-as-usual put an end to this promising experiment.)

By 1993, the measure had achieved such a vogue that it was featured on the cover of *Fortune* magazine. What's more, in a *Harvard Business Review* article around the same time, management guru Peter Drucker hailed EVA not as a new concept, but rather as a practical refinement of economists' well-established concept of "residual income"—the value that is left over after a company's stockholders and all other providers of capital have received their (often contractually specified) due. As Drucker also observed, EVA was the "first practicable measure of *total factor productivity*"—one whose extraordinary rise and popularity reflected the new demands of the information age. Companies that aimed to increase their competitiveness by decentralizing decision-making recognized that EVA could be a sensible basis for evaluating and rewarding the periodic performance of empowered line people, especially those entrusted with major capital spending decisions.

But as my fellow partners Joel Stern and Bennett Stewart liked to tell anyone who would listen (and as editor of the *Journal of Applied Corporate Finance*, I was not above allowing such claims to be made by contributors to our publication), EVA was more than just a performance measure. When fully implemented throughout a large organization, it was meant to be the centerpiece of an integrated financial management system that encompassed the full range of corporate financial decision-making—everything from capital budgeting, acquisition pricing, and corporate goal-setting to shareholder communication and management incentive compensation. By putting all financial and operating functions on the same basis, an EVA system could provide a common language for employees across all corporate functions, linking strategic planning with the operating divisions, and the corporate treasury staff with investor relations and human resources.

And for a good many companies, EVA succeeded in providing such a language— along with a shared understanding of the corporate mission and a value-driven culture. But EVA's influence began to wane with the "dotcom" bubble at the end of the '90s and the demand by investors for growth, especially growth in revenue. In fact, starting in or around 1999 until the bursting of the bubble in 2001, investors seemed to care *only* about revenue, and both EVA's cachet and the fortunes of Stern Stewart began to decline.

In what follows, I start by showing the shortcomings of the top-down, EPS-based model of financial management—a model that, however impressive the results when practiced by Jack Welch (and at least some of his many disciples), was in fact starting on its way out when Welch took control of GE in the early 1980s. Next, we view the rise of hostile takeovers—as well as the phenomenal success of LBOs just discussed—in the 1980s as capital market responses to the deficiencies of the EPS model. Then we turn to the EVA financial management system that, as we will see, borrows important aspects of the LBO movement—especially its focus on capital efficiency and ownership incentives—but without the high leverage and concentration of risk-bearing that back then limited LBOs to the mature sector of the U.S. economy. In the penultimate section, we present the outlines of an EVA-based incentive compensation plan designed to simulate for managers and employees the rewards of ownership. And in the final section, with the help of my former colleague Steve O'Byrne, who ran Stern Stewart's compensation practice from 1992–1998 (in what might be called "the heyday" of Stern Stewart and EVA), I offer some hints as to why the EVA financial system did not end up taking hold.

OLD-FASHIONED CORPORATE FINANCE: EPS-DRIVEN FINANCIAL MANAGEMENT

As Harvard Business School's legendary business historian Alfred Chandler has demonstrated in some of the most admired and widely cited books on corporate strategy,[2] the centralized top-down approach to managing large corporations was well suited to the relatively stable business environment—one we earlier identified as the era of "controlled capitalism"—that prevailed during the first two or three decades after World War II. The principal challenge of top management in those days was to achieve the huge economies of scale in manufacturing and marketing then available to companies seeking growth opportunities in the same or closely related businesses.

In that age of stability, the top managements of most large U.S. companies aimed to report steady increases in EPS by calling on each of their operating divisions to produce a given amount of profits each year. Because new capital appropriations for all the divisions—the total amount of which effectively determined the denominator in the EPS calculation—were usually tightly controlled from the top, a given amount of profits aggregated across all the divisions—the numerator in the calculation—enabled top management to hit its EPS target, barring a sharp economic downturn.

The strategy of corporate diversification that became popular in the late 1960s and 1970s (which Chandler himself later described as "both a disaster and an historical aberration")[3] can be explained in part as an attempt by top management to increase its ability to "manage" (many would call it "manipulate") its reported EPS. For one thing, the popular practice of buying companies with lower P/E multiples in stock-for-stock exchanges automatically boosted reported EPS—even though such "EPS bootstrapping," as the practice was called, was pure accounting artifice, with no economic substance whatsoever. Corporate diversification also helped produce less variable operating cash flows for the entire firm and so smooth reported earnings.

Also contributing to top management's ability to deliver steadily rising earnings, at least for a time, was the annual corporate rite of negotiating divisional budget targets. In a time-honored practice known as *sandbagging*, division heads with greater knowledge of their business prospects than corporate staffers would underestimate the profit potential of their own units when negotiating their budgets with headquarters. Having low-balled their estimates and negotiated easy targets, these division heads often "banked" excess profits for a rainy day—for example, by shifting revenues or costs across reporting periods.

This behavior can be readily explained by standard features of the corporate reward system. In most companies, the annual bonus awards of division heads were capped at a fairly modest fraction (say, 20–30 percent) of base salary, thus limiting their participation in exceptional profits. What's more, truly extraordinary performance in any one year could have the unwanted effect of sharply raising future years' budget targets, as well as casting doubt on the integrity of the managers making the forecasts.

Why didn't CEOs abandon this practice altogether and just give their division heads a fixed percentage of division profits? After all, this appears to have worked well for Jack Welch at General Electric, whom we've already identified as the most successful practitioner of old-fashioned corporate finance.

As some economists and management experts have rightly pointed out, excessive reliance on division profit-sharing plans can discourage cooperation among divisions. Purely "objective" division performance measures have the potential to undermine efforts to realize synergies among different business units—presumably the reason they are under the same corporate umbrella in the first place—by creating or fueling internal conflicts that end up reducing overall firm value.[4]

But another, more compelling explanation for the widespread use of negotiated budgets is that this budgeting process also helped top management produce the smoothly rising EPS intended to satisfy shareholders. Thus, while division heads were sandbagging their estimates for headquarters, top managements were in a sense sandbagging *their shareholders*, managing their investors' expectations while concealing the true profit potential of the business.

As Harvard Business School's highly regarded corporate finance professor Gordon Donaldson has argued, the understanding implicit in this management philosophy of the 1960s and '70s was that a company's shareholders represented only one of several important corporate constituencies whose interests must be served. Top managers saw their primary task not as maximizing shareholder value, but rather as achieving the proper balance among the interests of shareholders and those of other stakeholders such as employees, suppliers, and local communities.[5] In this view of the world, reporting steady increases in EPS was equivalent to giving shareholders their due.

This approach worked reasonably well—at least as long as product markets were relatively stable, and international competitors and corporate raiders remained dormant. By the early 1980s, however, the deficiencies of the top-down, EPS-based system were beginning to show in several ways. Strategically diversified conglomerates such as Northwest Industries, Beatrice Foods, ITT, and General Mills (which, as we saw earlier, proudly proclaimed itself the "all-weather growth company")[6] all saw their stock returns significantly underperform market averages, even as the companies were producing steady increases in EPS. The operations of such diversified firms began to be outperformed by smaller, more specialized companies. And as it became clearer that large, centralized conglomerates were worth far less than the sum of their parts, corporate raiders launched what became a U.S.-economy-wide deconglomeration movement.

At the heart of the failure of the top-down, EPS-based control system was its refusal to empower divisional managers, to make them feel and act as if they were stewards of investor capital. Business units whose performance was being evaluated mainly on the basis of operating profits had little reason to be concerned with the level of investment required to achieve those profits. The primary incentive of operating managers was to achieve (moderate) growth in profits, which could be accomplished in two ways: (1) improve the efficiency of existing operations or (2) win more capital appropriations from headquarters. Because most corporate measurement systems did not hold corporate managers accountable for new capital, managers quickly recognized that it was easier to "buy" additional operating profits by increasing their capital allotments and expenditures—even if the investment did not promise anything like an acceptable rate of return—than trying to wring out efficiencies. As one example, just before the company's takeover over by KKR, RJR Nabisco's CEO Ross Johnson reportedly approved a $2.8 billion outlay for a state-of-the-art cookie manufacturing facility whose projected pre-tax rate of return was a meager 5 percent.[7]

This standard capital budgeting procedure led in turn to what might be called the "politicization" of corporate investment, a process in which persuasive and well-positioned business unit managers received too much capital while their less favored counterparts received too little. The top-down EPS system also tolerated the widespread practice of corporate cross-subsidization, in which the surplus cash flow of profitable divisions was wasted on diversifying acquisitions or futile efforts to shore up unpromising divisions. The result was chronic overinvestment in some areas and underinvestment in others. In many cases, it was the more profitable but capital-starved business units that ended up being sold in LBOs to their own management teams, with the financial backing of outsiders like KKR and Clayton & Dubilier.

CORPORATE RAIDERS AND CAPITAL EFFICIENCY

But as we saw in chapter 4, the widespread corporate misallocation and waste of capital under the EPS-based system did not escape the attention of "corporate raiders" in the 1980s. In making their own assessments of potential value, the raiders used a performance metric that was quite different from EPS. They were concerned primarily with companies' ability to generate cash flow (not earnings) and with their efficiency in using capital.

LESSONS FROM THE SAFEWAY LBO

Consider the following testimony from Peter Magowan, who was the CEO of Safeway Stores both before and after the company's LBO by KKR in 1986:

> When Safeway was a public company, our reported earnings grew at 20 percent per year for five years in a row, from 1981 to 1985 . . . We thought all the while that we were doing quite well. Our stock tripled during that period of time, we raised the dividend four years in a row, and 20 percent earnings growth seemed pretty darn good . . .
>
> But we were still subjected to a hostile takeover in 1986—and deservedly so. We were not earning adequate rates of return on the capital we were investing to achieve that 20 percent growth. We were not realizing the values that were there for someone else to realize for our shareholders . . . For this reason, and with hindsight, it now seems clear why outsiders could come in and see a way of buying our company for $4.2 billion—which was way above its then current market value—and improving it so it was worth $5.2 billion a few years later. And I think that's an important lesson for corporate America.[8]

In many cases, as the legions of critics of takeovers pointed out, the push for capital efficiency led to cutbacks in corporate employment and investment. But in most such cases, downsizing turned out to be a value-adding strategy precisely because of the natural tendency of corporate management in mature industries that vexed Mike Jensen—the tendency to pursue growth at the expense of profitability, to overinvest in misguided attempts to maintain market share or, perhaps worst of all, to diversify into unrelated businesses. Which, again, is why the vast majority of leveraged restructurings in the '80s took place in industries with excess capacity—oil and gas, tires, paper, packaging, publishing, commodity chemicals, forest products, and retailing.

THE ROLE OF LBOS AND THE PUSH FOR A BETTER PUBLIC CORPORATE GOVERNANCE MODEL

Leveraged buyouts, as we saw in the last chapter, were among the most successful of the highly leveraged deals. And to set the stage for our discussion of EVA, let's briefly review some important differences between how LBOs operate, and the way most public companies were run, at least in the 1970s and '80s.

As newly private companies, those LBO firms that had once been public companies no longer had any motive for reporting higher EPS. This meant, for one thing, that LBO companies could increase their after-tax cash flow simply by choosing accounting methods that would reduce reported earnings, and hence corporate income taxes paid.

Even more important, where operating managers in many large U.S. companies tended to treat investor capital as a "free" good, the primary concern of especially the first wave of LBOs in the 1980s was to produce sufficient operating cash flow to meet their high required interest and principal payments. Besides making the cost of capital more visible to corporate managers, the heavy debt financing also provided what amounted to an automatic internal corporate monitoring-and-control system. If problems were developing, top management would be forced by the pressure of the debt service to intervene quickly and decisively.

But perhaps most important for the purposes of this discussion, operating managers in LBOs were also provided—if not required to purchase—significant equity stakes in their own businesses. Such ownership encouraged managers to resist the temptation, potentially strong in cases of high leverage, to produce "short-term" profits at the expense of the corporate future—and to devote the *optimal* level, neither too much nor too little, of corporate capital to investments with longer-run payoffs like advertising and plant safety and maintenance. And as we saw in the last chapter, the large equity stakes for operating managers, when combined with the active participation and ownership of LBO boards, appears to have produced consistently large increases in the efficiency and enterprise values of companies acquired by PE firms.

EVA: A NEW FINANCIAL MODEL FOR PUBLIC COMPANIES

The success of the U.S. LBO movement has had a number of important lessons for the structure and governance of public companies. For most large public companies, of course, it did not make sense to raise leverage ratios to 90 percent. Nor did many companies find it cost-effective to provide significant stock ownership for most of their line operating managers. What the top managements of a large number of public companies did instead was to come up with performance-measurement-and-reward systems designed to simulate the "feel" and "payoffs" of ownership. This was the principal aim—and insofar as its succeeded, the main accomplishment—of the EVA financial management system developed and popularized by Stern Stewart & Co. during the 1990s.

Like LBOs, an EVA-based performance measurement system makes the cost of capital explicit, and of some consequence, for those being evaluated. In its simplest form, EVA is net operating profit after taxes (NOPAT) less a charge for the capital employed to produce those profits. The capital charge is the cost of capital itself, or the required rate of return (the minimum needed to compensate all the company's investors—debtholders as well as shareholders—for the risk of the investment) multiplied by the *amount* of the investment, or the total capital tied up in the company (or business unit).

To illustrate, a company (or one of its businesses) with a 10 percent cost of capital that earns a 20 percent return on its $100 million of net operating assets has an EVA of (20 percent–10 percent) x $100 million, or $10 million. This means that the company is earning $10 million more in profit than the charge for investor capital, including the opportunity cost of tying up scarce capital on the balance sheet. In this sense, EVA combines operating efficiency and balance sheet management into a single measure that can be readily understood by operating as well as finance types.

For division heads and top management alike, EVA holds out three main ways of increasing shareholder value:

- increase the return on the assets already tied up in the business;
- invest more capital and aggressively build the business as long as the return at least equals the cost of that new capital;
- stop investing in, and find ways to release capital from, activities that earn substandard returns—by, say, turning working capital faster, speeding up cycle times, consolidating operations, and selling assets worth more to others.

The use of EVA as a guide to investment decision-making, besides encouraging managers to take account of capital costs, also has an important advantage over targets based on return on equity, or ROE: it avoids the temptation of companies (or their divisions) with already very high (well above the cost of capital) reported ROEs to turn down positive-EVA or value-increasing projects in mistaken efforts to preserve their high *average* ROEs.

What's more, the EVA measure itself can be, and generally is, "customized" for different companies or their businesses by incorporating a number of other adjustments intended to eliminate distortions of economic performance introduced by conventional accounting measures. One especially notable shortcoming of GAAP accounting comes from its requirement that corporate outlays with longer-term payoffs, such as R&D or employee training, be fully expensed rather than capitalized and amortized over an appropriate period. Though well suited to creditors' concerns about liquidation values, this kind of accounting conservatism can make financial statements unreliable guides to going-concern values. And to the extent GAAP's conservatism is built into a company's performance measurement and compensation system, it can unduly shorten managers' planning horizon.

In setting up EVA systems, companies can choose to capitalize (instead of immediately expensing) portions of their R&D, marketing, training, and even restructuring costs. To handle cases involving other "strategic" investments with deferred payoffs, capital can be kept "off the books" for internal evaluation purposes, and then gradually "readmitted" into the evaluated manager's internal capital account to reflect the expected payoffs over time. In each of these ways, EVA can be used to encourage a more far-sighted corporate investment policy.

In defining and refining Stern Stewart's EVA measure, the system's chief architect, Bennett Stewart, claims to have identified as many as 120 possible shortcomings in conventional GAAP accounting. Along with GAAP's inability to handle R&D and other corporate investments, we at Stern Stewart found ourselves addressing performance measurement problems ranging from standard accounting treatments of inventory costing and valuation to issues involving depreciation, revenue recognition, the writing-off of bad debts, and mandated investments in safety and environmental compliance. We also came up with adjustments for the valuation of contingent liabilities and hedges, transfer pricing and overhead allocations, captive finance and insurance companies, and joint ventures and start-ups. For most of these accounting challenges, Stern Stewart devised a variety of practical methods to modify reported accounting results with the aim of increasing the EVA measure's effectiveness in capturing economic income.

Of course, no one company was subject to all 120 measurement issues. Adjustments to the definition of EVA were recommended *only* in cases that met four criteria:

- Was it likely to have a material impact on EVA?
- Could managers influence the outcome?
- Would operating people readily understand the adjustment, and how to respond to it?
- Was the required information relatively easy to track and report?

For any given company, the definition of EVA we settled on aimed to strike a practical balance between simplicity and precision. To make the measure more user-friendly, we developed a management tool called "EVA Drivers" designed to help managers trace EVA through the income statement and balance sheet to identify the key operating and strategic levers for running their businesses. With the help of such a framework, management could diagnose performance problems and benchmark against peers, as well as projecting and planning their capital spending. And equally important, it helped people up and down the line appreciate their own potential role in increasing long-run efficiency and value. Such an approach also worked to guard against an excessive preoccupation with improving individual operating metrics to the detriment of overall performance. (Think of companies hellbent on winning the Malcolm Baldrige Quality Award with no expense spared!)

THE EVA FINANCIAL MANAGEMENT SYSTEM

As suggested at the outset of this chapter, the success of companies in today's Information Age is widely believed—even by many business strategists—to depend less on having a well-thought-out, far-reaching strategy than on re-engineering a company's business systems to respond more effectively to an environment of continuous change. Much as the information revolution was seen as creating a demand for business process re-engineering, it was also giving rise to a need to redesign the corporate financial management system.

What do we mean by a financial management system? As we at Stern Stewart—led, again, by EVA's principal architect Bennett Stewart—thought and talked about it, it consists of all the financial policies, procedures, methods, and measures that guide a company's strategy and operations. It addresses such questions as: What are our overall corporate financial goals and how do we communicate them, both within the company and to the investment community? How do we evaluate business plans when they come up for review? How do we allocate resources, everything from the purchase of an individual piece of equipment to the acquisition of an entire company to opportunities for downsizing and restructuring? How do we evaluate ongoing operating performance? And, finally, how do we reward our people?

As we saw the problem, too many companies had needlessly complicated, and in many ways obsolete, financial management systems. Many companies were using discounted cash flow analysis for capital budgeting evaluations—but measures like earnings, EPS growth, profit margins, and return on equity for other purposes such as setting goals and communicating with investors. The result was a confusion of, and "disconnect" between, cash-flow-based capital budgeting and accounting-based corporate goals. Making matters worse, bonuses for operating managers tended to be structured around achieving annually negotiated profit numbers.

The adoption of EVA was meant to help ensure that all principal facets of the financial management process were tied to a single measure, making the overall system far easier to understand and administer and providing clarity about the financial mission of the company. Even if the process of coming up with the right definition of EVA for any given company was complicated and time-consuming, the measure itself, once established, could become the focal point of a simpler, more integrated overall financial management system—one that would allow all important management decisions to be clearly evaluated, monitored, communicated, and rewarded according to how much value they were adding for the companies' shareholders.

Why was it so important to have just one measure? The natural inclination of operating managers in large public companies, as noted earlier, is to get their hands on more capital to spend and grow the empire. This in turn leads to an overtly political internal competition for capital—one in which different performance measures are used to gain approval for pet projects. Because of this tendency toward "empire-building," top management typically feels compelled to intervene excessively—not in day-to-day decision making, but in capital spending decisions—because they don't trust the financial management system to guide their operating managers to make the right decisions. With no real accountability built into the system, there is no effective incentive for operating managers to choose only those investment projects that are expected to increase value.

EVA was designed to strengthen accountability and incentives. As the centerpiece of a financial management system, it was meant to unify—in part by making clear the expected contributions to success of—*all* the varied interests and functions within a large corporation. And at the height of its popularity in the late '90s, it was providing an impressive list of companies around the world with a new model of internal corporate governance.[9]

THE CASE OF BRIGGS AND STRATTON

At the company's annual shareholders meeting in 1991, Chairman Fred Stratton of Briggs & Stratton noted that the company's stock was up 70 percent from the previous year, having outperformed the S&P 500 by about 40 percent. Stratton attributed the company's success in large part to the company's newly adopted "performance measurement and compensation system" based on EVA.

According to the assessment offered by President and CEO John Shiely,

Part of our problem in the early 1980s was an antiquated functional top-down structure. Nobody other than the CEO and the president was being held accountable for the profitability of our various lines. Under Chairman Fred Stratton's direction, we developed a plan to totally revamp the organization into discrete operating divisions.

(continued on next page)

(*continued from previous page*)

While the initial move was painful, the positive results were almost immediate. By pushing operating responsibility, including capital investment decisions, down to the level where they could be effectively managed, we accomplished a dramatic improvement in earnings and cash flow. Each of our seven new divisions now has its own functional management, resources, and capital. Each must develop very detailed strategic business unit plans. And each has an EVA incentive based on value created by the division.

Before moving to an EVA system, the company took pride in making almost all components in-house. We now buy premium engines, at significantly lower cost, from outside sources. Molded plastics and other components, once made in small batches in-house, now flow from suppliers in huge quantities. As a result, operating profits have risen while the amount of capital required to generate them has fallen sharply.

EVA AND THE CORPORATE REWARD SYSTEM

Incentive compensation was the anchor of the EVA financial management system. In place of the traditional short-term budget-linked bonuses and ordinary stock option grants used by most public companies, the original EVA ownership plan consisted of two main elements: (1) a cash bonus plan meant to simulate ownership, and (2) a leveraged stock option (or "LSO") plan that amplified the effects of conventional stock options.

The first Stern Stewart EVA bonus plans, much like the plan that General Motors introduced in 1918, set up bonus pools that were equal to a fixed percentage of EVA. (The GM plan set aside for its managers 10 percent of total company profits in excess of a 6 percent return on total capital.) Such "fixed sharing" plans worked well for those of our corporate clients that were already (or on the verge of) producing positive EVA. But for companies or businesses that were starting deep "in the red" with negative EVA, such plans provided little prospect for gain or motive for efficiency.

To deal with this problem, the second "generation" of EVA bonus plans developed at Stern Stewart (starting around 1992) made the bonus pool equal to a fixed percentage of EVA (if positive) *plus* a percentage of the increase, or "improvement," in EVA. Because most of these plans placed greater emphasis on (and offered higher rewards for) increasing EVA, the managers of businesses with sharply negative EVA were given clear incentives to engineer turnarounds.

Like true ownership stakes, EVA cash bonuses were potentially unlimited—on the downside as well as the upside—depending entirely on managerial performance. But to guard against the possibility of short-term "gaming" of the system, Stern Stewart also devised a "bonus bank" scheme that worked as follows: Declared annual bonus awards were not paid out in full, but instead "banked"—that is, held in escrow and at risk—with full payout contingent on continued successful performance. Each year's bonus award was carried forward from the prior year and a fraction—typically a third—of that total was paid out, with the remainder "banked" into the next year.

In good years, managers were rewarded with increases in both the cash bonus paid out and the bonus bank carried forward—much like shareholders who receive cash dividends and see capital appreciation. In bad years, however, the consequences—again, much like those facing shareholders—were shrunken cash distributions and depletions of the bank balance that had to be recouped before a full cash bonus distribution again became possible. And since the bonus paid in any one year was thus partly an accumulation of the bonuses earned over time, the distinction between a long-term and a short-term bonus plan became meaningless.

The Evolution of the EVA Bonus Plan. But as things worked out, such EVA bonus plans also turned out to have a major limitation. They posed problems for companies wanting to ensure that their pay levels were always "competitive" for managers or businesses that achieved *normal*, or expected, levels of EVA. The difficulty arose from the need to keep adjusting the two sharing percentages—the share of the EVA level and the share of the EVA improvement—from one year to the next.

To meet this challenge, Stern Stewart developed a new EVA bonus plan made up of two components: (1) a "targeted" bonus designed to provide "competitive pay" for meeting normal or expected performance targets—targets that ensured the firm would be earning at least its cost of capital; and (2) a fixed percentage of any amounts above that, or what we called "excess EVA improvement." With these two parameters now firmly in place, there was no longer any need to adjust the sharing percentage from one year to the next.

And thanks to its provision for fixed sharing of both *current* EVA and *future* EVA improvements, the new EVA bonus plan was seen as giving a company's managers a stronger ownership interest in their own businesses, creating what amounted to a more fair and durable "partnership" between the managers and the firm's shareholders. Under this "new deal," managers now understood that going forward, and year in and year out (with no need for further adjustments), they would continue to receive pay that was competitive with labor market norms as long as they met their EVA-based operating targets. And to the extent they exceeded the targets (and rewarded the firm's investors), managers would end up with their fixed "fair" share of the assumed gains to shareholders.

Leveraged Stock Options: Making Ownership Real. Along with annual EVA cash bonus plans meant to simulate ownership, Stern Stewart also helped its corporate clients design actual leveraged stock ownership plans, generally as supplements to the annual bonus plans. Bennett Stewart, also the principal designer of such options, found himself faced with a fundamental challenge: How can managers with limited financial resources be made into significant owners without unfairly diluting the current shareholders? Showering them with stock options or restricted stock was likely to be quite expensive for the shareholders. But expecting managers to buy lots of stock was asking them to bear too much risk.

The approach Stewart proposed as a way out of this dilemma was to encourage—and in some cases require—managers to purchase common equity in the form of special leveraged stock options, or LSOs. Unlike ordinary options, the LSOs designed by Stewart were initially "in-the-money" and not "at-the-money," and they made the exercise price go up over time at a rate that set aside a minimal acceptable return for the shareholders *before* management's payoffs kick in. Managers' purchases of the LSOs could be funded by them as one-time investments, or by diverting a portion of each year's EVA cash bonus, or some combination of the two.

To illustrate how an LSO operates, consider a company with a current common share price of $10. The initial exercise price on the LSO is set at a 10 percent discount from the current stock price, or $9, making the option worth $1 right out of the gate. But instead of just handing the LSOs to management, managers could be required to purchase them for the $1 discount, and that money is put at risk.

Another important difference between LSOs and regular options is that the exercise price was projected to increase at a rate that approximates the cost of capital—let's say 10 percent per annum. In this case, over a five-year period (and ignoring compounding for simplicity), the exercise price would rise 50 percent above the current $9 level to $13.50. Management would thus pay $1 today for an option to purchase the company's stock (currently worth $10) for $13.50 five years down the road.

The beauty of LSOs for the company's shareholders is that management comes out ahead only if the company's equity market value grows at a rate faster than the exercise price. If the exercise price rises at a rate just equal to the cost of capital (less dividends), the LSOs are designed to provide exactly the same incentives as an EVA bonus plan. They reward management for producing the amount of economic value represented by the spread between the company's rate of return on capital and the cost of that capital—as reflected in the rate of increase in the exercise price—multiplied by the capital used by management to buy the shares.

Perhaps a better comparison, however, is between the incentives held out by LSOs and those provided by leveraged buyouts. LSOs can be seen as putting management in the position of participating in an LBO of the company, but without requiring the actual transaction. By virtue of their being purchased 10 percent in the money, LSOs effectively replicate the 90 percent debt and 10 percent equity that characterized the capital structure of the LBOs of the '80s.

A number of Stern Stewart's clients adopted such LSO plans during the 1990s. Along with the above-mentioned Wisconsin-based Briggs & Stratton were North Carolina-based Centura Bank, Virginia-based railroad company CSX, Michigan-based pharma company R.P. Scherer, Canadian manufacturer Varity (formerly Massey Ferguson), and Fletcher Challenge, the largest industrial company in New Zealand. The effectiveness of such LSO plans can be traced to the performance demand imposed by EVA, the idea that management should participate only in those returns in excess of a company's required rate of return. Though conceptually identical to an EVA bonus plan, LSOs were likely to be an even more powerful motivator by amplifying the risks and rewards for management.

To get a sense of the incentive power provided by LSOs, if we assume that any increase in EVA that investors expect to be sustained over time is capitalized into the value of the shares, then a company with a cost of capital of 10 percent that increases its EVA by $1 million can expect to see its value appreciate by roughly $10 million. But for the managers holding the LSOs, such capitalized increases in value are themselves effectively further leveraged 10 to 1, thus creating $100 of added managerial wealth for each $1 increase in EVA. This leveraging effect made LSOs a potent way to concentrate management's focus on building EVA over the long haul.

THE DECLINE OF EVA

The rise and reign, however brief, of the EVA financial management system, when viewed as an attempt to institutionalize the running of a business in accord with basic microeconomic principles, deserves to be seen (even after taking account of the biases of this writer) as one of the success stories of modern corporate finance. When implemented wisely and well, EVA created what Stewart liked to describe as "a closed-loop system of decision-making, accountability, and incentives," a system that aimed to make entire organizations (not just CEOs) responsible for the successes and failures of the enterprise. It held out the promise of creating a self-regulating and self-motivating system of internal corporate governance. And when properly discounted for the inevitable bluster, such a statement seems to be a fair description of what actually took place at companies like Herman Miller, Ball Corporation, SPX, Vulcan Materials, and Manitowoc (a longtime favorite of *Mad Money* host Jim Cramer), in most of these cases over several decades.

But what ended up happening to the EVA financial management system? In 1999, Stern Stewart published a list of corporate clients that included 66 companies that professed to be guided by EVA. By 2008, however, only 39 of them were still independent public companies; and just six of those 39 claimed to be still using EVA—a shrinkage rate of over 90 percent.

Steve O'Byrne, who directed Stern Stewart's executive compensation practice during its heyday from 1992 to 1998, set himself the task of explaining EVA's fairly abrupt fall from prominence in a 2019 *JACF* article he called "Why EVA Failed."[10] Part of Steve's explanation focuses on the at least perceived complexity—or what also might be described as the "excessive ingenuity"—of the compensation systems that he himself, along with Bennett Stewart, had designed. But another part has to do with the accumulation of large "negative bonuses" in Stern Stewart-designed bonus banks. In the case of two of the most committed EVA companies, Herman Miller and Manitowoc, top management became so concerned about their companies' ability to retain their best operating managers that they chose to abandon the bonus bank practice altogether. The crux of the problem was that two years of terrible industry conditions had pushed the accumulated operating bonuses so far into the red that even the firm's best operating managers had little expectation of seeing a bonus payout in the foreseeable future. And in both of these cases, the EVA bonus systems had to be circumvented, if not short-circuited entirely.

As Steve himself now sees things, such problems with the EVA bonus plans could have been weathered with further adjustments. But in our view, there were deeper forces at work undermining EVA. What really sealed the fate of the EVA financial management system was the transition of the U.S. to a growth economy that moved into high gear at the very end of the 1990s. The inflating of the U.S. dotcom bubble, in which companies' revenue potential almost completely eclipsed their efficient use of capital as the main variable of investor interest and driver of value, effectively ensured that EVA would no longer be a good fit for the world's most valuable companies. To be sure, EVA might still be used to capture the value of, and serve as a guide for, steady-state companies with relatively limited growth prospects. But for companies on a clear growth trajectory with aspirations, the use of EVA could end up imposing a strait-jacket that prevented management from making bold bets on their future—from jumping into new markets the way Amazon did, with little concern about earnings, or at least near-term returns on capital, armed mainly with a strong conviction that the returns would materialize over time.

※　※　※

As Steve O'Byrne saw it, the big concern about EVA for companies with any appreciable growth prospects around the turn of the millennium was its failure to make sufficient accommodation for a well-known phenomenon that he called "the delayed productivity of capital." It's true that the EVA calculation could be adjusted—say, by capitalizing and amortizing (instead of immediately expensing) R&D and brand-building expenditures. But even with such tweaking, the EVA measure was still bound to understate the value of truly promising growth investments.

As if to confirm this, Steve's analysis of five-year S&P 1500 stock returns showed that whereas five-year changes in standard operating earnings (or NOPAT) explained almost half of the variation in stock returns during the periods ending with the years 1994–2007, the five-year changes in EVA accounted for little more than about 20 percent. And it was the capital charges associated with EVA that appeared to be the main culprit in understating corporate performance as perceived by the market.

To provide a remedy for this "delayed productivity" effect, Stern Stewart developed a kind of "strategic value accounting" adjustment that worked by phasing in capital charges gradually over time. Such a system might work as follows: Suppose a company makes an investment of $500 whose expected return is zero in the first year and gradually rises to 13 percent over the next six years. To prevent the capital charge from penalizing near-term performance and discouraging investment, the company defers the charge by putting it into a "strategic investment reserve"—a reserve that is then gradually transferred back into the NOPAT and EVA calculations and fully amortized by the end of the six-year period. With the help of such accounting, the company's (adjusted) EVA calculation ends up roughly reflecting the expected growth in the profitability of the investment in much the same way stock prices do.

The fact that Stern Stewart found so few public companies willing to be guided by this kind of analysis should not come as a surprise, especially during the heady days of the dot.com boom. But in the absence of such a calculation, what should corporate managements and boards have done? These were days, after all, when the entire value sector was trading at a mere five or six times earnings, and when even the legendary Warren Buffett seemed to have lost his touch.

WHAT, THEN, SHOULD CORPORATE DIRECTORS DO?

In theory at least, wise and experienced corporate directors and managers could conceivably have found ways to provide more effective incentives than formulas based on capital efficiency measures and industry adjustments. Even today, three decades later, a handful of companies like the Ball Corporation in Broomfield, Colorado and Vulcan Materials in Birmingham, Alabama continue to evaluate and reward their divisional managers using some variant of EVA (though Vulcan now identifies its performance measure as "Adjusted EBITDA Economic Profit"). Such loyalty reflects the reality that, for relative mature steady-state companies with predictable growth opportunities, the capital discipline provided by the EVA system is likely to remain quite valuable. And EVA also now reportedly appears to be achieving a foothold among private equity-controlled portfolio companies.

As for the EVA bonus bank system, although most of today's boards seem comfortable with single-year incentive formulas, most also appear to remain convinced that giving directors discretion over bonuses ends up providing more efficient and effective incentives than multi-year incentive formulas based on capital efficiency measures and industry adjustments.

But, as we will see in the next chapter, Steve's ongoing research suggests that although executive (including CEO) pay has contributed significantly to U.S. corporate productivity and stock returns, U.S. corporate directors' confidence in their own discretion has in some respects proved misguided. Thanks to a set of practices known as "competitive pay," measures of U.S. CEO pay-for-performance began to drop off sharply after World War II. And notwithstanding some promising changes in the '90s, such measures have made at most a partial comeback from the low point of the 1970s. Indeed, in Steve's reckoning, much of the success of U.S. private equity can be attributed to remaining problems with public company CEO pay—too much for mediocre performers, but too little for the best.

CHAPTER 9

THE PERENNIAL PROBLEM OF U.S. CEO PAY AND STEVE O'BYRNE'S QUEST FOR THE PERFECT PAY PLAN

S teve O'Byrne's now 40-year-plus career as a corporate compensation consultant has brought him up against a reality that has made his job considerably more difficult. The obstacle Steve continues to run into is that so few of today's U.S. public company directors—the people charged with approving and overseeing executive pay plans—seem to have any awareness that executive pay in corporate America during the first half of the 20th century was very different from what it is today.

Until the late 1950s or early 1960s, U.S. pay practices were guided by the principle of "fixed sharing," according to which management expected a fixed portion of a company's profits and the company's investors received the rest. The main basis for such sharing was a simple version of the EVA performance measure discussed in the previous chapter—a measure that took full account of the cost of investor capital when calculating managerial rewards.

Thanks to this collective amnesia, few of today's public company boards appear to have thought about the incentive consequences of giving up fixed sharing. By contrast, the investor-dominated boards of U.S. private equity-controlled companies have never had to confront this issue—because fixed sharing, mainly in the form of managerial equity ownership, has been one of PE's core principles, and a key contributor to its remarkable success, from its beginnings in the late '70s.

O'Byrne's career might be summed up as a search for what he calls "the perfect pay plan"—one whose design is meant to achieve a 100 percent positive correlation between not just long-run pay and long-run performance, but long-run *relative* pay (that is, how much more or less did you make over your tenure than the average for your industry and level of responsibility?) and long-run *relative* performance (how did your long-run performance stack up against that of others in your industry?).

Drawing on his decades of consulting experience, Steve has developed an analysis of historical pay data to provide estimates of what he, and most compensation and HR practitioners and consultants, have long viewed as the three most important features of a well-designed pay plan: *incentive strength* (or what might be thought of as incentive "bang for the bonus buck"); *alignment* with investor performance (do managers win only when investors do, and are they penalized when investors lose?); and performance-adjusted *cost* to investors (are managers' rewards disproportionately high relative to investors' payoffs?). The perfect pay plan Steve finally came up with, as we shall see, is designed to achieve an optimal balancing of these three basic aims—one that provides managers with clear and strong incentives to increase long-run efficiency and value, while limiting to acceptable levels the two main concerns of most of today's public company directors: retention risk and the shareholder cost of executive pay.

To the extent Steve has succeeded in his mission, his perfect pay plan holds out the promise of combining the strengths of the two very different approaches to CEO pay that have prevailed in U.S. public companies: the fixed-sharing approach that prevailed during the first half of the 20th century (and that has long been the norm in private equity), and the competitive, or labor-market-driven, pay practices of post-World War II corporate America.

DIAGNOSING THE PROBLEM WITH U.S. PUBLIC COMPANY CEO PAY

After earning graduate degrees in mathematics (at Northwestern) and law (at the University of Chicago), Steve got his start in compensation consulting in 1979 when he joined the Chicago office of the premier compensation consulting firm, Towers, Perrin, Forster & Crosby.[1] After he had spent a year working in the Chicago office, TPF&C asked Steve to transfer to New York to work with the firm's Compensation Data Bank, the unit that conducted TPF&C's executive compensation surveys.

The Data Bank used multiple regression models to predict "going rates" for every job or position reported in the survey. The models were based on measures of a position's scope and importance to the organization, such as business unit sales, number of employees supervised, and reporting level, as well as measures of the manager's experience, such as years of company service and corporate board memberships—all of which economists refer to as "labor market data."

This kind of statistical analysis was Steve's first brush with the concept of "opportunity costs"—basically, the value (or level of pay) associated with the next best use of a resource. To understand how a certain manager or employee (or an entire organization) was really performing, you had to know something about what the employee (or organization) was *expected* to do—and then focus on the difference between actual and expected outcomes. Identifying unexpected, or "abnormal," performance, as we saw in the last chapter, was what EVA is all about—providing investors more than their opportunity costs. Figuring out employees' expected rewards for an expected, or "normal," level of EVA performance became a major obsession in Steve's quest for the perfect pay plan.

THE CASE OF GENERAL MOTORS: THE GREAT "FALLING OFF" FROM FIXED SHARING TO COMPETITIVE PAY

Steve dates the beginning of his career-long education in the history of U.S. corporate pay practices to his first reading of Alfred Sloan's memoir, *My Years with General Motors.*[2] In an article called "The Evolution of Executive Pay Policy at General Motors, 1918–2008,"[3] Steve joined INSEAD accounting professor David Young in providing an account of the 60-year-plus rise and fall of what became the world's longest-running EVA-style bonus plan, a plan that was launched in 1918 and whose last vestiges disappeared in 1982.

The plan General Motors adopted in 1918 set aside for several hundred GM's managers and salaried employees a bonus pool equal to 10 percent of GM's total after-tax profit, but only after subtracting a capital charge equal to 6 percent of GM's net assets (equity plus debt)—a charge that was raised to 7 percent in 1922 to reflect an increase in interest rates. This calculation was essentially an early measure of residual income similar to EVA. By 1922, the plan covered 550, or 5 percent, of GM's salaried employees. And by the end of the 1920s, and after a decade of profitable growth, nearly 3,000 salaried employees were receiving such bonuses.[4]

But instead of the bonuses being paid out in the same year they were awarded, they were paid out in the form of GM stock in equal share installments *over a period of five years.* And one critically important aspect of the GM plan was a bonus reserve system that worked roughly as follows: Instead of granting share awards for the full amount of the bonus formula, a portion of the pool was reserved for payout in later years. The intent of this further reserve was to give the board the flexibility to provide managers with larger-than-earned bonuses in future years when residual income might be low or even negative because of industry or macroeconomic factors beyond the managers' control. Through the deferred share awards and the creation of a bonus reserve—much like the Stern Stewart bonus bank concept discussed in the previous chapter—boards could manage their companies' perceived talent retention risk while maintaining the incentive effects associated with a 10 percent fixed-sharing allocation over the long term.

The fact that this bonus plan, after the capital charge adjustment in 1922, ran for the next 25 years without any change in the sharing percentage or threshold return suggests that it was highly effective. Thanks to this EVA-like bonus scheme, GM's managers effectively became "partners" with the company's shareholders, sharing the wealth in good times (including most of the 1920s) but also the pain in troubled times (throughout the depressed '30s).[5]

And GM was by no means alone in taking this approach. Such formulas were common enough among large American public companies before World War II that a 1936 study reported finding that 18 of the largest 22 such companies gave management a fixed percentage of profits beyond either a stated dollar threshold or a specified return on capital.[6]

The strength of the GM board's commitment to fixed sharing became especially clear in the early 1950s when it added qualified stock options to management pay. Qualified stock options had been made irresistibly attractive by a tax law change in 1950 that treated option gains as capital gains instead of ordinary income. But because the options were difficult to value, most companies established separate bonus pools for options. And GM may well have been the only large U.S. public company to insist on maintaining its single bonus pool and, along with it, the fixed-sharing partnership concept.

But then finally in 1977, after having seen its residual income turn negative in two of the last three years, the GM board dropped the single pool concept. And five years later, in 1982, after three more consecutive years of negative residual income, the board dropped its use as a performance measure altogether and substituted measures of sales and earnings growth. In this fashion, the sharing philosophy and associated compensation practices were gradually but eventually completely supplanted by the emergence of what became known as "competitive pay" practices from the 1960s onward.

THE RISE AND DOMINANCE OF COMPETITIVE PAY IN U.S. PUBLIC COMPANIES

Although industry conditions clearly played a role in GM's decision to abandon fixed sharing, a likely more important contributor was the dramatic change in the stock ownership of GM's board of directors that took place in the three decades following World War II. From the vantage point of today's directors, it seems almost astonishing to think that, as recently as 1947, the median GM director received an annual director's fee of a mere $900 while owning 110,000 shares of GM stock, whose estimated value of $1.65 million back then would be worth $12 million in today's dollars. And the 77 million shares owned by GM's 28 board members in 1947 represented fully 28 percent of the outstanding shares and would be worth as much as $8 billion today.

By 1977, the median GM director owned just 500 shares of GM stock, worth a little over $30,000, while receiving an annual director's fee of $47,000. As this comparison should make clear, corporate boards that were once intensely interested stewards of shareholder wealth had become very much part-time hired hands with little financial stake in the effectiveness of their oversight. It's also hard not to see this fundamental change in board compensation playing an important role in the gradual abandonment of fixed-sharing at GM. If board members were unwilling to become, or prevented from being, major shareholders, what grounds would they have for advocating large equity stakes and fixed sharing by management?

⬤ ⬤ ⬤

In place of fixed sharing, the boards of GM—and most of America's largest companies—began to implement competitive pay policies and practices whose most notable and important feature was *annual recalibration* of the main terms of the pay package. To illustrate, suppose a company adopts a competitive position target—say, it wants its managers to be at the 75th percentile of total compensation relative to the rest of the industry. Then, at the start of each successive year, and taking into account performance in the past year, the board adjusts the bonus plan targets and the number of option or share grants to provide their top managers with "competitive" compensation at the targeted 75th percentile.

Now, as sensible as this all might sound without thinking much about it, the reality is that such a labor market-based, "competitive pay" practice of annually revisiting and revising key terms of the incentive pay contract ends up having effects that, however unintended, are deeply "perverse" (as economists like to call them). Although nominally designed to ensure that a large share of executives' pay is "variable" (as opposed to guaranteed payments like salary), such annually recalibrated plans work mainly to ensure that, at the start of each new year, the companies' top executives face what amounts to a full new set of market rewards *for that year*—but *only* for that year.

And as Steve's research has long attempted to show, this kind of system, for all its benefits in retaining (at least mediocre) managers, ends up providing all managers, effective and ineffective alike, with what amounts to a clean slate, thereby breaking any effective link between *multi-year* pay and *multi-year* performance. As Steve puts it, the competitive pay system has "no memory." Past failures are not only forgiven but actually *rewarded* with larger share grants—while success is in fact often penalized with smaller grants!

Let's use a simple example to illustrate how this "performance penalty" is built into the system. Suppose that a business unit manager's targeted operating profit for a given year is $10 million, and the target bonus is $1 million, or 10 percent of operating profit. But during that year, performance falls off to the point where the expected operating profit for the following year is revised down to only $5 million. In such a case, for the target bonus to remain the same $1 million, the targeted bonus paid for hitting the (now lowered) expected operating profit is effectively *increased* to 20 percent of that profit. By the same logic, if the stock grant required to provide the manager with an expected value of $1 million was 20,000 shares based on a stock price of $50, and the stock price falls in the second year to $25, the number of shares granted must be increased to 40,000 to provide an expected value of $1 million.

Now let's consider what happens if the manager's performance improves instead of deteriorating. In that case, and unless the board steps in and overrides the mechanism, competitive pay requires that the target operating profit actually be *raised* (or the manager's percentage of the profit be reduced) and the number of shares *reduced* to maintain the expected value of the bonus and stock grant at the targeted competitive level.

The net effect of such annual competitive "recalibration," which Steve's work has identified as by far the dominant compensation strategy of U.S. public companies, has been to sacrifice a large amount of longer-run pay-for-performance and accountability. As one particularly sobering example of what can (and has) gone wrong with this system, consider the case of John Akers, the CEO of IBM from 1985 to 1993. In Akers's first year as CEO, the IBM board gave him options on 19,000 IBM shares that could be exercised at the then current market price of $145. In the years that followed, as the stock price declined from $145 to as low as $50, the board gave him progressively larger option grants to offset the decline in the stock price and maintain the value of his annual compensation package at a competitive level. In 1990, when the stock price had fallen to $97, the board gave him an option on 96,000 shares exercisable at that price. The net result of this series of "competitive" grants was that, by the end of 1992, Akers's board had put him in a position to realize option gains of close to $18 million *just for getting the stock price back* to the $145 level that prevailed when he received his first option grant as CEO six years earlier. And adding to our sense of the board's failure to discipline Akers, during his nine-year tenure when IBM saw its stock lose nearly half its value, the broad U.S. market was up 135 percent!

HOW DID WE GET TO THIS POINT?—OR THE RISE OF MODERN HUMAN RESOURCES MANAGEMENT

A big part of the story, as we've already mentioned, was the dramatic drop in board stock ownership and incentives for effective oversight that followed the end of World War II. But along with this change, there are a couple of others worth noting.

As already mentioned, the preferential tax treatment of qualified stock options (as capital gains) resulting from the Revenue Act of 1950 created a strong incentive for companies to grant options. The growing use of stock options might have co-existed, as it did at GM, with the single-pool comprehensive sharing system that was popular before World War II. But the difficulties in valuing options (option-pricing models such as Black-Scholes were not developed until the early '70s) together with the rise of non-owner boards helped ensure that board efforts to retain fixed-sharing single bonus pools would be limited.

What most companies did instead was to create secondary pools containing only stock options, which had the predictable effect of weakening boards' commitment to maintaining fixed sharing. Faced with the inevitable tough times when profits were way down and the EVA bonus pool was negative, boards would continue to grant stock options without first reducing the option pool to recoup the EVA bonus pool deficit, thereby undermining the integrity and effectiveness of the EVA plan.

Together with (and no doubt partly as a result of) the drop in board stock ownership and commitment, the other major contributor to the gradual abandonment of single-pool fixed-sharing was the general shift in focus of public company boards and their human resource consultants toward identifying "job values" and providing "competitive pay," while at the same downplaying individual managers' contributions to value—a shift that began almost immediately after World War II. Though the replacement of sharing formulas by competitive pay practices in corporate America took place gradually over three or four decades, the HR movement had arrived in full force by the early 1950s, fundamentally changing the way everyone in business would be paid, including those at the very top.

The two critical turning points identified by Steve and David Young in their account of GM's 90-year pay plan were the first American Management Association (AMA) survey of executive compensation in 1950, and the introduction in the following year of the Hay Guide Chart for job evaluation. As Steve and David point out, the AMA surveys were designed by Arch Patton, a partner at McKinsey & Company and America's leading compensation authority at the time. Perhaps the best indicator of Patton's influence was his publication between 1950 and 1985 of fully 26 articles in the *Harvard Business Review*, many of them reporting the results of the latest AMA survey.[7]

In its first survey in 1950, which Steve and David describe as the most comprehensive examination of executive pay practices ever attempted, the AMA elicited responses from 664 companies. The survey reported finding that, after controlling for industry, the corporate level of profits (in dollar terms) was by far the most important determinant of executive pay,[8] a finding consistent with

Steve and David's claim that compensation programs in the early post-War period were generally effective in aligning the interests of senior management and shareholders.

But as they went on to note, while the first compensation surveys used profit as a measure of size, the AMA soon switched to revenue—and benchmark pay was defined in terms of revenue, not profit or value creation. The consequences of this seemingly minor change would be far-reaching. As the logic of competitive pay became increasingly dominant in corporate America, the incentives for senior managers would gradually shift from maximizing profit and shareholder value to growth and revenue.

And as Steve suggests in the last chapter, the pervasiveness of competitive pay policies helps explain why even pay systems based on EVA or economic profit often failed to deliver superior performance. Tying bonuses to EVA can end up accomplishing little or nothing if the targets are recalibrated each year to ensure competitive pay in the following year.

Once again, the critical flaw in the use of competitive pay targets was inherent in their aim of providing the same expected compensation year in and year out, regardless of a company's performance. And as we saw earlier, a system that has "no memory" ends up exacting little penalty for poor performance. When EVA falls, the drop in current year pay is largely offset by the higher future pay that results from the lowering of future EVA targets. And the converse effect may well have proved even more counterproductive: superior performance often led to increases in EVA targets that could end up penalizing energetic and committed managers.

This performance penalty unwittingly built into competitive pay policies and practices goes a long way in explaining Steve's finding that, during the period 1992–2008, the sales growth of U.S. public companies had a bigger effect than shareholder returns on their levels of executive pay.[9] What's more, the "perverse" incentives linked to competitive pay were openly acknowledged by even some of its own architects, including Arch Patton himself. As early as 1966, Patton noted that the relationship between top management pay and corporate profitability had eroded. Along with the shift from profit to revenue as the defining characteristic of "peers," he observed that setting pay targets without regard to performance had led to a growing disconnect between performance and pay to the point where most senior managements now faced incentives to invest in value-reducing growth. In Patton's own words,

The disassociation between pay and profits is a development of relatively recent years . . . The erosion of this profit-oriented relationship may well stem, at least in part, from the increasing management use of compensation surveys which gauge company size in terms of sales volume . . . [R]ewarding management for volume increases that are not reasonably matched by profit gains raises the specter of the 'profitless prosperity' that accompanies overproduction.[10]

When Patton died in 1996, his obituary in *The New York Times* expressed his regret that managers had "badly abused his survey and that this resulted largely from management assuming that all of its executives were above-average performers."[11] Thanks to the predominance of competitive pay, even mediocre managers would come to enjoy superior rewards—while the best performers would either end up being underpaid, or being recruited by private equity.

● ● ●

As for GM, the company ended up getting what its board paid for. Consistent with the company's gradual evolution from "pay for performance" to competitive pay, Steve's research found that, during the partnership period of 1950–1977, the total pay of GM's five highest-paid executives was strongly positively correlated with GM's shareholders returns—while, somewhat surprisingly, actually *negatively* correlated with the company's revenue growth. By contrast, in the years 1978 through 2008, Steve found both a large increase in the top five executives' pay as a percentage of GM's (for the most part steadily falling) EVA and, perhaps even more troubling, a "huge jump" in the correlation of executive pay and revenue growth along with a pronounced drop in the correlation of GM's total pay with its market-adjusted shareholder return.[12]

● ● ●

In a 2013 study, Steve and his former Stern Stewart colleague Mark Gressle looked for cases of U.S. company CEOs whose boards had put them in a position to gain the most from additional grant shares and lower option exercise prices that they were awarded *as a result of* drops in their stock prices. In their analysis of successive five-year periods, they found 15 CEOs who each stood to make $69 million or more just from their additional shares and lower exercise prices, provided they succeeded in simply getting their stock prices back to starting levels. Ten of these 15 CEOs ended up with actual gains of over $40 million from these arguably "undeserved" share awards, while presiding over such well-known companies as UnitedHealth Group, Sprint Nextel, Disney, Cigna, Cardinal Health, JC Penney, Georgia-Pacific, AT&T, and American Express.

Consistent with these undeserved CEO rewards, Steve's more recent work has shown that contemporary pay practices have ended up producing a very low correlation of pay and performance. In a 2018 study of the cumulative relative pay and relative performance of S&P 1500 CEOs over the period 2007–2016, he found that relative total shareholder returns explained a mere 10 percent of the variation in CEOs' relative realizable (or "mark-to-market") pay.

THE MISSING LINK: TOTAL WEALTH LEVERAGE

For corporate directors concerned about declining U.S. pay-for-performance, this finding should have been far from reassuring. But as Steve has learned the hard way, most of today's directors—or at least those who think about it at all—continue to believe that the dominant competitive pay approach provides a reasonable balance among its main objectives. It provides *alignment* between the interests of managers and their shareholders in the sense that bonus and stock compensation *for any given year* are typically tied to operating and market measures of shareholder value *for that year*. And it provides substantial pay *leverage* in that a large proportion of pay is dependent on current performance and therefore "at risk."

But perhaps most important for today's directors (especially those with modest shareholdings), competitive pay limits retention risk by giving executives competitive compensation opportunities *every year*. Competitive pay also manages the effective cost of executive pay to shareholders by limiting total compensation to that earned by the targeted percentile of the competitive pay distribution.

Steve's main response to competitive pay has been to show why having a large proportion of one's current year's pay at risk fails to provide incentives that are even remotely comparable to those of an owner holding lots of stock. On the strength of that analysis, he has urged corporate boards to focus on the value of executives' total *wealth*—as opposed to just their current income—and *its* relationship to *shareholder* returns and wealth.[13]

A CEO's total wealth can be thought of as the sum of the value of his or her *current investment* capital and the value of his or her *human* capital, which encompasses future projected earnings in all its forms—including not just salary and bonuses but also long-term incentive grants of all kinds, as well as pension benefits. In Steve's framing of the problem, corporate CEOs and other top executives are seen as aiming, like their shareholders, to maximize not just their current income but their career-long earnings and wealth.

In this framing, the best measure of the strength of the performance incentive provided by a compensation plan is the *sensitivity* of the CEO's wealth to changes in shareholder wealth, or the extent to which these two move together. This is the basic idea behind the concept Steve has taken to calling *wealth leverage*, which has become central to his thinking about CEO pay.

To illustrate the concept, if a 10 percent change in shareholder wealth changes management's wealth by 10 percent, then management's total wealth leverage is 1.0. It's important to recognize that 1.0 is meant to be viewed as the total wealth leverage of what Steve calls a "pure entrepreneur"—someone whose entire wealth is tied up in company stock. In such cases, any percentage change in shareholder wealth results in the same percentage change in the entrepreneur's wealth.

But because competitive pay policy has the effect of making expected future pay completely independent of current changes in shareholder wealth, a 10 percent change in shareholder wealth has no effect—zero!—on the *present value* of expected future pay. And because the present value of expected future pay is often a big (if not the largest) component of management wealth, this means that management's actual wealth leverage is often quite low—even when a significant proportion of management's *current* year's pay is at risk.

As one example, in a study published in 2010, Steve and David Young showed that ExxonMobil CEO Rex Tillerson's expected future pay had a present value of $141 million, which was almost two and half times the value of his stock, options, and current-year incentive pay. But although his stock, options, and current-year pay had wealth leverage greater than 1.0, the effective wealth leverage of his expected future pay was close to zero—even with 90 percent of his pay at risk—bringing his *total* wealth leverage down to just 0.3.[14]

The goal of Steve's analysis was to help companies come up with a practical approach to executive compensation that provides corporate executives with *entrepreneurial* incentives designed to make a substantial proportion of an executive's wealth sensitive to changes in investor wealth. The most important tools for increasing wealth leverage, as Steve's analysis made clear, are *front-loaded* grants of stock and options, fixed-share option and stock grant guidelines, and formula-driven bonus plans based on variables like EVA. The use of fixed share grant guidelines and an EVA-based bonus would have raised Tillerson's wealth leverage from 0.3 to something close to 1.0.

STEVE'S SEARCH FOR THE PERFECT PAY PLAN

Management wealth leverage might be described as Steve O'Byrne's *idée fixe*. But he developed a second major obsession, this one concerning possible refinements of the EVA performance measure he had begun exploring from his earliest days at Stern Stewart.

One major source of this obsession was Steve's conviction that the EVA bonus plan was the most sensible and promising of what he viewed as the four most important efforts in the last 70 years both to expand employee owner-ship and to improve economic performance by boosting employee motivation and morale. Along with the successes of the EVA approach described in the last chapter, Steve has found three other developments worth noting: (1) the growth of employee stock ownership plans, or ESOPs; (2) the explosion, particularly in the U.S., of franchise arrangements; and (3) the growth of worker cooperatives, both in the U.S. and abroad.

ESOPs have proved the most popular of the four in the U.S., with some 14 million employees participating in 6,500 ESOPs.[15] But one important limitation of ESOPs is their inability to provide ownership interests, as EVA plans do, at the "local" or business unit level.

Franchise contracts are the second most popular in the U.S., accounting for some 10 million employees in 500,000 franchisee establishments.[16] The downside of franchise contracts is their substantial upfront employee investment (by the franchisees) and elaborate legal contracts.

As for worker cooperatives, the world's largest and best known is the Mon-dragon worker cooperative in Spain, which has 75,000 employees in 141 subsid-iaries (each set up as its own cooperative). In the U.S., by contrast, there are some 500 mostly small worker cooperatives that employ less than 10,000 people in total.[17] The main limitation of worker cooperatives is their inability to access investor capital for growth, since the capital for cooperatives is provided largely (if not entirely) by their employees.

When set against these three other forms of what might be viewed as labor-capital partnerships, the EVA movement at the peak of its popularity in 1999 consisted of at least 66 public companies employing some 1.2 million people. As discussed in the last chapter, the typical Stern Stewart EVA bonus plan took the basic form of (1) a targeted bonus for expected EVA performance and (2) an incentive bonus intended to recognize and reward only the unexpected levels of EVA improvement.

Over time, though, with the dismantling of so many once-successful EVA programs, Steve began to sense that there was more work to do in getting a more useful measure of *expected* EVA improvement—more specifically, the *projected* EVA increases (or declines) that were currently being reflected in the company's stock price. To satisfy that condition, the expected EVA improvement measure had to incorporate investors' expectations for growth as well as current profitability.

It was at this point that Steve, now some 30 years into his career as a compensation consultant (and after-hours finance scholar), came to the startling conclusion that there might be such a thing as a "perfect" pay plan—one designed to provide a 100 percent positive correlation between *relative* pay and *relative* performance. After several years of using historical pay data to come up with workable estimates of the three critical variables of CEO pay plans—incentive strength, alignment, and performance-adjusted cost—Steve speculated that there might be a simple plan that provided not only a perfect correlation of relative pay and relative performance, but one with pay leverage—which is a simplified version of wealth leverage—of 1.0,[18] and what he referred to as "a zero pay premium" at industry average performance.

What he came up with was a simple *stock-based* plan consisting of annual grants of performance shares that met the following three conditions: First, the target grant value is not just market pay, but market pay *adjusted* for relative performance, since the start of the plan. When relative performance raises the stock price, the number of grant shares remains fixed, unlike a competitive pay plan where grant shares are reduced to offset the increase in the stock price.[19] Second, the plan uses a vesting multiple that is designed to remove the industry component of the stock return,[20] which in turn makes the vested stock value track the company's relative (not its actual or absolute) return. Third, the time horizon of vesting is stretched out to retirement, so that all cash paid out prior to retirement is treated as a draw against the value of the performance shares.[21]

Thanks in part to this vesting program, the perfect performance share plan has the same basic structure as the EVA bonus plan in the sense that the likely-to-vest value of the performance shares can, *at any point in time*, be expressed as the sum of cumulative market pay plus a share of the dollar excess return.[22]

So designed, Steve's perfect performance share plan can be seen as combining the strengths of the two dominant approaches to U.S. CEO pay in the 20th century: the fixed sharing that prevailed up through the end of World War II, and the labor-market-based, competitive pay concepts that became the norm in the 1960s and after.

One Step Back—to Semi-Perfect. To gain more insight into what Steve was trying to accomplish, it helps to note that he came to view the first EVA bonus plan he developed as head of Stern Stewart's executive pay practice—a plan designed for and put in place by a company called Continental Medical Systems in 1993—as a "semi-perfect" pay plan. It was only semi-perfect in the sense that the performance measure—the unexpected, or "excess," increase in EVA—was not really a measure of investors' *total* excess return, but only of the most visible portion of that excess return—the part that showed up in *current* operating cash flows and thus the corporate P&L. What was missing from this analysis were the changes in investors' perception of the companies' *future growth values* that often accompany, but are not always reliably reflected by, the changes in current cash flows, and thus by the changes in recorded EVA. The failure to recognize and reward valuable corporate investment in growth was the all too common complaint about EVA—and the fact that managers could increase EVA simply by cutting promising investment ended up creating skepticism about the entire financial management system.

As Steve came increasingly to recognize, if you really wanted to understand how a given year's performance affected a company's longer-run value, you would have to come up with not only the changes in current operating cash flow (those reflected in and measured by excess EVA), but also a second important variable:

any changes, whether negative or positive, in the future growth value that had accompanied the current-year changes in EVA. (Such changes in future growth value, as readers might recall, are a key part of both Merton Miller's valuation model presented in chapter 3 and the real option values introduced by Stew Myers and discussed in chapter 5.)

To sum up, then, a perfect pay plan would be one that captured changes in both a company's current operations value (or COV) *and* its future growth value (or FGV). The implicit assumption of the standard EVA models (and the semi-perfect plans that came with them) was that when EVA changes, FGV remains the same—in other words, the assumed change in FGV is zero. But the more Steve thought about it, the less likely it seemed that FGV would stay the same. What if shortsighted companies or managers were achieving their EVA increases mainly just by cutting valuable investment? In that case, even when managers were reporting stellar COV and EVA, their FGV was probably shrinking, and possibly significantly. Such changes can be seen in the recent performance of some pharma companies, like Gilead, where reported earnings have continued to grow even as the P/E multiple on the stock keeps dropping to new lows. Conversely, how could EVA even begin to capture the case of high-growth companies, like Amazon in its early stages, where current operating cash flow was hugely negative—and progressively more so with each year—while FGV was continuing to explode?

The task Steve set himself was thus to provide EVA-based systems with the flexibility and means to capture such possibilities, and so quiet the legions of critics of EVA who saw it as inevitably squelching even profitable growth. The way he did this was by creating a series of three EVA "equations" that work toward the perfect pay plan in stages. With the aid of this "EVA math" (and for those who feel up to the challenge of sorting through it, see the box below), the aim of Steve's perfect EVA pay plan is to reflect, and capture in the bonus awards, not only the changes in companies' current EVA but also any changes in companies' future growth values that accompany those changes in EVA— changes that are actually taking place while the managers are *still employed.* Steve's basic insight is that you don't have to wait for the future payoffs to materialize; you can detect, and reward, such increases in future growth value well in advance simply by identifying the current operating drivers of changes in future growth value.

A BRIEF PRIMER ON THE "EVA MATH"

The first EVA math equation, which Steve developed in 1993 early in his Stern Stewart career, expresses a company's market value as the sum of three components: (1) the book value of its total (debt and equity) capital; (2) the discounted present value of current EVA assumed to continue forever; and (3) the capitalized present value of expected future annual increases (or reductions) in EVA. The first two components were seen as constituting a company's "current operations value," or COV, while the third represented its "future growth value" or FGV. Such estimates of FGV were then used to "back out" the annual expected increases or "improvements" in EVA.[23]

The second equation, which Steve also formulated while at Stern Stewart, provided a more sophisticated way of backing out the EVA targets reflected in FGV—one that made the expected increase in EVA a function of two variables: the required return on FGV and the expected change in FGV. In this version, the capitalized future value of the expected or targeted increases in EVA was set equal to the required return on FGV *minus* the expected change in FGV. When current EVA performance targets are calculating taking account of the expected change in FGV, the targets for high-growth companies will be reduced in the early years—often to negative values—effectively stretching out required EVA improvement over time, deferring it to future periods when the profits from growth investments were expected to materialize.

The third equation, which Steve first published in 1997,[24] represents a refinement and extension of the second by expressing investors' excess return as the sum of two components: (1) the capitalized future value of unexpected EVA changes, and (2) the unexpected change in future growth value. In this formulation, the first component represents the variable of greatest interest to the managers being evaluated—namely, the capitalized value of their stream of unexpected EVA bonus awards.

ONE LAST LOOK AT THE PROBLEM OF CEO PAY

In an article published in 2002, *The New Yorker*'s longtime finance columnist John Cassidy went so far as to identify Michael Jensen's writings as the main incitement for the revolution in U.S. CEO pay that he, and many others, saw as beginning in the early 1980s.[25] Along with the negative stock returns of the 1970s, much of the impetus for this movement was traced to Jensen's earlier mentioned 1990 *Harvard Business Review* article with Harvard colleague Kevin Murphy, "CEO Incentives—It's Not How Much You Pay, But How."[26] Jensen and Murphy's basic argument was that, in the period leading up to the 1980s, the stock ownership of the CEOs of U.S. public companies had reached such a low level that, for every $1,000 increase in the market value of their companies, the CEOs stood to gain as little as about $3. As Jensen and Murphy saw it, the CEOs of America's largest public companies were being paid "like bureaucrats," while professional athletes and partners of law firms were making multiples of U.S. CEOs' annual pay.

In Steve's terminology, the wealth leverage of U.S. public company CEOs was negligible. For a CEO confronted with an acquisition opportunity that might double the size of the company (with commensurate increases in salary and perks) while reducing shareholder wealth by 10 percent, why not go for it?

In 1991, a year after publication of Jensen and Murphy's article, Steve published an article called "Linking Management Performance Incentives to Shareholder Wealth" that, instead of focusing on the dollar changes in CEO and shareholder wealth, looked at the *percentage* changes in CEO relative to percentage changes in shareholder wealth.[27] After using this measure to demonstrate that the typical CEO of a U.S. public company had a compensation package that effectively provided wealth leverage of about 0.4, Steve went on to show how such leverage could be increased by corporate boards to as high as 1.0 with a few fairly simple changes. Along with an increase in the proportion of incentive pay to total pay (from its then current level of 41 percent to close to 60 percent), the key steps were the adoption of fixed share (in place of competitive-pay) grant guidelines and a more leveraged bonus plan (achieved by using the cost of capital rather than recent performance as the basis for setting the profit target).

To be fair to Cassidy, his *New Yorker* piece was right to point out the effect of Jensen and Murphy's work on investors and directors—which may well have been a major influence on what became a large increase in U.S. CEOs' stock ownership and percentage of pay at risk. During the past three decades, the CEOs of

S&P 1500 companies saw their median percentage of pay at risk increase from 54 percent in 1992 to 79 percent in 2021—and the percentage of their total pay taking the form of stock or options tripled, from 19 percent to 57 percent. All of which is consistent with the idea that Jensen-fueled investor advocacy has brought about a revolution in executive pay.

But according to Steve, the revolution remains incomplete, with a major flaw that continues to undermine the effectiveness of U.S. executive pay. As reflected in Steve's analysis, the positive impact of the increase in percentage of pay at risk has been almost completely offset by corporate America's increased commitment to competitive pay concepts.

Using the simpler version of wealth leverage he calls "pay leverage"[28]—one that compares cumulative pay and *past* performance (while avoiding the need to project future pay)—Steve has shown that the big increase in percentage of pay at risk over the past 30 years has not led to stronger incentives. For the median S&P 1500 CEO, pay leverage has actually fallen over the past three decades, from about 0.8 during the five-year period 1992–1996 to 0.65 by 2017–2021. During the same 30 years, median grant date pay leverage—which focuses on the grant date (as opposed to the realized) values of stock and option grants and thus serves as Steve's proxy for *target* pay leverage—actually plummeted from 0.44 to a mere 0.08! At this level, the U.S. CEO pay system can be seen as approaching the "zero pay" leverage of a "pure competitive" pay policy—one in which all [CEOs] must—and do—have "prizes," with no effective rewards for good performance and no penalties for bad.

*   *   *

Twenty-one years after Steve's 1991 paper, two well-known finance academics, Alex Edmans and Xavier Gabaix, published a paper called "Dynamic CEO Compensation" that begins by suggesting that measures like Steve's wealth and pay leverage are likely to be far more effective in capturing incentive strength than Jensen and Murphy's dollar of executive pay per $1,000 of shareholder wealth.[29] Edmans and Gabaix then go on to propose what Steve has identified as another version of his own "perfect pay plan"—one that its authors call the Dynamic Incentive Account, or DIA.

The DIA is initially funded with the present value of the CEO's expected future market pay over his or her remaining years to retirement. The funds are assumed to be invested at some percentage (let's call it "X") in company stock and the rest $(1 - X)$ percent in cash. At the end of each year, a portion is paid out to the CEO, and the DIA is rebalanced to hold X percent in stock. When the stock price drops, the remaining cash is used to buy more stock—and when the stock price increases, enough stock is sold to add cash to the DIA so as to maintain $(1 - X)$ percent in cash.

As Steve has pointed out, the DIA provides constant wealth leverage, and the annual cash distribution, like the value of Steve's annual performance share grant, depends on the stock return from the start of the plan, effectively giving the system a memory. In so doing, it eliminates the performance penalty associated with competitive plans by ensuring that CEOs never get new grants with more shares when their stock prices have declined.

Much as private equity firms do with the CEOs of their portfolio companies, Edmans and Gabaix's DIA solves the competitive pay problem by effectively *front-loading* stock-based pay—though not, as Steve also does, by figuring out a better way to determine annual pay. But their proposal has elicited little interest from, and had little impact on, public company practitioners, presumably because it doesn't address the question of *annual* grants.

Along with the academic community, proxy advisory firms (which advise investors on how to vote their shares at corporate shareholder meetings) have failed to provide the intellectual insight needed to improve public company pay practices. In Steve's eyes, nothing has revealed this failure more clearly than the "no" vote recommended by the leading proxy advisor, Institutional Shareholder Services (ISS), on Microsoft's 2019 advisory shareholder vote on executive pay ("Say on Pay"). That rejection came in the face of the company's remarkable stock-price performance and its CEO Satya Nadella's compensation package that, by Steve's measures, had an enviable pay alignment of 97 percent and an eye-catchingly high pay leverage of 1.75—all with a pay premium of a *negative* 36 percent at industry average performance over his then five-year tenure as CEO. In other words, according to Steve's measures, Microsoft's shareholders were getting an extraordinarily good deal![30]

How did ISS miss the big picture so badly? Its own explanation for its "no" vote focused on the fact that Nadella's pay was deemed to be 105 percent above peer group median pay, and that he was given an additional $1 million in base salary that was not subject to performance conditions. It missed the big picture because it pays no attention to variables like pay leverage or alignment. Its pay premium of 105 percent was calculated *without any consideration* of Microsoft's performance, while the offending additional base salary amounted to just 3 percent of his total compensation.

Given the lack of guidance and insight offered by the academic community and proxy advisory firms, it's not surprising that U.S. public company pay has not embraced the main features of Steve's ideal plan, with its 100 percent pay-performance alignment and zero pay premium for average performance. Even when evaluated against the much lower bar set by his *semi-perfect* pay plan—defined as pay-performance alignment of at least 50 percent and pay premiums of no more than 33 percent—Steve's most recent assessment (involving over 32,000 five-year periods ending with the years 1996–2021) finds these criteria met *at least half of the time* by only 34 (or about 2 percent) of the nearly 1,700 companies with at least ten years of data.[31]

Notable for their consistently high pay-performance rankings are companies like (the old) Monsanto, Ingredion, Greif, Broadridge Financial, Airborne, Alberto Culver, and Del Monte. But even these stalwarts remain, according to Steve, prisoners of the conventional wisdom. As his analysis has shown, such companies get almost all of their higher alignment from their heavy reliance on equity compensation, and not from making their target compensation more sensitive to performance.[32]

IN CLOSING

The revolution in U.S. public company pay, to the extent there has actually been one, has come well short of accomplishing the goals that O'Byrne envisioned. The failure, or at least incompleteness, of this revolution can be seen most clearly in one very visible effect: the continuing dominance of competitive pay concepts and practices, with the result that the CEOs of the most ineffective U.S. public companies end up getting paid significantly more than they should. Somewhat less visible, but more troubling for the future of the dwindling numbers of U.S. companies, is the reality that the CEOs of the most productive companies remain undercompensated, as Jensen and Murphy argued, and often end up moving to private equity.

Coming on top of his failure to persuade many companies to adopt his proposals, then, perhaps Steve's biggest disappointment has been his limited success in getting academics in finance, economics, and accounting to see the weaknesses of conventional HR pay policy and lead the way to better pay plan design. Jensen and Murphy, after all, while deploring the absence of stock ownership by U.S. company CEOs, have shown no sign of recognizing the incentive problems arising from the "competitive" award process by which companies get more stock into management's hands.

● ● ●

With the current outcome in view, including the migration of many of America's best CEOs to private equity, Steve continues to speculate about how things might have been different. What if the academic literature in the wake of the Jensen and Murphy article had made a compelling case *against* the conventional HR wisdom and competitive pay practices? In that event, might some of the problems stemming from competitive pay have been headed off, and much of the damage limited, by influencing the proxy advisors and big index funds that have pretty much continued to support competitive pay?

We will never know the answer to that question. What we may come to find out, with more time and study, is that Steve's proposals for moving corporate America closer to his perfect pay plan will gain greater acceptance, perhaps first in the academy and then by proxy advisors and public company HR departments.

CHAPTER 10

MARTIN FRIDSON, THE EXTRAORDINARY SUCCESS OF THE HIGH-YIELD BOND MARKET, AND THE LEVERAGING OF CORPORATE AMERICA

I n 1970, there was no such thing as a market for publicly traded, *original-issue* high-yield bonds. Yes, there were a good number of "fallen angels"— once blue-chip companies whose fortunes and finances had fallen to the point where the two main credit rating agencies, Moody's and Standard & Poor's, no longer viewed their bonds as "investment grade." But such bonds were no longer considered suitable investments for small, presumably unsophisticated "retail" investors.

In those days, the managements of America's largest and most admired companies took enormous pride in their nearly debt-free balance sheets and their AA credit ratings. A handful of the bluest of blue-chip companies like General Electric and Kellogg even had AAA credit ratings, the same as that of the U.S. government (until its Treasurys were downgraded by S&P in 2011 to AA+).

In the post-War decades leading up to and including (most of) the 1970s, effective corporate financial management was widely believed to involve *minimal* use of debt. The idea was to work down your debt as quickly as possible, without disrupting your operations. Paying down debt would reassure outside investors of not only your probity, but also your ongoing profitability. By following this financing prescription, companies could avoid the fate of those hapless companies forced to borrow ever larger amounts they couldn't afford to pay back, and living more or less from bank loan to bank loan. Sound financial management, in other words—or what we have been referring to throughout this book as "old-fashioned" corporate finance—meant minimizing the possibility of financial trouble by maintaining balance sheets funded mostly if not entirely with equity.

With the stirrings of an original-issue, high-yield bond market in the early 1970s, this financing conservatism began to give way. From its initial trickle in 1970, annual issuance of high-yield bonds—or what rear-guard practitioners and journalists quickly dubbed "junk bonds"—had become a $1 billion stream by 1977. It is now a full-on flood, with over $400 billion of new issuance in 2020 alone in the U.S., and another $100 billion in Europe.

THE NOVEL IDEA OF ORIGINAL-ISSUE JUNK BONDS

By high-yield or junk bonds, we mean bonds whose corporate issuers lack either the size (in terms of annual revenues or assets) or the levels or stability of reported earnings to be assigned by S&P or Moody's to one of their investment-grade categories—that is, BBB or higher for S&P, and Baa or above for Moody's. (As an aside, the designation "high yield" was used by rating agency founder John Moody at least as early as 1919, but the myth was created—and never fully dispelled—that the term was a Drexel-coined euphemism designed to put a good face on inherently unsound investments.)

Publicly traded junk bonds were not unknown or even scarce in the early '70s. At the end of 1970, fully 23 percent of the bond issues rated by Moody's carried ratings below Baa. But the fact that 90 percent of such non-investment-grade bonds were rated Ba, and thus just one notch below investment grade, reinforces the reality that the vast majority of high-yield issues back then were companies whose debt had been rated BBB or higher when issued, but had been downgraded in response to falling profits (or even losses) or some other sign of increased financial risk.

Today, non-investment or speculative-grade ratings account for nearly half of Moody's rated universe of corporate bonds, or roughly double the fraction in 1970. What's more, only 25 percent of today's speculative-grade issuers fall into the Ba category, with the rest occupying riskier terrain, suggesting that growing numbers of smaller and less profitable companies—and their investors— have become increasingly comfortable operating with higher leverage than ever before. And the vast majority of today's speculative-grade companies are not fallen angels, but *issuers* of high-yield bonds, companies rated below investment grade from the outset.

For corporate finance theorists as well as practitioners, this has made it impossible to ignore not only the growing acceptance of financial leverage, but also the recognition of its value, by ever growing numbers of investors and corporate managers. And although this embrace of corporate debt financing may well have surprised even some of the "hard-core" Chicago School folks featured in this book, its import was not lost on Merton Miller, whose 1990 Nobel Prize address—which we revisit at the end of the chapter—was given a one-word title: "Leverage."

Within the investment-grade universe of public U.S. companies, the 1980s and '90s saw a steady migration, though by no means all voluntary, from the once prestigious and sought-after AAA to A categories to BBB. Triple-A ratings gradually faded from a coveted status symbol and sign of financial prowess to a telltale indication of management's failure to maximize value for its shareholders.

In response to this leveraging of an ever-broadening swath of corporate America, widely accepted notions of what constituted a prudent corporate capital structure began to give way. While companies like Amazon and Google continue to use debt sparingly (both companies have bond issues rated AA) and to shun dividend payouts, even once-meteor-like but now maturing growth companies like Microsoft and Apple have been forced to recognize the desirability of using large borrowings to fund stock buybacks. (In Apple's case, the spur for this recognition was activist investor Carl Icahn, whose agitation forced Apple to begin paying out part of its then vast and ever expanding hoard of cash.) More generally, in the new world of modern corporate finance—and at some point in the life cycle of even the best-run and most successful companies—leverage and capital structure have somehow ended up "mattering" to their shareholders.

THE ORIGINS OF HIGH YIELD (WITH A PRIMER ON DEBT COVENANTS)

In the early 1970s, most companies looking for longer-term debt financing and unable to qualify for investment-grade ratings found themselves resorting to the private placement market. Private placement lenders—most of them life insurance companies—insisted on restrictive debt "covenants" they considered necessary to assert their control and protect their principal if things went wrong. Many non-investment-grade issuers would have preferred to avoid the restrictions on their operating and financing flexibility imposed by such covenants. What's more, the inability to sell, and the resulting illiquidity of, private placement bonds also made them nonstarters for many investors.

That's why the opening of a truly public debt market to speculative-grade companies was such a watershed event. It gave corporate issuers without investment-grade size or profitability a way to issue bonds that were *not* subject to so-called *maintenance* covenants, the kind that could put a company into default if, say, its fixed charge coverage ratio (income before taxes and interest divided by interest and principal payments) temporarily dipped below a specified level because of a cyclical decline in its business. Most public bondholders, to be sure, were still protected by *incurrence* covenants, the kind that prohibit corporate issuers from taking actions such as piling more new debt on top of the old that would increase their credit risk beyond prescribed limits.

But, again, it was mainly the existence of a liquid resale market for high-yield bonds that appealed to investors concerned about a company's credit risk. Liquid markets gave such investors the option to vote with their feet. And speculative-grade bonds greatly expanded their opportunity to earn higher yields than those available in the traditional investment-grade public bond market, thus providing compensation for the lack of covenant protection.

THE LEVERAGING OF CORPORATE AMERICA

The emergence of the original-issue high-yield bond market in the 1970s played a key financial role in several major changes in American industry. The breakup of the AT&T Bell system through a 1982 consent decree spawned new telecommunications competitors that issued heavily in the speculative-grade market. High-yield bonds also financed much of the evolution of cable television operators from small regional businesses into national powerhouses that transformed home entertainment. When legalized gambling spread beyond Nevada, high-yield bonds financed much of the construction of both land-based and floating casinos. (Traditional lenders had been wary of the rechristened "gaming industry" because of its historical association with organized crime.) Independent oil and gas producers with new exploration and production technologies represented another large segment of the high-yield market's issuers.

Along with these industry-specific developments, many diversified conglomerates, either voluntarily or under pressure from corporate raiders, divested pieces of their business in order to narrow their operating focus. In many cases, the operations they shed were purchased by organizers of leveraged buyouts and financed with high-yield debt.

Although few denied that defaults were likely to increase in this new world of higher leverage, the vastly expanded market for public speculative-grade debt gave investors the opportunity to spread that credit risk over a diversified portfolio of speculative-grade issues and, in so doing, earn yields that more than offset the higher expected default losses. These opportunities were also available to individual investors in the form of mutual funds that specialized in lower-quality bonds. And it was the growth of such bond-laden mutual funds during the 1970s that encouraged investment banks to create investment opportunities for the funds by ushering speculative-grade companies into the public market.

ENTER MARTY FRIDSON, CICERONE OF THE HIGH-YIELD MARKET—AND THE CONCOMITANT RISE OF MICHAEL MILKEN AND DREXEL

What might be described as the modern era of high-yield finance commenced right around the time a newly minted MBA named Martin Fridson began his career in finance. Although Marty never heard the phrase "high-yield bond" during his two years at Harvard Business School, the subject of credit ratings had come up in his finance courses. So after graduating from HBS in 1976, Marty did not feel completely out of his depth when he got his first job as a bond trader and market commentator with a boutique investment bank called Mitchell Hutchins. There he began what has turned out to be a lifelong study of credit risk by focusing on the bonds of two less-than-investment-grade issuers, Savannah Electric and Metropolitan Edison. After Mitchell Hutchins was acquired by Paine Webber, Marty became a full-time credit analyst charged with covering what most analysts would find a staggering load of 136 industrial bond issuers.

While Marty was getting his professional start in credit analysis and research, a man named Michael Milken was developing a thriving business in speculative-quality bonds at a second-tier investment bank called Drexel Burnham Lambert. Milken got his start at Drexel's New York office trading in non-investment-grade fallen angels, a group that included the bonds of the bankrupt Penn Central Transportation Company and distressed real estate investment trusts (REITs). There he developed close relationships with a number of unaffiliated and highly active investors—among them Carl Lindner, Saul Steinberg, and Laurence Tisch—whose penchant for identifying and raising large amounts of debt financing for corporate takeovers in the late '70s and early '80s branded them (at least in the eyes of the financial establishment and media) as "corporate raiders." Also part of Milken's expanding circle were a number of bond mutual fund managers whose main focus was finding profit in heavily discounted, high-yield issues. Milken's operation quickly proved to be so successful that he was able to persuade Drexel's management to let him move his entire operation to his native Los Angeles.

En route to this success, Milken encountered one major obstacle that appeared to frustrate his plans to expand his lucrative business in deep-discount fallen angels. During the period 1974–1976, the universe of non-investment-grade public bonds was actually *shrinking* rapidly; indeed, the market contracted by as much as 40 percent during those three years, thanks to a combination of upgrades, defaults, and redemptions. To meet the growing demand on the part of bond mutual funds focused on high-yield opportunities, one of Drexel's rivals, Lehmann Brothers Kuhn Loeb, underwrote several original-issue high-yield issues. And in response to this competitive threat, Milken and Drexel's corporate finance chief Fred Joseph decided to enter this new business. By 1978, Drexel had become the leading underwriter of original-issue high-yield bonds.

A major part of Drexel's approach, and a significant contributor to its success, was Milken's effectiveness in establishing and then making use of the bank's network of corporate and investor clients—many of them playing dual roles as issuers and investors in what has often been described as a "daisy chain" of upstart life insurers and savings and loan associations that dared depart from the investing conventions that bound their competitors. The daisy chain label came from Drexel's practice of encouraging issuers to raise more debt than they needed for their own operations, and then hold the excess for possible investment in other Drexel high-yield deals.

In the case of savings and loans (S&Ls), the temptation to buy less-than-investment-grade corporate bonds was the prospect it held out for escape from what rising interest rates had made an obsolete business model. As many S&Ls discovered in the late '70s, it was hard to maintain the illusion of profitability when funding 30-year mortgages earning 5 percent or 6 percent rates with new money costing 7 percent or more, many of them using so-called brokered CDs. For a good number (though nothing close to a majority) of S&Ls, investment in high-yield bonds earning high single-digit returns represented a way of "gambling for resurrection." Making this escape route even more tempting was the (misguided) relaxation of regulations on S&L asset holdings enabled and encouraged by friendly members of Congress (on both sides of the political aisle).

In response to the squeeze between rising borrowing costs and embedded rates on long-term mortgages, many S&Ls had "demutualized" and then been acquired by entrepreneurs using mostly borrowed money. But for new and old owners alike, the ability of so many "underwater" S&Ls to take risks using other people's money created a moral hazard whose more or less predictable consequences—including nearly 1,000 failed S&Ls and an $800 billion clean-up bill for U.S. taxpayers—materialized over the next few years.[1]

THE MAJORS JUMP INTO THE MIX

In 1981, with Milken now enthroned as the "junk bond king," and his Drexel minions busily arranging new deals (while also quietly working out many that got into trouble), Marty was recruited as a corporate bond analyst at Salomon Brothers. By that time, the revenues being generated by high-yield bond underwriting—the lion's share by Drexel—had become too large for the "bulge bracket" investment banks to ignore. For the likes of Merrill Lynch, Morgan Stanley, First Boston, and Salomon Brothers, the high-yield business was particularly attractive because the underwriting fees as a percentage of the face amounts were substantially larger than those on investment-grade deals.

Salomon's position vis-a-vis the opportunity presented by high yield was initially tentative, given the firm's relatively recent ascent from scrappy trading-and-sales outfit to the ranks of the top underwriters. Morgan Stanley and First Boston, by contrast, had long enjoyed leading positions in bond underwriting, positions effectively conferred on them by the Glass Steagall legislation requiring them to separate from two of America's oldest and largest commercial banks. Both firms had developed their now substantial trading-and-sales operations not as profit centers in their own right (at least not at first), but mainly to accommodate their investors' demands for active secondary markets in the securities they purchased from the banks' syndicates.

The nightmare scenario for Salomon's leaders was one in which the firm, by underwriting deals for sketchy "junk" companies that then failed, ended up inflicting irreparable damage on the franchise that had been painstakingly built up through concerted due diligence on offerings associated with its name.[2] Morgan Stanley had similar reservations about getting into high-yield underwriting and trading—but once convinced of the opportunities, the firm moved decisively to capitalize on them. In 1985, the firm made a splash by hiring the "Michael Milken of the East Coast," Steve Judelson from L.F. Rothschild, to head its high-yield trading desk. This initiative amounted to a cultural shift for a firm that in those days did not allow alcoholic beverages to be served in its executive dining room. But there were limits to its risk-taking: Morgan Stanley was not about to start underwriting casinos, which were a major segment of the high-yield issuer universe.

When Marty found himself being interviewed for a new job there, the head of Morgan Stanley's high-yield underwriting told him that the firm's "sweet spot" was likely to be the highest-rated portion of the speculative-grade universe, rated BB on the Standard & Poor's scale. But even with such a cautious approach, the prestigious firm's initial foray into speculative-grade debt raised journalistic eyebrows, effectively compelling the media to comment on the incongruity of a "white shoe" firm sullying its hands with junk bonds.

The opportunity for Morgan Stanley would come from broadening the high-yield investor base by selling high-yield new issues to the mostly *mainstream* life insurance companies that had long been part of its franchise. The established life insurers also saw an opportunity because they were now being challenged by Drexel-friendly newcomer insurers that were not burdened by legacy portfolios from earlier, lower-interest-rate times. By purchasing high-yield bonds, the newcomers were able to offer higher returns to buyers of products that combined insurance and investment features, which put the incumbents at a serious disadvantage.

Complicating matters for the banks as well as their insurer clients, Drexel was clearly aiming for total domination of the market, which included efforts to block any competitor from leading a deal as large as $100 million. For insurers whose success was premised on identifying and managing risks, it was unthinkable to become involved in an asset class in which there was only a single market maker. The major life insurers were thus eager to see Morgan Stanley and other premier investment banks get into the high-yield business.

In addition to reputable underwriting and secondary market support, these potential new investors wanted credible research to back up their decisions about the public bonds of speculative-grade issuers. Drexel had a highly regarded team of company-focused credit analysts headed by Larry Post, who was one of Marty's former Salomon Brothers colleagues. The problem, though, was that Drexel's research on the asset class *sounded* to mainstream life insurers more like promotion than disinterested analysis.

THE BEGINNINGS OF SERIOUS HIGH-YIELD RESEARCH

In 1983, Morgan Stanley began to address its life insurer clients' demand for credible, independent research on the high-yield asset class by retaining Professor Edward Altman of New York University's Stern School of Business as a consultant. At that point, speculative-grade bonds had attracted little attention from the academy, but Altman had made a reputation for himself in a related area of credit analysis.

In 1968, Altman had introduced a statistical method for calculating default probabilities on corporate bonds that became known as the "Z-score."[3] Working with colleague Scott Nammacher, he provided high-yield investors with an extensive database identifying both the composition and the performance of their holdings, which created the ability to test different investing strategies that varied by the percentage of, say, high-grade junk—BB and B—and very low grade, all the way down to single-C. Nammacher's role in this collaboration was to redirect the focus of Altman's earlier work on the default rates of *all* corporate bonds (from AAA to C) to the more specific question of the expected default rates and eventual losses on *speculative-grade* issues—and their past and expected future rates of return.

As a further step toward raising the quality of its high-yield research, Morgan Stanley hired Marty from Salomon Brothers in 1984 to head its entire Corporate Bond Research Department. Marty was given a specific mandate to produce a research journal focused on high yield that he called *High Performance.* And as he recalls, his boss Robert Platt, then head of Fixed Income Research, urged Marty to avoid the temptation to become an *advocate* for this new asset class, and aim instead to uphold Morgan Stanley's (as well as his own) reputation as a "trusted adviser" with products and services designed to serve the interests of *all* the firm's clients, investors and issuers alike.[4]

Encouraged by the firm's endorsement of objectivity, which was far from the universal stance toward research on Wall Street, Marty began examining a

number of claims about high-yield then being propagated by Drexel and its satel-
lites. What first caught Marty's attention was the tendency of Drexel and others
to create the impression that high-yield bonds were not really as risky as Moody's
and Standard & Poor's were making them out to be. Although research back then
suggested that changes in corporate ratings tended to lag changes in bond prices
instead of predicting them,[5] as Drexel was correct in reporting, future research
would confirm Marty's own sense that the rating agencies had a reasonably good
record of downgrading issuers *in advance of* defaults.

Marty's work also called attention to the accuracy of ratings in general in
assessing default risk. For example, if Moody's downgraded an issuer from Baa
to Ba, that issuer's one-year probability of defaulting, based on actual defaults
during the entire period 1920–2021, increased by roughly a factor of four, from
0.26 percent to 0.99 percent. In this sense, ratings changes conveyed useful, even
if not the most timely, information.

Marty's research also challenged the Drexel-encouraged notion that companies rated speculative-grade when first issuing in the public market were over-
whelmingly the *rising stars* of American industry, while top-rated companies
were basically "dinosaurs" with only one way to go. Indeed, his research showed
that among original-issue high-yield bonds, defaults outnumbered upgrades to
investment quality. And in the case of fallen angels, the number of issuers returning to investment grade outnumbered defaults.

Finally, Marty questioned the appropriateness of debt for funding high-growth
companies. As academics like Stew Myers (featured in chapter 5) pointed out in
the late '70s (when Milken and Drexel were beginning their ascent), companies
whose value consists mainly of growth options tend to be financed primarily
with equity for good reasons—not the least of which was to avoid the possibility
of financial trouble forcing managements to make shortsighted cutbacks in strategic investment at critical moments in their development.

More generally, Marty's work was widely recognized by industry participants
as reinforcing and extending Altman's efforts to bring empirical evidence to bear
on prevailing credit research. As just one example, after cautioning credit analysts
against overreliance on fixed-charge coverage as a measure of credit risk, he urged
them to make greater use of operating cash flow analysis. And using an extension
of Nobel laureate Bob Merton's "contingent claims" model of corporate bond
valuation developed by Morgan Stanley colleagues,[6] Marty showed how changes
in stock prices might be used to assess the credit risk of high-yield issuers.[7]

HIGH YIELD AND THE MARKET FOR CORPORATE CONTROL

In 1984, the year Marty joined Morgan Stanley, the public controversy surrounding high yield reached a new level when high-yield bonds began to be used to finance hostile takeovers. The functioning of what finance academics began to identify as "the market for corporate control" was seen by the top managements of many highly regarded public companies as a threat to not only their organizations, but *their own reputations and jobs.*

The initial response of large-company CEOs, and the Business Roundtable that represented their (though not necessarily their shareholders') interests, was to discredit both high-yield finance and the market for corporate control. What's more, the largest, most reputable investment banks tended to view themselves as *allies*—and in many cases the *hired defenders*—of their besieged corporate clients. After all, the blue-chip corporations had provided mainstream banks like Morgan Stanley and Merrill Lynch with a large and reliable source of M&A and other advisory fees associated with their empire-building acquisitions during the era of conglomeration—as well as the divestitures that often followed when the promised synergies failed to materialize. Along with M&A advisory fees, the investment-grade bond offerings of Business Roundtable stalwarts were another source of fee income that involved comparatively little risk-taking for the most reputable investment banks.

So it's not hard to see why Wall Street's premier houses were generally keener on providing takeover defense strategies than advising on and raising funding for hostile takeover bids. And the media reinforced this preference by continuing to project the "morality play" in which greedy corporate raiders busted up community-minded companies, threw loyal employees out of work, and bankrolled it all with "fake wampum"—a term that political correctness would never countenance today—that was bound to inflict financial ruin on any endowment or pension funds with such holdings in their portfolios. For good measure, corporate CEOs took to railing against the perceived treason of *corporate* pension funds in holding the high-yield bonds used to fund such takeovers, even though the clear duty of pension trustees was to their plan's beneficiaries and not the companies providing the pensions for their employees.

But it was precisely because so many "hostile" acquirers were *unaffiliated* investors—people who needed to raise their own capital—that a well-functioning high-yield market became necessary. And when Drexel began backing hostile deals with its "highly confident letters," written guarantees of funding for acquirers' bids, the calculus began to shift, creating a dilemma of sorts for "white-shoe" banks like Merrill and Morgan. The top managements of their best corporate clients no longer seemed to be as insulated from the workings of the corporate control market as they were in the 1960s and '70s. The boldness of Drexel's claims to have put to rest any misgivings about the raiders being unable to pay for their proposed takeovers suddenly made it difficult, if not impossible, for corporate boards to "just say no," as they had in the past, to purchase offers representing 40 percent to 50 percent or more over their companies' prevailing stock prices.

Thanks to the operation of the high-yield debt market, the best, and indeed the only effective, defense against such takeovers was to have satisfied shareholders.

OTHER HIGH-YIELD CONTROVERSIES

By the end of 1986, high-yield bonds accounted for 14 percent of the value of the public U.S. corporate bond market. Around that time, Marty was contacted by the prize-winning financial journalist Connie Bruck, who asked to meet with him to discuss her plan to write a book about the high-yield bond market aimed at a general readership.

In prepping for the meeting, Marty pulled together facts and figures demonstrating the market's growth and performance, as well as its growing acceptance by mainstream institutional investors. He figured that a well-informed and constructive book by the winner of the 1984 John Hancock Award for excellence in business and financial reporting could only reinforce his efforts at Morgan Stanley to demystify high-yield bonds while helping bring them farther into the investment mainstream.

But as things turned out, Bruck made it clear from the outset of their meeting that what she meant by a book about the high-yield market was an exposé—the more sensational the better—of Drexel Burnham Lambert's unconventional practices. Where Marty had come ready to discuss the investment risks and merits of speculative-grade bonds, Bruck's interest was confined largely to the role of Drexel and high-yield bonds in facilitating hostile takeovers—and to the lengths the firm might go to attract and retain its network of clients.

Bruck's journalistic instincts proved, of course, to be right on the mark, clearly more commercially promising than Marty's. When released by Simon & Schuster in 1988, *The Predators' Ball: The Junk-Bond Raiders and the Man Who Staked Them* quickly rose to the top of the business bestseller list. Marty was forced to fall back on the consoling thought that he, unlike Milken (as reported in the book), at least never stooped to offering to pay Bruck *not* to write the book.[8]

SHEDDING MORE LIGHT ON HIGH-YIELD DEFAULT RISK

From the start, Milken and his team encouraged the belief that the yield spread on speculative-grade bonds would always more than cover losses from defaults. In Marty's view, Drexel routinely glossed over the difference between long-run average and annual default rates, sidestepping the question of what would happen during the next downturn, when defaults were bound to—and indeed did—rise to a cyclical peak. When that happened, moreover, Drexel had been disabled by federal prosecution for a variety of controversial practices, including alleged insider trading and "stock parking." And this meant that the firm's uncanny ability to work out the problems of troubled issuers (more on this shortly) no longer helped keep a lid on defaults and losses.

As Marty saw it, Drexel's near-exclusive focus on long-run "yield premium versus average default loss" also ignored the reality that high-yield fund managers were generally evaluated not just on their performance over many years, but also of course on their *annual* returns. In a bear market, high-yield returns drop not just because of defaults, but also because yield premiums tend to rise sharply—and bond prices fall—when both perceived credit risk and interest rates go up, as they did at the end of the 1980s. Such risks affect *all*, not just the defaulting, high-yield issues.

Default rate projections by high-yield enthusiasts at Drexel and elsewhere relied heavily on historical data. According to Moody's, default rates had averaged only about 2.7 percent a year during the period from 1970 to 1988. If one also assumed that recoveries on defaulted bonds would average 40 percent of face value, as they had in the past, the implied annual *expected* losses dropped to a mere 1.6 percent (2.7 percent x (1.00–0.40)). And with high-yield spreads over seven-to-ten-year Treasurys (based on Merrill Lynch index data) ranging from 2.9 to 5.7 percentage points during the period 1985–1988, high-yield seemed like almost a sure winner for investors with some appetite for credit risk.[9]

Encouraged by this kind of analysis, many high-yield investors seem to have convinced themselves that they truly were getting a free lunch, as sell-side cheerleaders for high yield regularly assured them. According to the accepted narrative, dumb-money nervous Nellies blindly overstated the risk of speculative-grade bonds, perennially causing the bonds to trade below their intrinsic value. And so the warnings then being issued by Modern Portfolio Theory types, Marty among them—that higher returns were likely to be accompanied by higher risks and, eventually, defaults and losses—went largely unheeded.

A NEW WAY TO IDENTIFY THE RISKS

But then an insurance academic named Irwin Vanderhoof took the novel step of viewing high-yield default risk through an actuarial lens—one that led him to analyze default rates in a way that, though it may seem obvious now, was far from the norm at the time. Vanderhoof calculated the default rates, both historical and projected, on the entire high-yield universe as the *weighted average* of the BB, B, and CCC through C rates. With that portfolio approach, it suddenly made a huge difference that the more default-prone B, CCC, and lower categories' share of the speculative grade universe had increased from 13 percent in 1976, the year preceding the takeoff in high-yield new issuance, to 52 percent in 1989.

And following Vanderhoof's reasoning, many investors may well have predicted the next peak cyclical default rate by reasoning as follows:

- Start with the rating-specific default rates of 1970, when defaults
  by several issuers under the corporate umbrella of the Penn Central
  Transportation Company boosted the overall default rate within the
  then-small universe of speculative grade issuers to almost 8.7 percent.
- Apply those rates to the speculative grade universe's 1989 ratings mix to
  calculate a weighted average.

The answer one arrives at using this procedure came close to 14 percent. But any analyst who dared project a 14 percent default rate for high-yield bonds at the beginning of 1989 would have been dismissed as a high-yield hater with no understanding of the realities of the asset class. After all, the entrepreneurs who had engineered the leveraged buyouts of the preceding years had significant fractions of their personal net worth invested in those companies, and such people were unlikely to allow that value to dissipate without a mighty struggle to preserve as much as they could.

But as we shall see, this "naïve" Vanderhoof-style calculation (of 14 percent) wound up being much closer to the mark than the blithe expectation that default rates would never again approach the anomalous 8.7 percent level of 1970.

THE ROLE OF HIGH YIELD IN THE S&L CRISIS
(AND ITS EXAGGERATION BY THE PRESS)

In 1988, the year *The Predators' Ball* was published, failures of U.S. savings and loan institutions reached their peak during the episode that became known as the S&L crisis. This financial calamity furnished yet another opportunity for the financial media to blame the carnage on high-yield finance. The big problem with the popular high-yield S&L story, however, is that more than 1,000 S&Ls failed between 1986 and 1995—and bad real estate investments were far and away the main contributor to those failures.

According to a 1990 *Washington Post* report, only 200 of America's approximately 3,000 S&Ls had invested in high-yield bonds at all, and most of them allocated comparatively small portions of their assets to the category. During the period 1985–1989, according to one study, the top 50 holders accounted for 95 percent of S&Ls' total high-yield investments—and a 1989 *New York Times* article reported that S&L holdings of high-yield bonds totaled $12 billion.[10] Whatever default losses these bonds experienced (between $1 and $2 billion) were thus at most a very small fraction of the General Accounting Office's assessment of the cost of the S&L bailouts at $160 billion.

But as Marty lamented in a recent article in a publication called *Financial History*,[11] although this information has long been readily accessible to journalists, another publication called *TheStreet* was still (as recently as October 2022) offering this kind of analysis in its potted history of the S&L crisis:

> In the 1980s, there was a financial crisis in the United States that stemmed from skyrocketing inflation as well as the rise of high-yield debt instruments, called junk bonds, which resulted in the failure of more than half of the

nation's Savings & Loans institutions . . . Deregulation allowed S&Ls to invest in even riskier instruments that would offer the high yields they needed: Junk bonds became the speculative vehicle of choice for financiers behind S&Ls in the hopes of offsetting the damage caused by fixed-rate mortgages.[12]

The good news, however, is that the terms "high yield" and "junk" do not even appear in the Federal Reserve's history of the S&L crisis, published almost ten years earlier.[13]

ANOTHER CAUTIONARY TALE OF MEDIA-INFLAMED CONFUSION

In 1989, three Harvard Business School finance professors—Paul Asquith, David Mullins, and Eric Wolff—published an analysis of original issue high-yield bonds that became widely known as the "the Harvard study."[14] The statistical approach and methods of their study differed little from earlier research by Ed Altman, yet somehow managed to create a media sensation by reporting a 34 percent *cumulative* default rate on bonds issued in 1977 and 1978. The authors emphasized that this rate was "substantially higher than reported in earlier studies."

Among the many problems with the Harvard study was its authors' failure to make clear that the main focus of the earlier studies was *annual* default rates, not *cumulative* default rates. To their credit, both *Fortune* and *Barron's* pointed out this problem, although they were largely alone among the major media in doing so. The 34 percent cumulative default figure that appeared so alarming, as the *Fortune* writer noted,

is about the same as the default figure arrived at last year in a study by New York University professor Edward Altman, long the reigning academic authority on junk. The Harvard study does not contradict the 2.5 percent annual default rate usually cited in discussions of high-yield bonds: The higher figures reflect how many bonds of all those issued in a particular period eventually default, while the lower figure represents the percentage of all junk bonds outstanding that default in a single year.[15]

In short, much ado about nothing!

HIGH YIELD'S NEAR-DEATH EXPERIENCE

But however misinformed and misguided, these media attacks on high-yield finance may well have had their desired effect. They coincided with the beginning of the period Marty has dubbed the "Great Debacle"—a period when overpriced and hence overleveraged buyouts, as we saw in chapter 7, began to fail in droves.

At the beginning of the first LBO wave in the early to mid-1980s, it made sense for LBO sponsors to pay substantial premiums over market value to acquire public companies, sometimes with as little as 10 percent equity. But as the sponsoring firms found themselves able to close deals while putting in ever less of their own equity, the purchase prices (expressed as multiples of operating earnings and cash flow)—and hence the amounts of debt needed to fund the deals—continued to rise throughout the decade. This, as Mike Jensen pointed out, was a prescription for way too many deals.[16]

LBO sponsors and their lenders were at huge risk of default if the economy turned down at some point, which it inevitably would. That point arrived with the 1990–1991 recession. By June 1991, the trailing 12-month default rate on U.S. speculative-grade bonds reported by Moody's had jumped from its cyclical low of 2.1 percent in 1989 to its peak of 12.3 percent, higher than at any point since the depths of the Great Depression in 1933.

The trouble started to show up well before the recession. As early as the second half of 1989, the perception of growing credit risk caused the high-yield index (then known as the Merrill Lynch High Yield Master II) to produce a total return of *negative* 2.9 percent! This was a considerable shock to the now large numbers of high-yield enthusiasts who had serenely assumed that the yield-spread-versus-default-loss cushion would *always* keep their heads above water.

But to understand how high yield default rates ended up exceeding 12 percent, it's important to note that, just as the market was showing signs of weakness, Milken pled guilty to securities and reporting violations—and Drexel filed for bankruptcy. The massive bear market shut down new issuance of high-yield debt for most of 1990. And the LBOs and the original-issue high-yield bonds that financed them appeared completely discredited in the eyes of many market participants.

THE PRIVATIZATION OF BANKRUPTCY (AND THE REGULATORY UNDOING THEREOF)

Up until that point, highly leveraged companies that got into financial trouble—as their sponsors foresaw many would—had powerful incentives to reorganize quickly, and so stay out of the (then especially) costly U.S. chapter 11 process, with all its inefficiencies and delays. Throughout much of the 1980s, this "privatization of bankruptcy," as recognized and hailed by Jensen himself, resulted in remarkably low default rates, even on LBOs leveraged 9 to 1. Before 1989, only three out of some 119 large LBOs (tracked by Steve Kaplan and Jeremy Stein) transacted during the '80s had defaulted.

One clear contributor to these low default rates was Drexel's practice of using *exchange offers* of equity for (distressed) debt to avoid disrupting what were still highly solvent and reasonably profitable business operations producing large amounts of (pre-interest) operating cash flow. Milken liked to refer to them as "good businesses" that now found themselves with "the wrong capital structure." As Harvard Business School's Stuart Gilson reported finding in his study of exchange offers in the early 1980s, the direct costs associated with default avoidance using exchange offers turned out to be as little as one-tenth of those incurred in formal reorganizations in chapter 11.[17]

Max Holmes, a former workout specialist at Drexel and later head of D.E. Shaw's distressed debt group, described the Drexel reorganization process as follows:

> In our exchange offers, the group of high-yield investors was small enough—and had enough confidence in Drexel—that we could persuade them to stretch out the maturities of the debt or, in some cases, convert part of their debt into equity. And I think that both the bondholders and the companies themselves were well served by this workout process.
>
> What we were really doing . . . was keeping an overleveraged capital structure from interfering with the operations of a fundamentally profitable company—and we were doing it in the most efficient way possible. At Drexel, people liked to say that the optimal capital structure changes over time. And I think the exchange offers we designed for our distressed issuers were an ideal vehicle for making those changes. It was our job as the workout guys to ensure

that the companies kept operating as if nothing had happened—and that's pretty much what happened, until the '90s changed everything.[18]

In the 1990s, and for a variety of reasons that include the ongoing prosecution of Milken and Drexel, the obstacles to reorganizing companies outside of chapter 11 became insurmountable. As Jensen described the situation,

> A private market correction to the overleveraging [of the '80s] was already well underway [at the start of the '90s] when new regulatory measures designed to purge our credit markets of "speculative excesses" greatly added to the difficulties in our HLT [highly leveraged transaction] markets. A series of misguided changes in the tax and regulatory codes and in bankruptcy court decisions blocked the normal economic incentives for creditors to come to agreement outside of chapter 11, thus almost putting an end to out-of-court reorganizations. The consequence was a sharp rise in the number of chapter 11 filings, and in the associated costs of financial distress.

In 1990 alone, almost $25 billion of high-yield bonds defaulted and wound up in chapter 11. The eventual number of defaults and bankruptcies, and the associated losses to investors, greatly exceeded what most market participants then thought possible.

THE GREAT RESTORATION

In the depths of the Great Debacle, many portfolio managers suspected that the "buy" recommendations of some sell-side analysts were motivated in no small part by the eagerness of their trading desks to unload damaged bonds from their inventories. Restoring the credibility of not only the would-be issuers and their bankers, but also of the supporting research, would play a significant role in the rejuvenation of the high-yield bond market that took place after the regulatory shutdown of high leverage in the early '90s.

In the middle of 1989—just as the market was going into the tank—Merrill Lynch had persuaded Marty to leave Morgan Stanley to head its High Yield Bond Research Department. When Merrill's team convened to discuss the future of the business, it was Marty who proved to be the greatest optimist in the group, projecting that the high-yield underwriting business might one day rebound to annual issuance as high as $10 billion. (His projections proved way too cautious in light of the $400 billion of U.S. non-investment grade issuance in 2020.)

Marty urged his team to follow the rule they'd all been indoctrinated with since fourth grade: *show your work!* The goal was complete transparency, proceeding step by step to the conclusion that the bond being analyzed was attractively priced. This way, the worst response from a buy-sider would be something like, "Though I disagree with some of your assumptions, your conclusion follows from them, and so your analysis looks like a genuine attempt to get to the right answer." That principle informed Marty's own work. With data becoming more widely disseminated, the point was to enable anyone who wished to replicate the work and determine its validity for themselves. The curtain had come down on the era of Wall Street strategists whose conclusions had to be accepted solely on the basis that everyone "knew" them to be geniuses.

Remaining faithful to Robert Platt's injunction to be an analyst and not an advocate, Marty also politely declined a suggestion from junk bond king Milken, after he resigned from Drexel, that Marty assume Milken's mantle in spreading the high-yield gospel. Marty replied that, however flattering he found Milken's suggestion, his service and value to his employer Merrill Lynch depended not on proselytizing, but on producing objective research that helped high-yield investors maintain and even boost their risk-adjusted returns. Marty viewed his research as part of a larger collective effort to increase the "information content" of high-yield prices and, along with it, the efficiency of the market in which they traded.

Taking full advantage of greater data availability, Marty tackled a variety of analytical issues, sometimes in collaboration with colleagues like Christopher Garman, Jón Jónsson, and Michael Cherry. Among his most notable insights was that senior bonds could carry larger risk premiums (spreads over Treasurys) than like-rated subordinated bonds if the subordinated bonds were obligations of higher-rated, and presumably more creditworthy, *corporate issuers*. It was not unreasonable to expect such issuers' lower default probabilities to more than offset the more senior bonds' higher expected recoveries in the event of default.

In another research initiative, Marty debunked the popular industry claim, by Drexel and others, that bonds systematically became underpriced when downgraded from investment grade to speculative grade. His price data showed that the values of such fallen angels were equally likely to continue falling as to rebound from the supposedly "oversold" levels resulting from forced selling by managers of investment-grade portfolios. Consistent with this finding, some of the largest pension plan sponsors told Marty that their investment rules gave them flexibility in timing their liquidations of fallen angels to avoid fire sales.

Another phenomenon that got Marty's attention was the stock and bond price changes accompanying "leveraging events"—say, large one-time distributions to shareholders—that led predictably to surges in stock prices (or returns) and plunges in the prices of existing bonds. Having identified this phenomenon, Marty devoted considerable effort to keeping bondholders informed about possible leveraging events that could inflict significant losses on their portfolios.

FURTHER VINDICATION BY THE ACADEMY

But as Marty himself has pointed out, probably the most important and credible piece of high-yield research—one that, with the 1980s "junk"-fueled takeover wars now over, likely did the most to help the high-yield market enter the mainstream of institutional investing—was a study published in the *Journal of Finance* in 1991 by Wharton School professors Marshall Blume, Donald Keim, and Sandeep Patel called "Volatility and Returns of Low-Grade Bonds."[19] The study analyzed the risks and returns of long-term speculative-grade bonds for the period 1977–1989 and found not only higher returns but also *lower* volatility for high-yield bonds relative to investment-grade bonds.

One effect of the Wharton study was to discredit the claims of the "Harvard study" that high-yield bonds become more default-prone as they age. But an even more important finding—and it's one that the finance scholars celebrated in this book would have predicted—was that speculative-grade bonds were neither systematically overpriced nor underpriced. Despite its lower volatility, high-yield investing clearly carries greater credit risk as reflected in the higher default rates and losses. The higher yields and eventual returns represent the expected compensation—neither too much nor too little—for bearing such risk.

And this is just what one would expect in a vigorous, highly competitive—and what we have been identifying as an *efficient*—market, a market that, in promising and providing higher returns for larger credit risks, would succeed in attracting legions of new investors. By providing investors with "fair," though not outsized or "abnormal" (of the kind sometimes claimed by Drexel and other enthusiasts), rates of returns, the high-yield market would ensure that corporate *issuers* would also perceive it as providing them with a fair deal and economic source of capital—at least when set against their main alternatives of private placements—and so keep returning year after year.

THE GREAT HIGH-YIELD REBOUND AND EXPANSION

After the Great Debacle of 1989–1990 and during the several-year hiatus of LBOs and other highly leveraged transactions that followed, access to high-yield financing expanded to a wider range of companies that were simply seeking funding for continuing and expanding their operations. In the decade from 1989 to 1999, the amount of U.S. high-yield bonds outstanding nearly doubled to $274 billion, of which over 90 percent was original-issue paper. In some quarters, the impression lingered that "junk" companies were all failing remnants of one-time blue chips, but the reality was that highly leveraged but clearly healthy—and even a good number of rapidly growing—companies began to account for a substantial portion of the total.

At the end of 1999, the largest industry within the ICE BofA US High Yield Index was telecommunications, whose issues then accounted for some 20 percent of total face value. Sensing that the growth of the industry had become too rapid, especially for debt-heavy financing, Marty began to warn investors that it was natural to expect a shakeout in the telecom industry.

While venture capitalists are accustomed to high failure rates offset by one or two big winners, high-yield bond investors have limited upside, and tend to look to an issuer's asset values to provide downside protection in the event of bankruptcy. But when the dotcom bubble burst in 2001, such protection did not materialize for the early-stage telecoms of the 1990s. Many of these enterprises were little more than "business plan" companies with no tangible assets or operating cash flows—just plans for constructing telecommunications networks and eventually obtaining customers. And in Marty's view, such growth companies had been able to raise capital in the high-yield market only because of the same "Fed-spurred" investment boom that was also encouraging and enabling dubious dot.coms to go public.

This "game" continued for several years before culminating in a high-yield "TMT" (telecom/media/technology) bust that paralleled the dot.com crash in the stock market. In 2001, telecom and broadcasting recorded the highest default rates among 35 industries tracked by Moody's. During the period 2001–2003, the US High Yield Telecom Index produced an annualized return of *negative* 25.1 percent, as compared to the positive 3.7 percent eked out by the rest of the High Yield Index. And telecom continues to hold the record for the lowest recovery rate (based on prices immediately after default) of the 35 industries for the entire 1983–2021 period.[20]

* * *

But the high-yield market would once again emerge from the wreckage to reach new heights. In the decade from 1999 to 2009, the face value of U.S. original-issue high-yield bonds once again more than doubled, to $618 billion. At the same time, the new issuers were joined by a growing host of newly fallen angels. Thanks to the Global Financial Crisis and Great Recession, and the large number of downgradings that came with them, the $618 billion of original-issue high-yield issuers now represented only 75 percent of the total high-yield outstandings, down from over 90 percent ten years earlier.

Nevertheless, in the decade that followed the GFC, the high-yield market showed remarkable resilience, with original-issue outstandings growing by almost 80 percent, to $1.1 trillion by June 2019. At that point they once again represented over 90 percent of the high-yield total, by then over $1.2 trillion. And at last count, these figures were 93 percent and $1.3 trillion.[21]

THE FIRST 40 YEARS OF HIGH-YIELD BOND ISSUANCE: A LOOK BACK AT THE MARKET'S ACCOMPLISHMENTS AND PROSPECTS

As Merton Miller wrote in 1988 when revisiting "The Modigliani-Miller Propositions After Thirty Years,"

> The significant innovation in recent years—and it is still a puzzle why it took so long—has been in the showing that, contrary to the conventional wisdom, junk bonds could in fact be issued and marketed successfully by design, and not just as "fallen angels."[22]

And the main aim and undertaking of Miller's Nobel Prize speech two years later was to dispel "the anti-leverage hysteria" that had "destroyed the liquidity of the high-yield bond market."[23]

Although he did not mention Michael Milken's role (in either the article or the speech) in the development of the original-issue high-yield bond market, Miller proved on several occasions more than willing both to appear in public debate with, and praise the accomplishments of, this convicted felon—a man he once described as "the victim of excess prosecutorial zeal," and whose social role in funding corporate growth and improving efficiency "would eventually be recognized."[24]

But having relied on Marty as our guide up to this point, let's now note his response when invited to respond to questions like the following:

WHAT DID MILKEN AND DREXEL GET RIGHT?

First, the idea that a company's value-maximizing capital structure is likely to vary over time, with changes in market conditions that were either favorable (or unfavorable) to corporate debt financing. (In fact, Milken coauthored a paper with one of his professors at Wharton on this subject.)

But his most important innovation—the notion that there could in fact be a market for new public issues of noninvestment grade bonds—wasn't Milken's. He had had no experience in investment banking before joining forces with Fred Joseph at Drexel. And Lehman Brothers Kuhn Loeb had been underwriting public high-yield issues before Drexel got in the game.

Nevertheless, Milken was the first to see the case for and insist that the trading and selling of high-yield bonds be housed in a separate department, as opposed to operating as a segment within the fixed-income desk. Trafficking in investment-grade bonds was pretty straightforward—largely a matter of interest rates, ratings, and spread-based arbitrage. By contrast, high-yield traders and salespeople had to be prepared to immerse themselves in and master the financial and operating intricacies of the corporate issuers. In other words, they really had to understand corporate finance and how the company was expected to make money, both in the near term and in the future. The bonds of companies with the same rating, capital structure priority, and maturity often had risk premium differentials of hundreds of basis points. Milken and his team made huge profits for Drexel from developing a clear sense of the economic basis for such differences, and how long they were likely to remain.

WHAT DID MILKEN GET WRONG?

Drexel's worst offense, in Marty's view, was to continue to flog the findings of a study by economist Braddock Hickman that purported to show that high-yield bonds were systematically undervalued.[25] The Hickman study presented the simple finding that speculative-grade bonds returned more net of default losses than investment-grade bonds, with no attempt to determine if the return differential was large enough to compensate investors for the larger credit risk. As Marty saw it, the Drexel crowd skated over the fact that the return premium existed only if the sample included bonds that the Hickman study referred to as "irregulars"—those created in distressed exchanges. This meant that the results they were touting were not relevant for or applicable to newly issued noninvestment grade bonds (without an implied reorganizer like Drexel backing them). What's more, Hickman took charge of the study at a comparatively late stage, and presented noninvestment grade bonds in a more favorable light than the originator of the study, Harold Fraine.

Perhaps equally troubling to Marty (though less so to this writer), Milken's efforts to present his own commercial activity as a social calling or form of public service, however justified it may turn out to have been in terms of its actual economic effects, was almost certain to put most people off. Whether Milken truly views himself as guided by a higher social purpose is largely irrelevant to Marty's more immediate concern: "Is the bond you're showing me, or the asset class you're trying to attract me to, likely to be a good investment?" As Marty once told me, "Maybe Milken really did go into finance because seeing the Watts riots in LA firsthand led him to conclude that the most reliable way to lift Black people out of poverty is to 'democratize' capital. But I was taught in college to avoid the goddess of true motives."

Marty also claims to have been put off by Milken and Drexel's failure to respond to an op-ed by prominent economist Herb Stein, formerly chief of Richard Nixon's Council of Economic Advisers, challenging the logic underlying Milken's claims. Stein's argument went roughly as follows: assuming that the total of investor capital is a largely fixed commodity, the fact that more of it is devoted to Drexel-funded enterprises, no matter how productive, must inevitably mean that less capital is available for all others. A nation's GNP, which Stein—like most of his macro brethren—appears to believe captures everything worth knowing about the social benefits of a nation's commercial activity, must therefore remain largely *fixed*, almost wholly unaffected by all of Milken's efforts, however exceptional.

But since Milken for whatever reason didn't care to respond to Stein, I'm going to take a shot at it here. As should become clear in the next two chapters of this book—one on the enormous problems with Chinese corporate governance and public finance, the other on problems with GNP as a gauge of national economic performance and much macro thinking in general—it ought to matter hugely whether capital is being employed productively or not. The hands that capital ends up in, and under what conditions and constraints and for what purposes, should also be expected to have potentially large effects on a nation's general economic and social well-being. To assume otherwise is to assume away all the problems that corporate finance theorists (Jensen first and foremost) and practitioners (above all, Milken) have devoted their careers to thinking (and in Milken's case, doing something) about.

* * *

Productivity gains matter. Contrary to the logic of Herb Stein and many other macroeconomists, productivity increases don't just fall from trees. The financial system has to be designed—and in some cases, actually evolve—to keep giving rise to ever more productivity. Such a system, as we have been suggesting throughout these pages, appears to be the *most* (and may well be the *only*) reliable basis for economic and social progress.

CHAPTER 11

CARL WALTER AND EXPOSING THE BRITTLE FAÇADE OF CHINESE CORPORATE AND PUBLIC FINANCE

After the collapse of the Maoist revolution at the end of the 1970s, a 30-year old named Carl Walter was among the first American graduate students to be allowed to study in China since 1949. Along with fluency in Mandarin, he was able to acquire enough material during his first stay in Beijing—which earned him a certificate in "advanced study" from Peking University—to complete his Ph.D. dissertation back at Stanford in 1981. The subject was the workings of China's central bank.

But rather than an academic, Carl became an investment banker. After several years in Taipei and then Tokyo, he moved in 1992 to Beijing, where he lived and worked for the next 20 years. During that time, he played a leading role in China's first IPO, Brilliance China Automotive, which had a "blow-out listing" on the New York Stock Exchange in October 1992. Then, after establishing Credit Suisse First Boston's China office in Beijing, he helped "lead-manage" the first listing of a state-owned enterprise, Shandong Huaneng Power, on the New York Stock Exchange in August 1994.

The next moves in Carl's career brought him as close to becoming an "insider" in Chinese finance as any Westerner is likely to get. After joining Morgan Stanley in 1999, he became a member of the Management Committee of China International Capital Corporation (CICC), China's first and most successful joint venture investment bank. In that role, he not only supported debt and stock offerings by Chinese companies, but served as an informal adviser on a number of reforms of Chinese capital markets and corporate financial practices.

But as will become clear in what follows, these attempts at adopting Western-style markets and corporate practices have fallen well short of what their planners and promoters—Carl not least among them—had envisioned and hoped for.

THE RISE OF RED CAPITALISM
(OR THE TRAPPINGS, WITHOUT THE SUBSTANCE,
OF MODERN CORPORATE FINANCE)

My introduction to Chinese corporate finance took place in the summer of 2014, when I first met Carl at a conference held on the campus of Hong Kong Polytechnic University in Kowloon. He was the keynote speaker, and both the occasion and the matter for his opening talk were provided by his 2010 book *Red Capitalism*, co-written by fellow banker Fraser Howie and bearing the provocative subtitle, *The Fragile Financial Foundation of China's Extraordinary Rise.*[1]

The main argument of the book—which was recognized by both *The Economist* and Bloomberg as "A Best Book of the Year"—is that despite the best intentions of would-be reformers, China has ended up adopting the forms, but not the substance, of Western capital markets. With considerable help from U.S. investment banks like Goldman Sachs and Morgan Stanley, China has succeeded in replicating the entire panoply of institutions that support public capital markets, from stock exchanges to regulators and auditors to listed companies large enough to justify the costs of raising public equity capital.

But as Carl's book shows, the profitability and underlying fundamental values of most of China's publicly traded companies—two thirds of them state-owned enterprises (or SOEs)—are largely an illusion created and sustained by two things you rarely see in today's Western markets: (1) government-granted monopolies and protection against foreign competitors; and (2) a seemingly endless supply of cheap capital provided entirely by China's state-owned banks, whose main mandate, as established and enforced by the Chinese Communist Party, is to promote domestic growth, full employment, and the financial stability of the SOEs.

As a consequence, and despite the attempts of "private" companies like Alibaba and Tencent to break out of this mold, Carl's account of the situation in 2010, and written a decade ago, remains largely true today:

> For the most part China's National Champions remain state-controlled enterprises and act like them. Beijing plays every role from issuer, to underwriter, to regulator, to controlling investor and manager of the exchanges. The state in its many guises still owns nearly two-thirds of domestically listed company shares.

And so few will be surprised to learn that the Chinese conception of the rights and role of shareholders has turned out to be very different from what we see in the U.S. and most Western economies. Whereas the shareholders of companies in the West—and even increasingly in Asian nations like South Korea and Singapore—play important roles in disciplining inefficient management teams, the minority shareholders of Chinese SOEs have long been, and continue to be, viewed in Beijing, as a powerless and largely voiceless source of very cheap capital. Most Chinese managers, as Carl reports, view outside public equity, especially from foreign investors, as a kind of perpetual bank loan with more or less optional payments of interest (called "dividends) and no foreseeable redemption date.

What's more, there's remarkably little attempt by the CCP and its policy makers to conceal this reality. As openly conceded in a government-authorized book published in 1999 to celebrate the 50th anniversary of the People's Republic,

> Looking at the current situation in our country, no matter whether the regulators, government departments, or the listed companies, all treat public offerings and listing of shares as a cheap source of funding.[2]

U.S. public equity markets, to be sure, also continue to be viewed by both the American and overseas public companies that use them as an inexpensive source of capital, but for mostly different reasons: For issuers in U.S. stock markets, public equity's affordability reflects mainly the diversification of its enormous investor base *and* the strengths of the U.S. governance system. For Chinese companies, the attraction of Chinese equity markets involves a different role for governance. Thanks to the laxness of the Chinese governance system, there's little that dissatisfied investors can do to increase their odds of getting a return—which makes the capital virtually free (until the companies have to return for more).

THE STRANGE PHENOMENON OF CHINESE IPO UNDERPRICING

Another peculiar feature of Chinese capitalism is what Carl characterizes as a *shocking* degree of IPO underpricing—orders of magnitude larger than what we have become accustomed to in the U.S.—that has prevailed throughout the entire post-Mao 1998–2021 period. In 1998, for example, there were 92 IPOs of Chinese SOEs on the Shanghai Exchange that experienced an average first-day price jump of 149 percent, as compared to the roughly 15–20 percent "pops" that accompanied U.S. deals the same year. In these Chinese IPOs, moreover, 62 percent of all so-called investors dumped their shares on the first day the shares were deemed tradable. By 2010, the picture was similar, but with an average first-day price jump of only 47 percent—the maximum then allowed by new regulation—and 69 percent selling their shares.

Chinese "investors" accordingly scramble to get as many IPO shares as they can—typically using illegal bank loans—and then sell out immediately to repay those loans and so minimize both their legal and economic risk. As Carl describes the phenomenon, "This is not investing, it is speculation encouraged by the state, and coming at the expense of the state."[3]

All in all, then, it's not hard to see why the interest of most Western institutional investors in Chinese companies—again, with a handful of exceptions like tech giant Alibaba—has continued to fall steadily since the flurry of successful banking IPOs in the mid-2000s, not to mention a seemingly endless series of accounting and governance scandals that started soon after the onset of the Global Financial Crisis. And with the state still holding a clear majority of domestically listed shares, as Carl points out, "Outsiders cannot help suspecting that state entities largely control the share price movements of even Hong Kong-listed Chinese companies."

And so for overseas investors contemplating investments as minority shareholders in Chinese companies, there are not one, but *two* main sources of uncertainty that are likely to prevent the companies' stock prices from reflecting their fundamental values. First are questions about who's really buying the stock: Are there large inflows of government capital ready to prop up the values when useful or expedient. (Remember Merton Miller's comments in chapter 2 about the investor skepticism created by the covert buying and selling of Japanese stocks by the Japanese Ministry of Finance.) And then there is the uncertainty about the companies' fundamentals: will the government continue to protect the monopolies and favored access to public assets and cheap capital on which much of the profitability and value of such companies depends? Once such protection goes away, and with investors virtually powerless to intervene should things go wrong, what's left to motivate the top managers of Chinese SOEs to work to increase or just preserve the values of their enterprises?

A look at Chinese stock returns during the past 30 years (since the re-opening of Chinese markets in 1993) is revealing. Even during the 15 or so years before the Global Financial Crisis, the annual returns of the shares of Chinese companies that could be bought and sold by foreign investors, as reported in Jay Ritter's study (also cited in chapter 2), averaged a *negative* 5 percent![4] In the decade since the global crisis, the Chinese market has continued to produce returns statistically indistinguishable from zero, leading one political economist to describe China's massive increases in GNP during that period as having been accompanied by "no net gains in productivity and social wealth."[5] And since the outbreak of the COVID pandemic in 2020, these numbers have turned sharply negative.

All this raises questions that we explore in the rest of this chapter: Even if the performance of its SOEs and financial markets is deeply suspect, how has China succeeded in lifting hundreds of millions of its citizens out of poverty in such a short period of time? And is Chinese economic and social progress likely to continue? As we asked back in chapter 2, can a nation with a failing corporate finance system continue to create the economic and social wealth on which rising standards of living depend? Though it's now fashionable to blame much of China's economic problems on the strictness of the government's COVID lockdown, Carl's work addressing the cracks in China's entire financial system has been pointing to this outcome for well over a decade.[6]

HOW, THEN, EXPLAIN THE CHINESE ECONOMIC MIRACLE?

Since the death of Mao and the return to power of Deng Xiaoping in the late 1970s, the Chinese government has succeeded in engineering nothing short of an economic miracle. "No other government," as economists Randall Morck and Bernard Yeung proclaimed at the same Hong Kong conference I attended in 2014, "has achieved anything remotely comparable."

In their attempt to explain how this feat was accomplished, Morck, a finance prof at the University of Alberta, and Yeung, Dean of the National University of Singapore's NUS Business School, began with the provocative statement,

"Economics surely has more to learn from China than China has ever learned from economics." They went on to say that China's remarkable success appears to defy the conventional wisdom of developmental economists that institutions like the rule of law, well-defined property rights, and well-functioning capital markets provide the most reliable—and possibly the *only*—path for nations intent on achieving long-run growth and prosperity.

Morck and Yeung made a plausible case that China's transformation into a modern industrial economy may in fact have been accelerated by the CCP-controlled government's deliberate *suppression* of such institutions. They pointed to the writings of Paul Rosenstein-Rodan, a mid-20th-century development economist (credited with having designed and launched the World Bank), who argued that the main challenge for most of today's developing economies is finding a way to overcome what he identifies as "coordination failure"—that is, the challenge of creating the networks of suppliers and manufacturers required for large-scale production. The solution to this problem—and Rosenstein-Rodan's main contribution to development economics—is what he calls the "Big Push," a government-orchestrated effort to plan and carry out the simultaneous development of networks of companies across a range of industries.[7]

The best illustration of the "Big Push" in action, according to Morck and Yeung, is China's recent growth. And given the country's desperate circumstances from the 1970s up through the late '90s, they suggest that it may well have been the *only* way of accomplishing the goal in such short order.

But after praising China's leaders for pulling off this "greatest economic feat in history," Morck and Yeung expressed two major reservations about the "Big Push." First, such initiatives don't have to be planned or carried out by governments. Research (much of it their own) on Japanese and Korean economic development provides compelling evidence that *private-sector* coordination—by networks of firms called *zaibatsu* in the case of Japan, and *chaebol* in Korea—has generally proved more effective than central planning in building an industrial economy and national wealth.

The second, and probably more important, concern is that although the "Big Push" has raised China from the bottom to the middle ranks of the world's economies, the odds are stacked against its success in taking China to the next level. China's per capita GDP, at about $6,000 in 2014 (and about $12,000 today), remains a modest fraction of Japan's nearly $40,000, and greatly overshadowed by the $70,000 or more in the U.S. and other "high-income" countries. Economic history, as Morck and Yeung point out, is littered with cases of initially rapid ascents by developing countries like Brazil and Argentina that, with almost predictable regularity, become mired in what economists now refer to as "the middle income trap."

What are the main causes of this trap? At the top of the list is the tendency of well-entrenched "elites" to suppress competition and tilt the system toward their own interests—and at the expense of almost everybody else.[8] Recognizing the special means and potency of the CCP (whose members Carl identifies as China's *only* elites) to suppress would-be competitors, Morck and Yeung end up expressing major doubts that China will continue its rise into the world's economic upper ranks until it gets serious about adopting the substance as well as the form of those "missing institutions" that are "the only well-marked path to high-income status."[9]

The most memorable advice to Chinese policymakers at the conference I attended in 2014 was offered by British-born David Webb, one of Hong Kong's leading investor activists and authorities on Chinese corporate governance. After observing the remarkable similarities between China's corporate ownership and governance system and the domination of the UK economy by state-owned enterprises in 1980, Webb urged the Chinese government to follow the bold example of Margaret Thatcher: Sell down, or *privatize*, the government's massive holdings of SOEs as quickly as possible, while providing the greatest possible encouragement for foreign investors and banks to expand their participation in Chinese capital markets.

But that alas has not been happening. In the nearly a decade that has passed since then, there's no indication that the CCP has become any more receptive to the idea of privatization than it was in 2014 . . . or 1993 . . . or 1970 . . . or 1949.

THE POST-GFC DETERIORATION OF CHINESE PUBLIC FINANCE

But let's now turn to what is in some ways an even more important question—one that, although raised briefly in chapter 2, we have yet to take head on in this book: Is there a necessary link between the efficiency of a nation's publicly traded private-sector, the strength of its public finance, and its general economic growth and prosperity? Can a well-run (or at least well-heeled) public sector somehow compensate for the deficiencies of its publicly traded private sector? And can a nation like China continue to make significant economic and social progress *without* well-functioning financial markets and public companies dedicated at least in part to increasing their own efficiency and long-run values?

These are the questions Carl Walter raised in his recently released (2022) book, *The Red Dream: The Communist Party and the Financial Deterioration of China*. As part of the book's account of the long-run effects of China's alternating embrace of and clampdown on Western-style capitalism during the past four decades, Carl constructs a rough financial balance sheet for China's current (2022) state sector—a reckoning the Chinese government has been unwilling, or possibly unable, to provide. And Carl's balance sheet reflects a number of important quirks and possibly troubling realities.

First and foremost is China's highly unusual, "ad hoc" fiscal system in which Beijing has for decades negotiated with local governments the amount of tax revenues to be turned over in return for subsidies—all the while preserving social stability by redistributing part of its "excess" revenue from these exchanges with the municipalities to the poorer provinces. The problem here stems from the reality that, although the tax revenues from the municipalities have increased dramatically over time, their subsidies from Beijing have been hugely outrun by the local government's assumed responsibilities and spending. And because these governments have been left with less money and more social obligations (again, those imposed but not funded by Beijing), they have ended up creating a "shadow" fiscal system—one in which the accumulating debts of the local governments do not show up in the national income accounts.

The second critical factor has been the dramatic increase in foreign investment, starting as a trickle in the mid-1990s, but becoming a torrent with China's entry into the World Trade Organization in 2001. Thanks to such foreign investment and related supply chains, the Chinese export sector became the envy of the world. And as a direct result of such investment and export success, the bank deposits of Chinese private companies and households—by far the main forms of Chinese savings—have exploded. This in brief is how China succeeded during the first decade of this century in developing a middle class, the first in its history, consisting of some 300 million Chinese.

Helping to fuel all this activity and growth, stock markets both domestic and international generated tens of billions of U.S. dollars in capital for Chinese state-owned enterprises. But since the Global Financial Crisis started to abate in 2009, China has embarked on what became a decade-long financial stimulus program, a binge of social spending made possible and effectively funded by the household wealth stored as savings accounts in China's (all state-owned) banks.

And the main finding of Carl's new book can be summed as follows: the Chinese state's net worth, even after taking account of its very large trade surpluses with the U.S. and the rest of the world, has largely disappeared under a mountain of debt that has been extended to parts of the state sector itself. On the basis of the most recent available Chinese government data—whose endpoint is 2018 (and thus pre-COVID)—Carl's analysis leaves us with the suggestion that the value of China's state assets today may not be enough to meet its obligations to Chinese households—most of them, again, in the form of deposits in state-owned banks with arguably negative net worth themselves.

How does Carl account for the rise of such a Byzantine financial structure and its ability to continue dissipating China's national wealth? China's Communist-Party-driven government, by first introducing, and then reversing many of, its economic reforms, has made a more or less deliberate national economic policy decision to sacrifice efficiency and economic value to maintain what the CCP values most: social stability and its own power and control.

REVISITING THE MYSTERIOUS CASE OF CHINESE IPO UNDERPRICING

As we saw earlier, when selling minority interests in its SOEs to the public, the Chinese government has allowed underwriters to offer the shares at "shocking" discounts to their economic values. But the question is, why? Who benefits from what amount to these massive wealth transfers from the state (and Chinese taxpayers) to the privileged few who manage to get, and then quickly dump, the shares?

Carl's attempt to explain this peculiar practice is worth quoting at length, if only as a way of getting at the CCP's view of the social role of the financial system:

> The state may have seen itself as protecting retail investors from the rapacity of underwriters, and as protecting underwriters—all owned by the state of course—from losing money. And Beijing, it's true, has always sought, but largely failed, to control the level of the market index to prevent crashes and the associated social unrest. But all that considered, the state would appear to benefit least from the huge first-day price jumps coupled with heavy turnover thereafter. While the listing company succeeds in raising capital with the underpriced shares, some

investors get to walk off with fortunes. There is no doubt but that the listing enterprise is the biggest loser in this arrangement—and, as the owner of such enterprises, so of course is the state. And though the loss on a single enterprise IPO may seem immaterial, over time and with thousands of IPOs, the loss of value to the state becomes enormous.

But the underlying rationale of Chinese policymakers becomes at least a little clearer when one goes on to consider the following:

Such IPO underpricing amounts to a huge transfer of real wealth from the accounts of ordinary Chinese citizens to not just a handful of lucky retail investors, but to a galaxy of "Friends of the Family" who might be related in some way to the state sector. But from a public finance perspective, the critical point is that the gains from underpriced IPOs of these investors . . . are not going to be invested back into the state. Even while recognizing this dissipation of SOE value through IPO pricing, my analysis is premised on the assumption that the state's ownership position is maintained at roughly 60 percent of total domestic A share market capitalization. Beijing has always by policy and regulation insisted on holding at least a majority (over 50 percent) stake in its enterprises.

To repeat Carl's main insight and message, then, Beijing's dominant interest and top priority is in maintaining social stability and control, with economic efficiency and value a distant second. And the big question is, to what extent is such an approach likely to prove self-defeating and even destabilizing?

THE PROGRESSIVE DETERIORATION OF CHINESE PUBLIC FINANCE

The Chinese state-owned sector today generates as little as 30 percent of China's GDP.[10] If the social stability sustained by full employment is the key, then it's important to recognize that SOEs provide only one out of every six Chinese jobs; the rest are in the non-state sector.

Largely missing from conventional analysis of the Chinese financial system and public-sector solvency is recognition of the concentration of wealth and risk in the Chinese banking system that has taken place during the past two decades. As mentioned earlier, the net exports stemming from foreign direct investment have been *the* chief driver of wealth and liquidity in the Chinese economy, and of the massive growth of corporate and household bank deposits.

As early as 2004, China began running a current account surplus—exports less imports—with the world that is widely understood to have led to its huge foreign exchange reserves. But one less recognized effect of China's remarkable export growth has been the huge amount of Chinese currency, or RMB, released into the system. These massive flows of RMB went first into *corporate* bank deposits, including those by foreign enterprises as well as Chinese SOEs and private companies. But much of this money was paid out in salaries to China's workers, most of which has found its way into state-owned Chinese banks, and with negative consequences that, until recently, have gone largely unnoticed.

But one clear effect, then, of China's economic miracle and new middle class has been the massive increase in deposits held by Chinese banks, again most of them owned by the state, and the concentration of national wealth in bank assets. The ratio of China's bank assets to its GDP in 2022 was an astonishing 3.1 times, as compared to the 1.0 or less that has for decades been the norm in countries like the U.S. (In 2022, the U.S. bank asset-to-GDP ratio was 0.9; and even in Japan, with its historical heavy reliance on banks, the ratio was only 1.2.)

What accounts for China's disproportionate reliance on banks and banking?

The short answer is that Chinese people, however fabled as savers, have long had few attractive investment alternatives to bank deposits. Of the few possibilities, most, like the Chinese stock market, are seen as too erratic and risky for anyone but insiders.[11] And as Carl points out, Beijing policy has been "designed to encourage Chinese households to put their money *into banks.*" But the experience of most ordinary Chinese savers—those without ties to the CCP—is that, given the negative returns on Chinese stocks, the bulk of their money has long been in low-yielding bank accounts that, in real terms, have long been losing value.

The Rise of "WMPs." One response of Chinese banks, during the aftermath of the GFC in 2009, was to offer higher-yielding investments for their depositors called "wealth management products," or WMPs. Though originally blessed by Beijing, these investments—which are effectively three- to six-month bank CDs backed by a mix of highly risky investments like private equity and loans to municipalities—have proved to be possibly more toxic than the U.S. mortage-backed securities issued just before the Global Financial Crisis. And like the U.S.-originated MBS, WMPs several years ago became the center of a looming national fiscal disaster—but one that went largely undetected and unreported by Western as well as Chinese media.

WMPs were extremely popular among Chinese depositors as long as they believed there was an implied government guarantee backing them. But by 2017, when their large losses became impossible for regulators and policymakers to overlook (much like the U.S. home mortgages backing MBS in 2007), Chinese regulators not only shut down bank originations of WMPs, but ordered banks to start buying them back. (And although we will never know for sure, such WMPs almost certainly experienced even higher losses than the 10 percent losses currently estimated on U.S. MBS.)

What about the State Balance Sheet? But this brings us back to the question we posed earlier: what has been the cumulative impact of this private-sector (SOE) and public mismanagement on the Chinese government's finances? With the aim of answering this question—and since China, unlike most developed economies, does not publish a government balance sheet with the IMF—Carl, as mentioned earlier, devotes a good part of his new book to using government statistics to construct a rough balance sheet for the Chinese state.

And given the glowing press reports about the world's second largest economy that, at least until the onset of COVID, we'd grown accustomed to hearing, readers are likely to be surprised by the main finding of this analysis—namely, that the liabilities incurred by the state in the past two or three decades may well exceed the value of its assets. As Carl states his conclusion,

> though the state's absolute net worth . . . has increased somewhat, the weight of the debt it has taken on has largely offset any increase. By 2018, Chinese state liabilities in both calculations were roughly 18 times net worth; in other words, there were $18 of claims against the state for every $1 of state equity. In this sense, the state since 2018 has been technically bankrupt.

But given the remarkable and much publicized success of the Chinese export sector, with its massive benefits for both Chinese companies and employees, how could something like this have happened? The short answer is that most of the wealth built up by China's growing middle class has ended up financing the massive state lending program in the last 20 years.

To see how this took place, we have to go back to the dramatic increase in both household and corporate bank deposits that followed China's (foreign investment-financed) export boom. As Carl makes clear, China's citizens have experienced an enormous increase in prosperity since 2001. Nevertheless, and as a result of such prosperity, household *claims on the state*, including those in the form of deposits and investments in state-owned banks and companies, had increased to the point that, by 2018, they accounted for fully 17 percent of total state assets. And as Carl sums up the situation,

> the excessive borrowing by the state has left Chinese households (and a handful of foreigners) as the de facto majority owners of state sector assets. And this is not just Communist rhetoric, folks, the people today really are the effective owners of the China's socialist state—and the party itself is bankrupt!

THE DEEP FISCAL PROBLEMS OF LOCAL GOVERNMENTS—AND THEIR ROLE IN THE COLLAPSE OF CHINA EVERGRANDE

But to see how things have been allowed to reach this pass, it helps to go back to the first attempts at reform. Following the enactment of China's first Budget Law in 1994, the local government budgetary revenues supplied by Beijing were deliberately left insufficient to meet expanded budgetary responsibilities. To finance gaps in their budgets and investment, local governments were allowed to borrow from banks (again, mostly state-owned) directly or indirectly. But though such investments ended up being classified as bank loans, most were "consumption-oriented" spending on things like public health, education, and social security, with little expectation of ever being repaid. The municipalities simply expected the loans to be rolled over and refunded when the next wave of funding from Beijing came in.

But at some point, there has to be day of reckoning. The recent troubles of China Evergrande Group, at one time the most valuable real estate developer in the world, do a wonderful job of shedding light on the fiscal difficulties of local governments. Since around 1997, the sale of land use rights to developers has been a major source of revenue for municipalities and all levels of local government.

And so a company like Evergrande could long count on being warmly welcomed and embraced by local party officialdom in most parts of China.

But real estate development by itself has not been enough to produce revenue; local government have had to provide the infrastructure-related investment for projects. On top of that, they have had to pay relocation money to whomever was living on the land. Evergrande played a critical role in the entire process involving the coordination of developers, banks, trust companies, construction companies, and utilities, each of which had a strong interest in keeping the process rolling. It became a kind of Ponzi scheme in the sense that the revenue from the sale of one piece of land was typically used to cover the expenses of the last development. The prevalence of such a process throughout China helps explain why the China Household Survey conducted in 2017 found that 65 million, or over 20 percent, of the country's apartments were empty.[12]

But now that local governments are being expected to complete projects that Evergrande cannot, where are they finding the money? At the behest of the CCP, banks and enterprises are stepping up to help, adding to the state's mountain of debt.

Although the extent of Beijing's knowledge of and complicity in all this is not clear, such overbuilding has been going on for the past 20 years. Analysts have estimated that real estate development as an industry has long contributed overall close to 30 percent of China's GDP (as compared to estimates of 15–18 percent in the U.S.).[13] Carl's best guess is that Beijing simply looked the other way until the problem became too large to ignore. And as he points out, this has proven to be "an expensive way to provide social stability." Though it adds to GDP growth, it effectively contributes little or nothing to the state itself. Once the land use fee has been paid, local governments receive little else since there is no real estate tax in China, at least not yet.

THE CASE OF CHINA HUARONG: THE CRACK IN THE FOUNDATION?

Throwing even more light than Evergrande on the workings and underlying insolvency of the Chinese state was the fairly recent case of China Huarong, one of the four original "bad banks" that were created as part of the restructuring of the four state banks over two decades ago. In April 2021, Huarong was unable to provide audited financial statements as required by the Hong Kong Listing rules.

To see why this event came as such a shock to so many, it helps to go back to the fact that when Huarong was created in 1999, the Ministry of Finance owned 100 percent of the shares. After its public listing in October 2015, the ministry's share fell to 61 percent as shares were sold to a number of state and foreign "strategic" investors (including Goldman Sachs) as well as public investors.

But in April 2021, such investors were reportedly stunned by Huarong's inability to submit its financials to the exchange. The reported explanation was even more astonishing, and in some ways unthinkable: the failure of a state-owned enterprise like Huarong to secure a loan to fill a balance sheet gap.

Chinese press accounts of the government's actions placed all responsibility for Huarong's financial difficulties on its Chairman and CEO, Lai Xiaomin. Lai was placed under investigation in 2018, removed from the party the same year, accused and convicted of lurid dealings, and finally executed! But raising doubts about the public accounts, some 200 million *yuan* in cash was found in his apartment—which isn't easy to manage, since the largest bill in China is 100 *yuan*! What's more, as many skeptics of the public reports noted, Lai was a man who placed first in China's tough college entrance exam and was a senior official in the central bank before being sent by the party's Organization Department to Huarong.

But as Carl points out, perhaps the biggest problem with the official story is that the Ministry of Finance had majority ownership and control of Huarong, and so *the Ministry itself* was responsible for overseeing it. But from April to August 2021, the Ministry refused to make clear how it would respond. What Carl refers to as "the drawn-out volleyball game between government departments on how to handle Huarong's default" was a clear indication (to Carl at least) of not only the state's technical illiquidity, but of its possible insolvency. The fact that all of Huarong's debts are direct, central government obligations cast doubt on not just the state's willingness, but on its *ability*, to make good on its debts.

The real problem, however, as Carl goes on to point out, is that even if the MOF had the capital, it was effectively prohibited from helping. Any large contributions of state funds to Huarong by the MOF would have required the approval of the National People's Congress (NPC) as part of the national budget. And the fact that the need for a bailout of such a high-profile Chinese institution would have proved an embarrassment to the CCP goes a long way in explaining why the

Ministry tried to bury these obligations in the Chinese sovereign wealth fund or other state entities.

As of this writing, the matter has been resolved (for now) by saddling the China Citic Group—a state entity which is able to borrow without the NPC's consent—with the debt needed to clean up the Huarong mess. But, as Carl suggests, Citic cannot be a long-term solution because it too will eventually be forced by the low quality of Huarong's "assets" to borrow even more to support what the Chinese media euphemistically call "equity."

CLOSING THOUGHTS: HOW TO REFORM CHINESE CORPORATE FINANCE AND RESTORE THE SOLVENCY OF THE STATE

In the late 1990s, Zhu Rongji, then the head of the Chinese Ministry of Finance and leader of the reform efforts, made the decision to shut down or sell many smaller state-owned enterprises. Although that decision cost 35 million workers their jobs, many of them—and, more important, their children—found better ones in a burgeoning Chinese "private" sector. The small SOEs that Zhu turned over to the workers became the export dynamos that continue to flourish on the east coast of China. Though few are publicly listed, such companies are estimated to account for nearly 60 percent of China's current GDP—while agriculture provides another 10 percent. This "private" sector has long since proven it can both employ and pay more for Chinese workers, while making a profit as well.

And the lesson in all this, as Carl says in closing, is that

> Beijing needs to do more than start a deleveraging campaign, it needs to decide to restructure its financial system as was done in 1997—or else inflate the problem away or actually privatize state assets. The decades-long Chinese experiment to render state assets, banks, and enterprises more profitable has clearly failed.

But these, as Carl is the first to concede, are the views of an outsider, and perhaps take too little account of China's economic and social gains since Deng Xiaoping initiated the country's experiment with Western-style capitalist markets some 30 years ago. Thanks to Deng's vision and efforts, China today has a first-rate infrastructure supporting a national market for capital. And for good or ill, it has succeeded in using its control over the Hong Kong market to promote greater economic (and political) integration with the mainland. This effort has created national corporations that compare favorably in market capitalization with the world's largest multinationals. Moreover, the operations and performance of these corporate behemoths are more transparent than ever before, thanks to the legal and accounting standards they must maintain. The sale of minority stakes in these companies has raised as much as $1 trillion to support their activities.

That's the good news. The bad news is that the public listings of Chinese companies, whether in China, Hong Kong, or the U.S. and overseas, have rarely worked to raise Chinese corporate governance and management standards. And this means that China's National Champions continue to behave and perform like state-controlled enterprises. The IPO lottery process described earlier limits the participation of retail investors, as it does in the U.S., by favoring large institutional investors. But where the U.S. book-building process arguably works to increase the values of the stock (and net proceeds) raised by the corporate issuers, in China the outcome is a clear giveaway, a more or less direct transfer of wealth to largely state-owned institutions and the politically connected.

And so we should not be surprised to find that the returns to the Chinese stock market, which again consists largely of state-owned enterprises, have been zero to negative since the Global Financial Crisis. But, as Carl points out,

> this is the way the party seems to like it. The new government, bent on eliminating corruption, seems unable to figure out exactly what it wants to do with this piece of China's reform effort. When Zhu Rongji supported the listing effort back in the early 1990s, the hope was that the markets would create state enterprises able to compete on the same footing as their international competitors, while at the same time raising capital without requiring privatization.

But China's 30-year experiment in adapting Western capitalist markets to its own circumstances has clearly failed to produce the results Rongji and other early promoters had hoped.

On the other hand, 30 years, as Carl reflects in closing, may be too short a time for a nation like China to change—or even to suggest that Deng's decision to Westernize was misguided. The capital the Chinese state has succeeded in raising from

Western as well as domestic capital markets, and through what has amounted to an involuntary commandeering of Chinese corporate and household deposits in state-owned banks, has been directed almost entirely to the state sector.

Less than 20 percent of the state's total assets today take the form of loans for mortgages or small businesses. The state's investments in its SOEs have clearly failed to become productive or profitable enough to generate the new capital and jobs required to continue driving the economy forward. This task has thus been left almost entirely to unlisted domestic Chinese companies.

The failure of China's SOEs begs the question: What might have happened to companies like China Telecom if foreign investors had been allowed to acquire large enough stakes to exercise some degree of influence or control? And what if a well-functioning Chinese M&A and corporate control market had been allowed to develop, at least in some sectors of the economy?

Had China instead chosen in the 1990s to follow Margaret Thatcher's example and gradually privatize its state-owned enterprises, the Chinese economy—and its public finances—might look very different today. The Hong Kong and Shanghai exchanges might now be populated by the likes of Foxcomm and Taiwan Semi-conductor Manufacturing Company instead of the state-owned zombies we now see.

But as Carl sums up the matter,

> China's government values control and stability over efficiency, and has paid dearly for it. But at some point, efficiency in the use of capital will have its say. Capital, after all, is a limited commodity even in China.

To the extent this assessment of the state of China's public finance is a reliable guide to the future, China's supply of capital may soon become even more limited than it now appears to be. And as we suggest throughout this book, letting capital have its say is likely to be the best prescription for a healthy corporate sector and a prosperous citizenry.

CHAPTER 12

JAMES SWEENEY AND MICRO-BASED ATTEMPTS TO MAKE MACRO RELEVANT

Westerners have long been impressed by China's remarkable economic growth, by its ability to report the largest uninterrupted series of increases in GDP during the past 30 years. But as we saw in the last chapter, such growth has failed notably in providing returns for those Western and Chinese investors willing to entrust their savings to listed Chinese companies.

Figuring prominently in that story, the gargantuan assets and suspiciously large and consistent reported profits of today's Chinese state-owned banks seem to be telltale signs of a kind of Ponzi scheme—one designed to conceal a still rising mountain of bad debt, continuously rolled over and backed by assets with small and disappearing values. (Think of Evergrande's unfinished buildings, and all the others that have been demolished without ever housing tenants.)[1]

But how could so many presumably smart and interested people, including investors and the regulators appointed to protect them, have fallen for such a scheme? A big part of the answer, as we argue in this chapter, has to do with major limitations of the macro statistics that are routinely compiled and released by government officials everywhere, and received and reported by many business economists (and most of the business press) as holy writ.

GDP AN UNRELIABLE GUIDE TO THE WEALTH OF NATIONS

In a book published by Cornell University Press in 2018 called *Unrivalled: Why America Will Remain the World's Sole Superpower*, political economist Michael Beckley begins by telling us what any American who's been to China is likely to be aware of—that the United States continues to be "several times wealthier" than China. But more surprising, and counter to the received (certainly pre-COVID) wisdom is Beckley's report of the progressive widening of the wealth gap between the U.S. and China since the onset of the Global Financial Crisis in 2007, a gap that Beckley estimates has been *growing* by "trillions of dollars every year."[2]

But how, Beckley asks, can this wealth gap be growing when China

> has a bigger GDP, a higher investment rate, larger trade flows, and a faster economic growth rate than the United States. How can China outproduce, outinvest, and outtrade the United States—and own nearly $1.2 trillion in U.S. debt—yet still have substantially less wealth?

The answer, in a nutshell, is that GDP and other standard "macro measures" of national economic performance are incapable of capturing the reality that China's economy is "big but inefficient," and that its vast output is produced at enormous expense. As Beckley puts it,

> Chinese businesses suffer from chronically high production costs, and China's 1.4 billion people impose substantial welfare and security burdens. The United States, by contrast, is big and efficient. American businesses are among the most productive in the world, and with four times fewer people than China, the United States has much lower welfare and security costs.

Calculations of GDP effectively ignore such costs by, for example, counting production costs as output. "Spending money," as Beckley goes to point out,

> almost always increases GDP, even if the funds are wasted on boondoggles. In fact, the most common method of calculating GDP is called the "expenditure method" and involves simply adding up all of the spending done by the government, consumers, and businesses in a country in a given time period.[3] Hiring workers always increases GDP, even if they spend all day getting drunk in the break room. Boosting production always increases GDP, even if the goods rot on the shelf and tons of toxic waste are released in the process. In fact, a country can increase its GDP by dumping toxic waste in the streets and hiring millions of workers and spending billions of dollars to clean it up.

What's more, because GDP also effectively counts most welfare payments and associated costs as output, and "money spent feeding people is counted much the same as money earned selling supercomputers on world markets,"

> populous countries generate considerable economic activity simply by existing. Even a nation caught in a Malthusian hell, in which all output is immediately devoured and living standards and technological progress are stagnant, will post a large GDP if it has a big population.

And since GDP also counts most security costs as output, and a "$100 million gulag shows up the same as a $100 million innovation center," GDP fails to account for the economic costs of ongoing "internal unrest and international conflict."

So, what happens when we try to adjust for these distortions of national income accounting? How productive is China's economy?

The answer Beckley comes up with is remarkably consistent with Carl Walter's account in the last chapter. Since 2007, nearly all of China's growth in GDP has come from two sources: hiring workers and spending money. During the same period, however, China's growth in productivity has been "not only unspectacular, but virtually nonexistent."[4] In the U.S., by contrast, productivity increases have been estimated to account for roughly 20 percent of U.S. economic growth in not just the past decade, but most of the past century.[5]

As Beckley sums up the case,

> Even without visiting China, one could conclude from these productivity figures that much of China's GDP is a mirage based on fruitless investment. It is only when one tours China, however, that the sheer volume of waste becomes apparent.[6] China has built more than 50 "ghost cities"—entire metropolises composed of empty office buildings, apartment complexes, shopping malls, and, in some cases, airports.[7]

MICRO-BASED ALTERNATIVES TO MACRO NATIONAL INCOME ACCOUNTING?

By failing to take account of such costs, then, GDP and other standard macro measures have long contributed to the widespread impression that China is overtaking the United States. A more realistic picture of the Chinese economy, such as those provided by Beckley (and Carl Walter in chapter 11), would show a nation that "is barely keeping pace as the burden of propping up loss-making companies and feeding, policing, protecting, and cleaning up after one-fifth of humanity erodes China's stocks of wealth."

But to get such a picture, what might analysts consider using instead of the conventional national income accounts? And what could macro and business economists do to address the clear shortcomings of GDP?

One proposed solution is a national "economic balance sheet" that at least begins with the kind that Carl Walter worked up in the last chapter, with assets on one side of the ledger and liabilities on the other. And such a measure might then be expanded to reflect not just the financial, but the social value, of all kinds of assets and liabilities. Under this kind of social accounting, as Beckley quite reasonably proposes,

> if a country cuts down a forest to build a new office park, the value of the forest would show up as a loss on the country's balance sheet. If a country spends $50 billion imposing martial law in one of its regions—or growing food to feed its people or cleaning up toxic waste or hosting the Olympics—then $50 billion would be deducted from its stock of assets. In short, there would be no free lunch.

And as Beckley points out, both the World Bank and the United Nations have in fact begun compiling and publishing rough estimates of countries' wealth stocks in three main areas: (1) *produced capital* (man-made items such as machinery, buildings, infrastructure, and software); (2) *human capital* (the population's education, skills, and working life span); and (3) *natural capital* (water, energy resources, arable land). Alongside the information provided by these two sources, Beckley also sets estimates of over 100 different countries' private stocks of financial wealth compiled and published annually by the investment bank Credit Suisse.[8]

The story told by each of these three approaches, each using different data and methods, is reassuringly similar: The United States, as already mentioned, is several times wealthier than China. And far from getting smaller, as the popular press has long been suggesting, the gap between the two nations' stocks of wealth has not been shrinking but growing "by trillions of dollars each year." Also important to keep in mind, this growing divide between U.S. and Chinese wealth was taking place well before the onset of the pandemic in 2020.

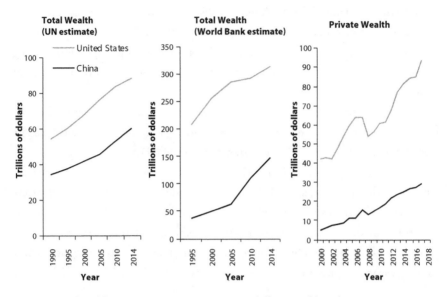

12.1 Stocks of wealth. UN estimate in constant 2005 dollars. World Bank estimate in constant 2014 dollars. Private wealth data in current dollars.

Source: UNU-IHDP 2018; Lange and Carey 2018; Credit Suisse 2018.

What's more, this division can also be seen clearly in measures that go well beyond the financial, in everything from air quality to employment opportunities for new college graduates. Which tells us that the U.S. advantage in virtually all these social dimensions—with the notable exception of opioid and alcohol addiction—was expanding during the years *leading up to* the outbreak of COVID. Since the pandemic, and without making light of America's own problems, the growth of this inter-country wealth and welfare divide between the U.S. and China has clearly accelerated, to the point of becoming itself a source of political tension.

ENTER JAMES SWEENEY AND THE ATTEMPT TO MAKE MACRO REFLECT U.S. ECONOMIC REALITY

We have just finished showing some among the many ways that GDP and other macro statistics can be used to misrepresent national economic performance and, even with best of intentions, end up misleading policymakers, the press, and the body politic. But the distortions thus far have been those noted in Chinese, not American macro accounts and accounting. But what about U.S. GDP and other macro variables: are they giving us the information we think they are; and could they be reworked, or at least reinterpreted, in a way that tells us more about what we really want to know?

In the lead article of the Fall 2020 issue of the *JACF*, James Sweeney, then Chief Economist of the investment bank Credit Suisse, began by expressing his thought that "the prestige of our National Income Accounts has peaked."[9] But what did he mean by that, and why might it matter?

For one thing, it suggested that the dismal assessments of real U.S. GDP and wage growth we've been hearing from most macro and business economists for the past three or four decades should be taken with not just a grain, but maybe truckloads, of salt. Such conventional macro statistics, and the media who breathlessly report them, are invariably wielded by both political parties—Trump's campaign in 2016 no less than Biden's in 2020—as grounds for handwringing over calamitous and irreversible drops in U.S. productivity and standards of living.

But in the meantime, U.S. stock prices had been continuing their decades-long practice, especially pronounced since the '80s, of going up instead of down, even reaching new highs just six months into what the pundits were viewing as a global-economy-destroying pandemic. Which raises the question that this chapter is meant to put in front of Sweeney's macro colleagues:

How can stock markets keep pushing higher when GDP, job growth, and other "fundamentals" are all down and on their backs, and many companies find themselves unable or unwilling to offer guidance?[10]

A big part of the answer to this question, as James suggested in his article, has to do with the limitations of conventional macro measures in capturing two critical determinants of both economic growth and stock prices: inflation and productivity. And let's start with inflation: How and what do we really know about how much the prices of a representative basket of goods and services go up in a particular year?

To answer this question, Sweeney begins by providing an amusing account of a 1996 Federal Open Market Committee meeting in which Fed Chair Alan Greenspan is pressed by future chair Janet Yellen to define his goal of "price stability." Greenspan's response: "zero percent inflation, when properly measured." Then, after Yellen cites the well-known imprecision of the inflation measurement process as grounds for the Fed's continued use of its standard 2 percent inflation target, Greenspan just shrugs and says, "Okay, let's leave it at that, and move on."

This exchange between these two highly regarded Federal Reserve leaders was consistent with, and likely reflected, the findings of studies of inflation like the Boskin Commission's in the mid-1990s. What such studies found was an upward bias of some 100–150 basis points in the annual CPI estimates during the '80s and '90s. And it's not just the failure of the CPI to track and reflect things like consumers' tendency to find cheaper substitutes in response to price hikes. More important—and far more troubling when measuring productivity—is the inability of macro stats to account for changes in the "quality" of goods and services. If the car you bought last year is in most respects twice as effective in meeting your "wants and needs" as the one you bought five years ago for half the price, then its inflation would in fact be roughly the *zero percent* that Greenspan claimed to be aiming for.

But if reliance on national income accounts has likely led for years to a significant *over*statement of U.S. inflation, it has almost certainly resulted in a much larger, and more misleading, *under*statement of U.S. productivity. And the question that productivity measures purport to answer is an especially important one. Indeed, for this book—and for many economists from Adam Smith on—it's likely to be the most important of all, the key to national wealth: To what extent, it asks us to keep finding better ways to figure out, is the value of the goods and services produced by U.S. companies each year rising faster than the cost of the inputs, including investor capital, used to produce such goods?

One major limitation of the national income accounts in answering this question is that our estimates of inflation and GDP are based mostly on *transactions*— and so they reflect mainly just the dollar amounts paid and received. The value of goods or services provided *gratis*, or at prices significantly below what consumers might or would pay for them, go unrecorded in GDP or inflation.

What this suggests, then, is that our measures of *nominal* GDP and wage growth are giving us reasonably reliable indications of aggregate spending on final goods and services. But in the case of our *real* measures, the systematic overstatement of U.S. inflation and failure to reflect increases in quality (and gains in "consumer surplus") have not only exaggerated the extent of slowdowns, but may have prevented us from seeing actual *increases* in productivity—and even real wages—in recent decades.[11]

All this raises the tantalizing possibility that such under-the-radar productivity increases have a lot to do with the efficiency and stock price gains of U.S. companies during the past four decades. And although Sweeney himself cautions against taking this idea too far—after all, he still has his own macro credentials to defend—I like to hold up his own favorite illustration of an increase in the quality of *his* life. His example is Google's Waze app, whose vast benefits to all and sundry continue to elude the national income accounts. And in what is probably the most telling indicator of our basic problem with our macro measures, James goes on to note that, "In my meetings with CEOs, my suggestions of a productivity slowdown in corporate America almost invariably gets laughed out of the room."

GETTING MACRO TO RETHINK WHAT
CONSUMERS REALLY VALUE

Now, as James will be the first to tell you, none of what you've just been told is *news*. These shortcomings of the macro data have long been understood, and acknowledged, by serious macro and business economists themselves. Where the problems arise is from the uninformed and uncritical acceptance of macro numbers as providing reliable representations of things most of us care deeply about, like living standards, the cost of living, worker efficiency, technology growth, and general social welfare. All of these concepts and concerns, needless to say, play a major role—but also alas end up getting seriously distorted—in today's policy debates and public assessments of the health of the economy.

If the most trusted and widely reported data reinforce the wrong message, the data itself can be a cause of genuine mischief, including misguided public policy as well as distorted private decision-making. As one example, the very real possibility that the equality of income distribution has actually improved in recent decades could easily be lost in the handwringing over subpar growth.[12] Or take the claim that "real median income has fallen for decades." Would the median household really prefer the opportunities available to them in 1980 to what they can have now with the supposedly same real income?

After urging economists to be more tentative in their uses of conventional macro statistics, Sweeney notes the promise of alternative measures, some spawned by the pandemic, that are improving how some business economists now track the economy in real time and, in so doing, make possible "a deeper, more accurate, and more realistic view of economic activity."

* * *

But all this said, a more fundamental solution to the inflation bias has to begin by recognizing the ways in which the problem has shown up in the past. Robert Gordon, in his much-acclaimed account *The Rise and Fall of American Growth*,[13] argues that the cluster of new technologies that came to market in the early part of the 20th century led to a very large upward bias in reported inflation and inflation measures generally—and, *because* of the resulting overstatement of inflation, to a huge *under*statement of productivity gains (and social and economic progress). As Gordon points out, there was simply no way that macro statistics could begin to capture the enormous economic and social benefits of inventions like automobiles and electricity—and, so, any attempts to adjust for quality when measuring inflation were bound to fail.

But in what is somewhat of a puzzle for Sweeney, Gordon shows little inclination to view today's technological advances in the same light, famously dismissing IT innovations as improving the lot of a small subset of consumers. But while conceding Gordon's point that the "quality adjustment bias" was more pronounced and distorting in the pre-war period than today, James goes on to insist that the inflation bias—and hence the extent of the unseen productivity and social benefits—associated with today's evolving digital economy are far greater than those we experienced during the 1980s and '90s. All of which suggests that, even if recent technologies have not been as transformative as the innovations of the late 19th century or early 20th century, new developments like artificial intelligence, robotics, genomics, and a host of others have brightened the outlook for companies and consumers in innumerable ways that do not show up in GDP.

To see these unapprehended social benefits of innovation more clearly, Sweeney asks us to consider 2018 Nobel laureate William Nordhaus's famous analysis of the historical cost, and its changes down through the centuries, of a lumen of light:

> a comparison of the pure price of light with a traditional light price indicates that traditional price indexes overstate price growth, and therefore understate output growth, by a factor between 900 and 1600 since the beginning of

the nineteenth century. This finding suggests that the "true" growth of real wages and real output may have been significantly understated during the period since the Industrial Revolution.[14]

Following Nordhaus's message, then, what we should really be seeking from our national income accounts, and the macro economists who use and report them, are new ways to measure the price not of lightbulbs, but of light itself. In other words, to understand the value of the goods and services created by an economy, we would need to know the demand curve for specific quantities of what consumers really want and need, like lumens of light.

REWORKING MACRO MEASURES TO CAPTURE LUMENS OF LIGHT

One promising idea that shows up in philosophy and psychology, but is seldom seen in economics, is that of an "affordance."[15] An affordance might be thought of as something that not only gives people the ability to accomplish some kind of task, but also improves their lives by, for example, changing the entire surrounding environment. The invention of fire was an affordance that made cooking possible, which in turn dramatically changed and improved human life by stimulating the search for ever new and better ways to find and prepare all kinds of foods fit for human consumption and nourishment.

The smartphone is a modern-day affordance whose permanent loss would, for many if not most of us, be unimaginably painful. Expensive phones and data eat up household budgets, and low-income households struggle, work more, and incur debt to pay for their phone and data. Although this new affordance has led to increases in some kinds of measured economic activity, comparing "living standards" before and after smartphones (or fire) is not as straightforward as GDP data might suggest.

GDP's conceptual problems, as Sweeney makes clear, will never be eliminated entirely by better data, better models, and better thinking. But even so, he is encouraged by the prospect of a range of alternative measures working gradually to replace (or at least supplement) official GDP, inflation, and productivity measures, especially when thinking about economic performance under special circumstances and conditions.

At the outset of the pandemic in March 2020, data on broad trends in individuals' body temperatures, foot traffic to various types of establishments, web traffic, road traffic, and the exact timing of stimulus and other benefit checks to individuals all proved helpful when trying to understand how economic activity was behaving in real time. And the actual tracking of COVID transmission and hospitalization data and correlates turned out to be remarkably useful to some business economists when assessing economic prospects. For example, in the third quarter of 2020, after the extreme drop in GDP that had occurred in many countries the quarter before, this kind of information predicted a general rebound whose strength surprised many analysts.

Other alternatives seen as having promise are several attempts at "happiness indices," ad hoc-constructed "quality of life" indices, and direct measures of innovation. In many OECD economies, the growth of patents and general spread of published information have shown no signs of falling off. As most of us understand, the development and spread of the internet has accelerated the dissemination of information, increased the possibilities for collaborative research, and generally made once arcane knowledge widely available. New technologies like machine learning, robotics, and advances in biology are clear drivers of promising innovation. And although the development of the CRISPR gene editing technology has the potential to profoundly shape the future, its significance will not be captured with patent data or reflected in GDP any time soon.

Now if we insist on sticking with measures of real or "hard" data, one possible alternative to GDP is industrial production (IP), whose measurement took place well before GDP came into being. IP measures physical goods that can usually be stored and traded. One virtue of such indicators is that they require financing, which ensures that IP data are highly correlated with financial market measures.

But when all is said and done, the most reliable, forward-looking indicators of future income and productivity may well turn out to be stock prices, particularly those reported on U.S. stock exchanges. As noted earlier, the stock returns of U.S. public companies were remarkably high during the post-GFC period from 2009 until the 2020 pandemic. And after a short-lived plunge in March 2020, both the S&P 500 and Nasdaq have recovered strongly in the face of the Fed's series of interest rate hikes.

On the other hand, and possibly sobering for macro and business economists, studies have been hard-pressed to find evidence of a *positive* relationship between

GDP and equity returns. In fact, as we saw earlier, the studies cited in chapter 2 actually find a *negative* cross-sectional correlation of –0.4 percent between equity returns and the per capita GDP growth rate of 19 advanced or "developed" countries over the entire 112-year period from 1900 to 2011.[16]

What's more, the "disconnect" between the value creation being projected in today's stock prices and the stagnation suggested (at least until fairly recently) by the conventional macro indicators of productivity and growth provides yet another alert to the differences between concepts and statistics that James's work has been pointing to for many years.

* * *

To be sure, there are other sources and stores of private-sector wealth than the public equity market. U.S. private equity, as we saw in chapter 7, has been flourishing and outperforming public equity for almost 40 years, and now reportedly accounts for a stock of wealth equal to 10 percent of the total market cap of all companies listed on U.S. stock markets. And, of course, the owners of U.S. real estate have also seen those assets appreciate significantly. All of which is consistent with a sharp increase in U.S. private-sector net worth in recent years that is clearly at odds with the slow growth in GDP, providing yet another indication that something is amiss in our macro measurement system.

To sum up, then, at least some macro economists are beginning to think "differently" about how to capture the performance of national economies. As one of those economists, James Sweeney, has described the situation,

> We don't know much about the future and never have. As for the present, we have large and troubling income and wealth disparities, global imbalances, amazing new technologies, slower-than-usual nominal growth, high corporate profits relative to nominal GDP and labor income, unusual monetary policy, changing demographics, debt/budget concerns, political economy tensions, and a broad sense of discomfort reported and no doubt experienced by many households.

And as James points out in his closing sentence, "Condensing all that into a single productivity or GDP statistic does not begin to do justice to the complex reality of the U.S. economy."

But if you want a better indicator, and at the risk of belaboring the point, let me leave you with the suggestion that one could do worse than look at changes in stock prices. Especially in the U.S., where they are less subject to manipulation by the Ministry of Finance or other government agencies, such prices are likely to reflect the collective wisdom, with all its limitations, of a lot of smart, and intensely interested people, something the macro data alas seem to be routinely failing to do.

EPILOGUE

Sustainable Financial Management (and the Promise and Pitfalls of ESG Investing)

Public corporations have always faced pressure to be good corporate citizens. But the globalization of business during the past 50 years, together with the recent COVID pandemic and ever more visible effects of climate change, has increased the popular demand for business to play a bigger role in addressing environmental and other social problems. And today's public companies, while expected to do more to protect the environment and support local communities, continue to be subjected to greater capital market pressure to increase their own operating efficiency and long-run value.

All of which raises the question: how can public companies make significant contributions to "sustainability" while remaining profitable enough and creating enough value to keep attracting the investor capital that will enable them to sustain themselves?

●   ●   ●

But what do we mean by *sustainable* financial management, and how comfortably do its precepts and methods fit with the movement that has been embraced in some quarters—and reviled in others—as "ESG" (short for Environmental, Social, and Governance)?

As became clear during the much-publicized case of Twitter (now called "X") and Elon Musk, most U.S. public companies are continuously "for sale." This is what happens, and is supposed to happen, in a well-functioning market for corporate control. U.S. public companies that aim to preserve their independent existence have to show at least the promise of producing high enough returns on capital to keep the support of their investors. Otherwise, their managements and boards run the risk of being supplanted by investors and management teams armed with the conviction that they can do a better job—and willing to back their claim by paying a significant premium over the company's market value for the right to try.

Study after study suggests that the operation of this market leads to increases in corporate efficiency and longer-run value. It is these efficiency gains—some of them regrettably from polluting activities—that provide us with the social wealth to fund institutions and activities that most of us put a high value on, including the security provided by a strong military, clean-up of industrial waste sites and polluted rivers, and investments in healthcare and education.

But in a marketplace premised on meeting the demands of outside investors and serving the interests of "capital," how do we ensure that employees, local communities, and other corporate stakeholders get *their* due? Short of banning all commercial activity that harms the environment and exploits workers, how do we encourage public companies to think harder about funding initiatives that aim to limit damage to the environment and expand opportunities for mid- and lower-level workers? And how far should policymakers and investors feel comfortable in urging (or prodding) companies to depart from business as usual—and perhaps even consider modest sacrifices of shareholder returns—when making such investments?

SUSTAINABILITY AND *ENLIGHTENED* VALUE MAXIMIZATION

The globalization of business and remarkable growth of large multinationals that began in the 1970s provided the main impetus for the "corporate social responsibility" movement that got its start in the late '70s and '80s, and whose "CSR" programs proliferated in the 1990s. But it was in the early 2000s that the specter of global climate change materialized, and began to get serious attention. And in a process that started around 2005, the widespread CSR programs dedicated in large part to cushioning the effects of local poverty began to be supplemented, if not largely replaced, by environmental "sustainability" initiatives at corporations of all sizes and operating in a broad range of industries.

Such initiatives began by taking the form of the recycling and energy conservation efforts adopted by almost all public companies, and many private ones. But apart from these now nearly two decades-long efforts to harvest "the low-hanging fruit," what does it mean for public companies to be "sustainable," or to pursue the goals of "sustainability"? And how is this different from what many of the world's most admired companies have been doing for well over half a century?

At the end of chapter 4, we saw Michael Jensen, unabashed apologist for the market for corporate control, proposing an expansion of the mission statement for public companies that, for this writer, captures the essence of sustainable financial management. Jensen's proposal appeared in an article we ran in the *JACF* in 2001, when the perennial debate between "stakeholder value" and "shareholder value" advocates was heating up once more in academic and policy circles. The title Jensen gave his article—by far the most cited in the *JACF*'s 40-plus-year run—was "Value Maximization, Stakeholder Theory, and the Corporate Objective Function."[1] And the article's aim, in keeping with Mike's characteristic modesty of scope (and not a little intellectual naivete),[2] was nothing less than the once-and-for-all resolution of this seemingly endless debate.

Jensen's answer was to introduce the concept of "*enlightened* value maximization," thereby once again invoking the writings of Adam Smith.[3] As Jensen defined it, enlightened value maximization means devoting sufficient corporate time and resources to *all* important stakeholder groups that can affect the efficiency and long-run value of the firm. Among such groups are the usual suspects: a company's customers and employees, for sure, and also its creditors and suppliers. But in a somewhat new twist (at least for financial economists), management also now had to take more serious account of both the environment and local communities as well as legislators, regulators, tax collectors, and other representatives of the "public interest."

And Jensen's message to top managements was a fairly simple one: to maximize long-run value, you have to start by gaining at least the tacit support, if not the emotional allegiance, of *all* these corporate constituencies while still providing competitive returns to your shareholders. In fact, meeting at least the minimal requirements of all these stakeholder groups is likely to be the *only* way you can end up satisfying your shareholders.[4]

* * *

But if enlightened value maximization is a useful way to think about including sustainability in the corporate mission statement, it leaves management with some tough decisions. First of all, how much and what kind of stakeholder invest-ments are likely to increase long-run value? As the CEO of any large commercial enterprise will tell you, conflicts between shareholders and stakeholders—and among different stakeholder groups themselves—are everywhere. Recognizing and then managing such conflicts is, after all, what Jensen and Meckling's theory of "agency costs" is about: how does management navigate the legion of con-flicts that are bound to arise, and make the well-reasoned tradeoffs required to address them?[5]

A big part of Jensen's answer was CEO vision and leadership. As Mike saw it, perhaps the most important task of the CEO is to communicate his or her vision of the corporate mission and strategy in a way that proves convincing to all stakeholders, making as clear as possible their expected benefits from as well as their expected contributions to the success of this collective enterprise.

But along with effective leadership, the long-run success of a large collective business enterprise also depends on the making the *right* allocations of capital and other corporate resources—not too little, but not too much—to each import-ant stakeholder group. Having decided to commit investor capital to stakeholder investments that are going to reduce near-term earnings, top management and boards must then also find ways to convince skeptical investors about the lon-ger-run payoffs from such investments.

To the question of how companies should evaluate these investments in stake-holders, Jensen's short answer was to "follow the old net present value rule": invest another dollar today in all important corporate constituencies, but only up to the point it has an expected payoff of at least a dollar.

Making such calculations is, of course, easier said than done, involving far more intuition and art than science. The payoffs from stakeholder initiatives are especially hard to project because they often don't take the form of near-term increases in revenue or earnings. Indeed, the main purpose of such investments may be to strengthen the commitments of *non-investor* corporate stakeholders—employees, suppliers, regulators, and local communities—all with the ultimate aim of increasing a company's long-run value, social standing, and staying power.

But this raises another tough question: if the longer-run benefits expected from more engaged employees and more loyal customers, and from more favor-able treatment by the media, legislators, and regulators, generally don't show up right away as higher revenue or earnings, then how is the value of such invest-ments reflected in corporate market valuations?

The answer proposed in these closing pages is that, thanks in part to the workings of the ESG and sustainability movements (to which we now turn), the expected benefits of such stakeholder initiatives and investments are likely to materialize sooner than companies expect, in some cases almost immediately. But rather than increases in near-term revenue and profits, such benefits are likely to take the form of reductions of investors' perceived risk and, hence, of the corporate cost of capital.

The claim being made here, then, is that well-designed (and reasonably cost-effective) stakeholder initiatives are likely to tap into investors' willingness and propensity—identified in this book as the "magic of finance capitalism"—to assign higher valuation multiples (and P/E ratios) to the earnings reported by commercial enterprises and activities in which there is "far more to admire than to despise."[6]

* * *

But how do companies convince their shareholders that such investments are likely to increase long-run efficiency and value? Think about Walmart's decision several years ago (and well before the onset of the pandemic) to raise its employee wages more or less across the board. In the next earnings call after the decision was announced, when earnings predictably fell short, the company's CFO described the wage increase as an "investment." Although investors were initially unconvinced, the expected payoffs began to materialize over the next series of earnings reports, along with gradual market appreciation of the farsightedness, and longer-run cost-effectiveness, of the strategy.[7]

THE WALMART SUSTAINABILITY SUCCESS STORY

Walmart is one of America's and the world's largest private-sector employers, with 2.1 million employees (including 1.6 million in the U.S.), that operates 10,500 retail stores in 28 countries. The company's founder, Sam Walton, when accepting the Presidential Medal of Freedom in 1992, described the company's social goals entirely in terms of its benefits for its customers: "If we can, why, we'll lower the cost of living for everyone—not just in America,

(continued on next page)

(*continued from previous page*)

but we'll give the world an opportunity to see what it's like to save and have a better life for all."

To this day, the company's stated purpose—"*to help people save money so they can live better*"—continues to focus on what economists like to call "consumer surplus." And economists' current best estimate of this elusive social benefit of Walmart's operations for the average U.S. family of four is something like $5,000 a year, with the savings for Walmart's overseas customers likely to be even larger, at least relative to the lower incomes.

But the focus of the company's sustainability efforts has expanded well beyond providing affordable products to customers whose weekly visits are now said to number in the hundreds of millions. Among the company's top three environmental and social priorities, first is increasing economic opportunities for Walmart's employees—through not only competitive wages and benefits, but expanded workforce training and education, including generous college tuition programs, and hiring-from-within practices, all designed to increase employee morale and loyalty and professional mobility. Walmart's second major ESG priority is ensuring the sustainability of its supply chains through extensive supplier monitoring and support programs emphasizing the safety and livelihoods of workers. The third is preservation of the environment through a variety of approaches and programs, including the world's largest private-sector coalition to limit climate change, and packaging reforms that work to reduce plastic waste.

As experiences like Walmart's have made clear, one of management's biggest challenges in launching and funding its sustainability programs has been to gain the confidence and commitment of a group of investors who are not only responsive to the ideals that inform these decisions, but also sophisticated and far-sighted enough to see the possibility of combining social and economic goals in this way. The challenge for the corporate finance—and specifically the investor relations (or IR)—function here is getting the Warren Buffetts of the world to see, and then join in on, what it is you're setting out to do. This is where today's troubled ESG movement is likely to prove most valuable for—and where it has demonstrated at least the potential to help—well-managed and well-meaning corporations, while also persuading others to rethink some of their principles and practices.

THE PROMISE OF ESG INVESTING (WITH MORE ON THE MAGIC OF MODERN CORPORATE FINANCE)

Up to this point, we have viewed the sustainability and ESG movements pretty much from the *corporate* vantage point—that is, in terms of the possibilities that such developments hold out for public companies, and how corporate CEOs and CFOs can respond effectively to make the most of them for their shareholders. Now let's turn to the perspective of capital market investors themselves, who have long provided the impetus for and impressive energy driving the ESG movement.

Despite all the political controversy that now surrounds the movement (to the point where many supporters have chosen to abandon the term ESG, though not the mission), the most visible sign of its success to date is the astonishing growth in the number of institutional investors—and in their assets under management—that at least claim to use ESG criteria as part of their investment decision-making process. From 2006 to 2022, the number of investors endorsing the United Nations-backed Principles for Responsible Investment (UNPRI) jumped from the initial 100 signatories to almost 5,000, representing over $120 trillion assets under management.

The world's leading authority on ESG investing is a self-described "recovering playwright" named Steve Lydenberg, who for decades has guided social and environmental research at an investment firm called Domini Impact Investment. In an article we ran in the *JACF* in 2014, Steve provided a "taxonomy of responsible investors" that shows wide variation in such investors' approaches and degree of commitment.[8] At one end of the continuum are the admittedly very large numbers of investors whose main support for ESG takes the bare-minimal form of *compliance* with internationally accepted ESG norms and standards. (And as with most if not all forms of compliance, there is bound to be a good deal of window-dressing and "green-washing.") At the other extreme is the willingness of some "impact" investors to accept below-market returns to support social causes.

THE OUTPERFORMANCE OF "SIN" STOCKS

In the early days of corporate social responsibility, many CSR investors committed their capital with the understanding that they were volunteering to accept somewhat lower returns to promote social goods such as more nutritious snacks and soft drinks, less gun violence, and protections against the most exploitative kinds of child labor. In most cases, these aims were achieved mainly by "screening out" the worst corporate offenders from their investment portfolios.

One of the less welcome and somewhat unrecognized effects of such "disinvestment" strategies has been its contribution to a well-documented phenomenon known to investment veterans and academics as the "outperformance of sin stocks." In brief, the shunning of tobacco companies and gun manufacturers—by university endowments as well as CSR investors— has had the presumably unintended and unwanted consequence of *increasing* the returns to those investors less influenced by CSR considerations.

Is there anything deplorable or nefarious at work here? No, just the forces of capitalism in one of its more ordinary, but less magical or endearing, manifestations. When the more or less concerted selling by investors drives down the price of sin stocks, their now higher expected returns attract investors undeterred by the disapprobation and greater risk that tends to be associated with public and political disapproval. The net result of all this is higher returns for possibly riskier investments.

But somewhere in the middle of these two groups are two other kinds of "responsible" investors that deserve most of our attention. First are those investors who use industry-specific ESG ratings and rankings—like those used in compiling the Dow Jones Sustainability Indexes—when choosing companies to invest in, although with little conviction, as Steve suggests, that such rankings give them an investing edge. Notably different from this group are the smaller number of "deep-dive, fundamentals-based" investors who have made ESG analysis a critical part of their stock valuation process. These are people, it goes without saying, who are predisposed to see significant economic as well as social value in corporate ESG investments.

•   •   •

For well-run public companies with significant sustainability programs, the knowledge that these four kinds of investors have long been a significant, and likely still growing, part of the market should be reassuring. But perhaps most encouraging for such companies is the presence, and possibly outsized influence, of the last of these four. This group includes people like Dan Hanson, a self-described "intrinsic value business investor" in the tradition of Graham and Dodd (and their best-known follower, Warren Buffett), who describes himself as "a buyer not of stocks, but of high-quality businesses" and now runs the ESG portfolio at the investment firm Neuberger Berman. While citing Buffett's famous prescription that "it's far better to buy a wonderful company at a fair price than a fair company at a wonderful price," Hanson also makes a convincing case that the basic principles of ESG investing have long been at work in the world of fundamental investing he invokes as "Graham & Doddsville." In other words, as Hanson goes on to say, the world's best "business value" investors, starting with Graham and Dodd in the 1930s, have routinely incorporated what we today call social and governance considerations into their investment decisions.

Why have they done it? Because much like today's "business value" investors, they were looking for "reliable signs that management is thinking about the company's future, about what the organization will look like 25 years from now."[9] And as Hanson continues, "communicated in a credible way to the investment community, a company's ESG policies and investments are likely to be helpful in assessing the durability of its competitive advantage."

EARLY SIGNS OF ESG SUCCESS

Among the most encouraging signs that ESG might be working as hoped is the accumulating evidence that, as Warren Buffett loves to tell people, "companies get the investors they deserve." In an article we ran in the *JACF* in 2015 called "Integrated Reporting and Investor Clientele," Harvard Business School's sustainability expert George Serafeim provided some interesting documentation of this investor sorting mechanism at work.[10] George's work confirmed that companies filing sustainability reports during the past decade experienced significant increases in the proportion of "dedicated holders"—that is, institutional investors with small numbers of large equity positions and longer-than-average holding periods—in their shareholder base. In other words, companies professing to be, and widely viewed as, committed to sustainability have long been attracting the Warren Buffetts and Dan Hansons of the world.

Even more encouraging for sustainability and ESG, in a 2021 article called "Corporate Resilience and Response to COVID-19," Serafeim teamed up with three State Street analysts to present what may well be the most compelling evidence to date of the stock market's recognition of the value of corporate sustainability programs and initiatives.[11] The outbreak of the pandemic was seen as providing a test case of such value in the sense that, by making significant and credible commitments to their stakeholder relationships—say, by limiting layoffs, providing flexible work schedules, and offering paid sick leave—companies were given the opportunity to "signal" both their humanity, and their resilience, to investors.

And that's basically what Serafeim and colleagues found. Using measures of media sentiment to evaluate corporate responses to the pandemic, their study reported that those companies seen as strengthening their human capital and supply chain relationships experienced significantly less-negative returns during the crisis. This finding stood up clearly after taking account of differences in the companies' pre-COVID profitability and financial condition.

Of course, by volunteering to help limit their employees' exposure to the pandemic and other hardships, companies might also be viewed as simply cushioning their own market values, even as their earnings were disappearing, against much greater collapse—in other words, preserving their own long-run value. And this begs the larger question: if our public companies continue to be encouraged to seek profit and maximize long-run value, how do we accomplish a *social* goal like the economy-wide transition from fossil fuels to renewable energy that even most Republican pols have finally acknowledged the need for?

The near-universal prescription of economists, which has also gained the support of all large, publicly traded oil companies, is the imposition of a carbon tax, thereby establishing a "carbon price" that encourages companies and consumers to cut back on the use of fossil fuels. But as has become painfully clear, there is almost no political will to levy such a tax, especially now that inflation has pushed gas and power prices back to higher levels.

* * *

The good news here—and this might come as a surprise to many—is that modern corporate finance, operating in concert with a discernible trend in capital market pricing of public companies, may well end up providing the best answer to this arguably most urgent of today's social questions. Some supporting evidence for this possibility comes from recent work by Columbia's Patrick Bolton, a former President of the American Finance Association. What Bolton, working with colleagues at Lazard's relatively new Climate Group, found was basically this: After large public companies in 77 countries were divided into two categories—high and low carbon emitters—the realized average stock returns of the high-carbon-emitting companies during the period 2005–2017 were significantly *higher* than those of their low-emitting counterparts.[12]

But what are we supposed to make of these higher returns? Not, as most ESG enthusiasts love to tell people (and way too many persist in believing), that the market "rewards" corporate virtue with higher rates of return, and punishes corporate misdeeds with lower returns. That's not how capital markets work. Companies perceived to have higher political and regulatory risks are generally "priced" in such a way as to provide *higher*, not lower, expected (and actual) returns. And the higher realized returns for the high-carbon companies reported by Bolton et al. are thus best viewed as the "risk premiums" *required* by investors to compensate them for bearing the "transition risk" now faced by energy corporations.

But, again, there is good news in all this—namely, that the market prices risk in a way that ends up imposing a higher *cost of capital* on the high-carbon emitters, which in turn means a *lower* valuation and price-to-earnings multiple for a given level of earnings or cash flow. Before the massive COVID-19 stimulus spending and Russian invasion of the Ukraine led to a spike in oil prices, lower valuations (again, per dollar of earnings) were sending a clear message to companies like Exxon to cut back their exploration and production budgets. And the U.S. majors in Texas were doing exactly that, though with considerable prodding by shareholder activists like D.E. Shaw—and some pain to the Houston economy.

But as many U.S. oil company executives must now be thinking to themselves, no good deed goes unpunished. Since the recent surge of oil prices and general inflation, the oil execs have lately found themselves in the midst of a political whipsaw, now urged to *increase* their output by the same politicians who had just finished flogging them over their emissions. The good news for both the environment and oil company shareholders, however, is that the companies have largely stuck to their commitments to their investors to limit their capital spending.[13]

What this new development suggests, then, is that contrary to a long-established tenet of economic theory, private capital markets may now in fact be performing a social function widely believed to be achievable *only* through government action—namely, limiting the "negative externalities" associated with climate change by *pricing* them. In effect, the stock market can and should now be seen as imposing its own "carbon tax" on high-carbon emitters—a tax that economists have been imploring legislators to pass for years.

This is just another example of what we have been referring to throughout these pages as the magic of modern corporate finance at work. However obscure and undetected its operations and benefits have remained to policymakers and (even most) macroeconomists, it's a reality of capital markets that has long been suspected by people studying and working in corporate finance.

MORE ON THE END OF ACCOUNTING—AND ITS POSSIBLE IMPORT FOR ESG

Another fairly recent development—one mentioned earlier in chapter 3—that might be seen as boding well for the U.S. corporate sustainability movement has been dubbed "The End of Accounting" by distinguished NYU accounting professor Baruch Lev. During the past 50 years, as we saw when reviewing the work of Merton Miller and his Chicago colleagues, the correlation between annual changes in U.S. companies' reported GAAP earnings and their annual (market-adjusted) stock returns has plummeted from a level as high as 50 percent in 1970 to the point where the "relevance of earnings" is now said to be statistically undetectable.[14] And as we also noted, this dramatic drop in earnings relevance can be traced directly to an economy-wide rise in corporate investment in intangibles—in R&D, and in market- and brand-building outlays that GAAP requires be expensed rather than capitalized and put on balance sheets.

But if the value of such intangible assets does not show up on corporate balance sheet . . . then how or where does it get recorded—and how or where does it make itself known? As we also saw in chapter 3, both reflecting and contributing to this near disappearance of earnings relevance has been a truly astonishing jump in the proportion of U.S. public companies—now estimated to be as high as 30 percent—with persistently negative earnings and *operating* cash flow. In other words, thanks in large part to the GAAP requirement that companies expense virtually all their investments in intangibles, close to a third of today's U.S. public companies *appear* to be losing more money with each additional dollar of investment and revenue—while their market valuations continue to grow![15]

And as also noted earlier, if one is looking for an explanation of this transformation by U.S. capital markets of persistently profitless "zombies" into highly valued growth companies, perhaps the best place to start is with the 50-year trend in both corporate R&D and selling, general, and administrative expenses, or SG&A—the category, by the way, where most corporate ESG spending shows up. For U.S. public companies, Dave Denis has reported that SG&A as a percentage of total assets jumped from 25 percent in 1970 to a remarkable 55 percent in 2017. And the lion's share of this growth in SG&A spending represents increases in categories such as marketing and promotion, and investments in other intangible assets that fall under today's rubrics of human, brand, and reputational capital.

What's more, as Denis goes on to note, the remarkably strong positive correlation between this U.S. economy-wide increase in both R&D and SG&A "investment" and general corporate market valuations—to the point where such spending seems to mirror directly the long-term upswing in stock prices—contains an important message for corporate managers and their investors: The stock market now appears to be pricing most U.S. companies with very high levels of R&D and SG&A as if they are funding substantial profitable growth opportunities. And those companies have predictably responded to such market pricing by continuously increasing their investment in intangibles—including their ESG initiatives and budgets—and finding investor recognition and rewards for so doing.

So, for those concerned about both the outlook for U.S. corporate competitiveness *and* commitments to sustainability, the good news from Denis's (and others') analysis is that U.S. public companies have been investing heavily in both their individual and collective futures. As we saw earlier, total R&D spending by U.S. public companies for the past five decades has been rising even more sharply than SG&A, from just 1 percent of total assets in 1970 to 20 percent in recent years. And since most of what public companies now view as part of their ESG investment also falls under this SG&A umbrella—or maybe a better metaphor is under the market "halo" it seems to be casting—corporate sustainability fans should be heartened by this development in market pricing.

THE LIMITATIONS AND PITFALLS OF ESG

But having explored the considerable promise of ESG, let's now take a brief look at the pitfalls, some of which are quite deep (and inviting).

First and most obvious is the once-widespread claim that ESG investing is a reliable way for well-meaning and socially conscious investors to earn not lower, but *higher* rates of returns than their less enlightened counterparts. Under the banner of ESG, investors have been lured in droves by the claim that such investors can do not only well, but *better than most*—while and *by* doing good!

But this chimera has been proven to be real only in the following sense: Companies that experience a significant, and often fairly sudden, upgrade in their ESG status and reputation have shown a tendency to outperform their less ESG-conscious peers, at least for a while. But this outperformance is best viewed as a one-time upward adjustment in value, at which point the most reputable companies then begin to hold out *lower*, not higher, expected returns to new investors, to reflect their now perceived lower risk—and lower cost of capital.

And, yes, a lower cost of capital is a social boon for those companies when evaluating their own performance, and when contemplating new ESG projects—but *not* for investors intent on profiting from their shareholdings. ESG investors can and should expect to earn competitive, *risk-adjusted* returns going forward, no more no less. To the extent corporate ESG initiatives have increased companies' values by making them less risky in investors' eyes, their own shareholders' returns in the future are likely to be lower, not higher. Again, that's how capital markets work.

●   ●   ●

A more troubling, and potentially far more destructive, misconception common among ESG enthusiasts and activists is that virtually any and all ESG campaigns are "good for society," regardless of their effects on corporate competitiveness, efficiency, and longer-run value.

In 2022, ShareAction, a UK-based non-profit and ESG activist, filed the first "living wage" resolution in the UK against Sainsbury's, one of the UK's large supermarket chains. Although the resolution was intended as ShareAction's opening salvo in a battle with the *entire* UK supermarket sector, it was directed only at Sainsbury's and the company's largest shareholders—many of them, like the well-known British asset manager Schroders, with their own well-earned ESG credentials to uphold. Placing emphasis on the "S" in ESG, the resolution was presented by ShareAction to the institutional investors whose support it was seeking as a kind of litmus test of the genuineness of "their social commitments amid the cost-of-living crisis"—a crisis that, given the extraordinarily high inflation rate in the UK (as much as double that in the U.S.), is considerably worse than the challenges now being endured by U.S. workers.

But when the matter was put to a vote at Sainsbury's Annual General Meeting on July 7, 2022, the Living Wage resolution was *rejected* by roughly five out of six Sainsbury's shareholders, and for a number of reasons. Far from promising to improve employee morale and productivity, as the Walmart general wage increase mentioned earlier was intended (and appears to have accomplished), the ShareAction resolution appeared to be undermining Sainsbury's competitive position by expecting the company to move first, without being joined by any of its competitors. Had the ShareAction-sponsored proposal succeeded, the outcome may well have been not only losses for Sainsbury's shareholders, but possibly much greater hardship suffered by its employees and other stakeholders in the event of the company's lost market share and profit.

In other words, the proposal demonstrated ShareAction's willingness to sacrifice much of the value, and possibly the future, of Sainsbury's to promote its own vision of economic equality. Having shown its indifference to the company's economic viability, the ESG activist then went on to question the commitments to social progress of the other large reputable investors, including Schroders, who voted down their proposal.

In sum, ShareAction's methods and rhetoric hardly seem the ticket for getting others—whether it's the investors whose support you need, or the managements whose buy-in you probably ought to at least seek before proceeding—to help realize your goal of economic equality.[16]

The Engine One-Exxon Case. Another, even more highly publicized, proxy contest also took place in 2022—in this case, a campaign that was waged, won, and celebrated with great fanfare. Cast as a classic engagement of a corporate Goliath by a plucky David-like investor holding a mere 0.02 percent of oil giant Exxon's outstanding stock, the success of tiny ESG activist Engine One in persuading Exxon's largest holders—the BlackRocks, State Streets, and Fidelitys of the world—to elect two of the three new directors on Engine One's slate was hailed by ESG enthusiasts as both (1) unexpected and (2) having major consequences for Exxon's long-run strategic direction and performance (financial and otherwise).

The election of two Engine One's directors was certainly unexpected in the sense that it beat the odds. Hundreds of ESG shareholder resolutions claiming to advance social goals (at the expense of corporate profitability, to a greater or lesser degree) are introduced each year by "gadfly" activists who hold at least the $25,000 minimum required position in the stock. The vast majority of these resolutions are voted down by larger, presumably better-informed investors, again including BlackRock and Fidelity.[17]

And most are voted down for a good reason: Attempts to address broad social issues by training the spotlight on—and trying to "punish"—a handful of the perceived biggest private-sector "perpetrators" tend to suffer from a major "free-rider" problem. Letting a few big guys take the fall for what is a society-wide challenge is likely to look and feel good. But, as economists have long pointed out, these kinds of "externalities" are generally addressed most effectively through government regulation and enforcement that ensure widespread sharing of social burdens.

Still, while many if not most of us would agree that it's good to see the largest U.S. institutional investors expressing their concerns about climate change, it's not clear that the Engine One victory will have much of an impact. How, if at all, will the presence of two new directors change Exxon's strategic direction and future performance, including its climate posture and initiatives?

Well before Engine One showed up, the plummeting of Exxon's stock price (and P/E ratio) and the amassing by hedge fund D.E. Shaw of a large position had already communicated the market's message to management: cut back capital spending on drilling and exploration, sharpen your focus on operating efficiency, and start returning excess capital through dividends and buybacks. And as we saw earlier, up until the Russian invasion of the Ukraine and the recent bout of oil price inflation, that's pretty much what Exxon's management was doing.

But at the same time, under the direction of a board that had managed several years earlier to attract both well-known ESG activist investor Jeff Ubben (founder of first ValueAct and, more recently, Inclusive Partners) and highly regarded former Merck CEO and chair Ken Frazier (as Exxon's lead director), the company was also investing heavily in several major "green" initiatives—carbon sequestration, low-carbon "blue hydrogen" and, most recently, lithium—while staunchly resisting the temptation to get into renewables like wind and solar. (The sheer waste of shareholder capital and loss of value experienced in the past few years by companies like BP and Royal Dutch Shell should serve as a cautionary tale against misguided attempts to stretch fossil-fuel-based core competencies into renewables.)

So given these green initiatives already in place at Exxon, it seems more than fair to ask, what difference are Engine One's two new directors likely to make going forward? And in fact, I got the chance to pose this question to Jeff Ubben himself at a recent conference on climate change held by investment bank Lazard.

When I asked this Exxon director—famous for having brought about significant change at companies like Microsoft and coal-burning American Electric Power—if he thought the Engine One proxy contest was a "constructive" event, and whether Exxon's two newest directors were likely to make significant changes, Ubben sort of laughed. Then, after offering the bromide that "it's always good for companies to refresh their boards," he went on to praise Exxon's competence and capabilities in carbon sequestration and blue hydrogen in what I found a remarkably impassioned defense of one of the most vilified companies in America. But as Ubben also said in closing, for Exxon's green initiatives to succeed, the company needed "help" from the federal government in the form of a carbon tax, or other laws or regulations, that could make these technologies a major source of revenue.

THE CASE OF AMERICAN ELECTRIC POWER (AND THE FATE OF *ITS* CARBON SEQUESTRATION PROGRAM)

To get a clearer sense of the limits of much ESG activism, and of even the most well-intended private corporate sustainability initiatives, it's useful to consider the story of American Electric Power (AEP), a mainly coal-burning

(continued on next page)

(*continued from previous page*)

electric utility that identifies itself as "the largest user of coal in the western hemisphere" and "the largest emitter of carbon dioxide among U.S. electric utilities."[18]

AEP has long had a well-developed and highly regarded "stakeholder engagement" program in which it regularly seeks input from customers, local communities, and regulators in the eleven different U.S. states where it operates—along with an ongoing program to shift its use of coal to natural gas and renewable energy sources like nuclear and hydro. In 2009, AEP made a major investment in a carbon capture and storage facility in West Virginia. According to then-CFO Brian Tierney, "The project was the world's first integrated CCS," one that succeeded in capturing "more than 51,000 metric tons of carbon dioxide and stored more than 37,000 metric tons underground between September 2009 and May 2011."[19]

But when the company requested increases in rates that would allow it to recover costs and earn a competitive return on its investment, it was turned down by the state utility commissions in both Virginia and West Virginia. Why? Because the two states were understandably reluctant to shoulder the entire financial burden and risk of a project they believed should be shared by all of AEP's customers. The result was a $76 million write-off—and unhappy shareholders. And as Tierney noted with some disappointment, "AEP has discontinued plans to move forward with a second commercial-scale phase of CCS due to the absence of a working market for carbon credits, and the reluctance of regulators to allow cost recovery for CCS operating costs."

The lesson from the AEP story is the importance of "getting regulation right." As the rulings of both state utility commissions suggest, the best way of meeting AEP's request for rate increases would probably have been to spread the burden of higher rates across all the eleven states in which AEP operates.

The problem with such a solution, however, is that it would have required unprecedented coordination among state regulators. And as already suggested, the broader solution—one that would extend to Exxon and other energy companies—is a national carbon tax. But our politicians have thus far predictably failed to see—or at least get behind—it.

TOWARD A 21ST-CENTURY SOCIAL CONTRACT

How, then, do we get our political and economic systems to work together in encouraging private-sector companies like Exxon and AEP to make "environmentally friendly" investments? And how do we continue to make strides in reducing global as well as U.S. poverty, and racial and economic inequalities?

In an article we ran in the *JACF* in 2012, Carl Ferenbach, longtime chairman of the Environmental Defense Fund (and a cofounder of the PE firm Berkshire Partners), teamed up with his colleague Chris Pinney in proposing a "21st-century social contract."[20] Such a contract amounts to a new understanding between business and government that begins by recognizing the distinctive capabilities of each and aims to bring about a productive collaboration between them. The goal of such collaboration is to make the most of the economic and social benefits of the globalization of commerce, while working to limit its disruptive effects on labor, local communities, and the environment.

For business, this new understanding is expected to continue to lead to greater investment of corporate thought and other resources in addressing social problems like the environment and local poverty. It is also meant to encourage more and better corporate sustainability reporting of the kind that got its start after the Global Financial Crisis, along with other attempts to communicate the value of such investments to investors and other stakeholders.

For governments, however, the 21st-century contract involves more of a break with the past. As Ferenbach and Pinney see it, global business has a long history of adapting to and thriving in the face of change. Governments, on the other hand, have shown far more resistance to change and been slow to respond to today's even more than usually pressing social imperative for efficiency—with the result that already heavily indebted government treasuries continue to face ever-higher levels of public spending on retirement, healthcare, and education.[21] The new social contract calls for greater recognition of the need for laws and regulations that encourage both corporate efficiency and investments designed to address social problems—once again, by allowing companies to earn the returns that will enable them to continue attracting capital from their investors.

* * *

Ferenbach and Pinney have, of course, been far from alone in making the case for and envisioning a more effective business-government collaboration. In 2017, a book with the unfashionably optimistic title, *Climate of Hope: How Cities, Businesses, and Citizens Can Save the Planet*—and co-authored by the unlikely team of Michael Bloomberg, billionaire founder of Bloomberg LP and former mayor of New York City, and Carl Pope, former executive director and chairman of the Sierra Club—had a message and tone strikingly different from those of most other writings on the subject.

One of the main reasons for the optimism projected by Bloomberg and Pope is the limited role they see for national governments in developing and carrying out effective responses to climate change. In place of federal policies and top-down directives, the authors' main focus is the efforts of local organizations—especially state and city governments, often working with for-profit companies—to come up with solutions to specific local challenges, such as providing clean air and water. Cities and states are praised for negotiating contracts with local utilities to produce steadily growing amounts of renewable energy. Water-treatment plants, rapid transit programs, and other infrastructure projects have increasingly been funded by combinations of public and private capital. And making the good news even better, such practices have often worked to strengthen the financial condition of city and state governments while helping to protect the environment and human health.

Perhaps the best news held out by Bloomberg and Pope is their recognition of the ever-expanding role of the private sector *even when in pursuit of profit* in the battle against global warming. More and more companies—large and small, private as well as public—have been finding ways to reduce waste and their carbon footprint, while increasing their own bottom lines. At the same time, large public companies like Nestle, Unilever, and Coca-Cola have continued their longtime practice of making major investments in maintaining and improving water supplies in communities where they produce as well as sell their goods and services.

What's more, the fact that even staunch critics of the private-sector like David Leonhardt (mentioned earlier) and Paul Krugman seem willing to acknowledge gains in the war against poverty and racial inequality is grounds for guarded optimism. Such developments, particularly the remarkable post-pandemic return of the U.S. economy to full employment (even in the face of a record series of Fed rate hikes),[22] are likely to be important since value-seeking companies and their investors may well turn out to be the most effective force in producing investments of sufficient scale and practical efficacy to meet the challenges of both climate change and global as well as local poverty.

* * *

To encourage more public companies to harness the power of financial markets for social good, there are a number of challenges that need to be addressed. Among the most formidable is persuading our politicians and policymakers to rethink laws and regulations with an eye to encouraging both corporate efficiency and new or better solutions to our arguably two most pressing problems: climate change and global poverty.

What we are talking about is a new—or if not wholly new, at least better—kind of public-private partnership. Government will continue to set the rules and provide the necessary oversight, along with much of the resources, to help the less fortunate cope with the disruptions of modern corporate finance and its creative destruction—while the private sector, as described in these pages, continues to use the principles and methods of modern corporate finance to provide most of the capital, and create most of the jobs and wealth on which most of us depend.

NOTES

PROLOGUE: THE MAGIC OF FINANCE CAPITALISM

1. *Financial Analysts Journal*, Vol. 31 No. 1 (1978), pp. 31–37.
2. A number of the Stern Stewart founding partners, me included, did MBAs in finance at the University of Rochester, often described as "the eastern annex" of the University of Chicago.
3. Joel continued to use this term long after being advised by a number of our Texan clients that herds are led by cows.
4. The term was coined by well-known legal scholar Henry Manne, while working with Jensen at the University of Rochester in the early '80s.
5. See Edmund Phelps, "*Mass Flourishing: How Grassroots Innovation Created Jobs Challenges and Change*, Princeton University Press (2013).

1. INTRODUCTION TO CORPORATE FINANCE: WHAT IS IT, AND WHY DOES IT MATTER?

1. Michael Jensen and William Meckling, "Specific and General Knowledge and Organizational Design," *Journal of Applied Corporate Finance*, Vol. 8 No. 2 (Summer 1996).

2. THE CAUTIONARY TALE OF JAPAN INC.—AND THE LINK BETWEEN CORPORATE FINANCE AND SOCIAL WEALTH

1. This quotation from Miller's speech, and all succeeding ones in this chapter, are taken from Merton Miller's article, "Is U.S. Corporate Governance Fatally Flawed?" *Journal of Applied Corporate Finance*, Vol. 6 No. 4 (Winter 1994).
2. Carl Kester, "The Hidden Costs of Japanese Success," *Journal of Applied Corporate Finance*, Vol. 3. No. 4 (Winter 1991).
3. See Joichi Aoi, "Mitsui Life Roundtable on US vs Japanese Corporate Governance," *Journal of Applied Corporate Finance*, Volume 6 No. 4 (Winter 1994).

4. For a representative expression of macroeconomists' continuing inability to explain, or propose effective solutions for ending, Japan's now well-over-30-year recession, see Paul Krugman's "Rethinking Japan," *New York Times* (October 2015).

5. Jay Ritter, "Is All Economic Growth Good for Investors?," *Journal of Applied Corporate Finance*, Vol. 24 No. 3 (Summer 2012).

6. Ibid.

7. See James Manyika et al, "Growth and Renewal in the United States: Retooling America's Economic Engine," *Journal of Applied Corporate Finance*, Vol. 23 No. 1 (Winter 20011).

8. See Tyler Cowen, "Why So Many Economists Were Wrong about Recession," *Bloomberg* (Dec. 23, 2023).

3. MERTON MILLER AND THE CHICAGO SCHOOL THEORY OF VALUE

1. Peter Bernstein, *Capital Ideas: The Improbable Origins of Modern Wall Street* (New York, The Free Press, 1992), p 164.

2. Bernstein (1993), cited above.

3. Markowitz was the Chicago colleague whose Nobel Prize was awarded the same day as Miller's.

4. Bernstein, cited earlier.

5. Ibid.

6. Bernstein, cited earlier.

7. Williams's ideas of earnings power and conservation of investment value ended up attracting few followers in his day. The best of the conventional wisdom was projected by Columbia Business School investment gurus Benjamin Graham and David Dodd in their classic investing textbook, *Security Analysis*, the first of whose many editions came out in 1932. But here, as with even the best fundamental analysis, the main focus was not so much "intrinsic values" and "earnings power" as vigilant attention to corporate balance sheets (generally the less debt, the better) and earnings stability. Such focus in turn became the most reliable key to investing success: readiness to pounce on and profit from the bouts of "market irrationality and mispricing" that, at least in Graham and Dodd's eyes, seemed to come about with almost predictable regularity.

8. Franco Modigliani and Merton Miller, "The Cost of Capital, Corporation Finance and the Theory of Investment" *American Economic Review* (1958).

9. Originally published in the *American Economic Review*'s *Journal of Economic Perspectives* (Fall 1988), and then in somewhat abridged form in the *Journal of Applied Corporate Finance* (Spring 1989).

10. Merton Miller and Franco Modigliani, "Dividend Policy, Growth, and the Valuation of Shares," *Journal of Business* (1961).

11. Miller (1989), cited earlier.

12. Shyam Sunder, "Optimal Choice between FIFO and LIFO," *Journal of Accounting Research*, Vol. 14 No. 2 (Autumn 1976).

13. Hai Hong, Robert Kaplan, and Gershon Mandelker, "Pooling vs Purchase: The Effects of Accounting for Mergers on Stock Prices," *Accounting Review* (1978).

14. Eric Lindenberg and Michael Ross, "To Purchase or to Pool: Does It Matter?" *Journal of Applied Corporate Finance*, Vol. 12 No. 2 (Summer 1999).

15. Given the tendency for poolings to be funded largely with acquirer stock rather than cash, Lindenberg and Ross attributed part of this somewhat surprisingly negative response to the market's well-documented reservations about companies when announcing new equity offerings—and stock-financed deals have much the same potential for unwanted dilution as new secondary issues. To "control" for this stock issuance effect, the authors created a third category of deals—a relatively small group of stock-for-stock *purchases*. In this case, the average market response to the 120 announcements was indistinguishable from zero, as compared to the 4 percent positive reaction to 357 cash-only purchases. But when set against the negative 4 percent reaction to all poolings, investors clearly view stock-financed *purchases* as more promising than stock-financed poolings.

16. Indeed, when Welch retired in 2001, GE had long had the highest market cap of any listed public company in the world. See William D. Cohan's fascinating account, *Power Failure: The Rise and Fall of an American Icon* (Random House, 2022).

17. As recounted in Cohan's book, Jeff Immelt, when taking the reins from Welch in 2001, discovered that many of GE's largest institutional investors had *no idea* how the company made money, or even what businesses the company operated in. It was only when 9/11 put an abrupt end to GE's miraculous earnings growth that such investors began to ask questions. In most cases, many of them simply sold the shares—and asked questions later—causing a frustrated Immelt to describe the company's investor base as "bordering on moronic." (Cohan, p. 301)

18. John McConnell and Chris Muscarella, "Corporate Capital Expenditure Decisions and the Market Value of the Firm," *Journal of Financial Economics*, Vol. 14 No. 3 (1985).

19. Su Chan, John Martin, and John Kensinger, "Corporate Research and Development Expenditures and Share Value," *Journal of Financial Economics* (1990).

20. See Baruch Lev and Feng Gu, *The End of Accounting and the Path Forward for Investors and Managers* (John Wiley & Sons, 2016).

21. David Denis and Stephen McKeon, "Rising Intangibles, Negative Cash Flows, and Corporate Funding Practices,"*Journal of Applied Corporate Finance*, Vol. 34 No. 4 (Fall 2022), pp. 42–43.

22. David Denis, "Is Managerial Myopia a Persistent U.S. Corporate Governance Problem?," *Journal of Applied Corporate Finance*, Vol. 31 No. 3 (Summer 2019).

23. Ray Ball, "The Theory of Stock Market Efficiency: Accomplishments and Limitations," *Journal of Applied Corporate Finance*, Vol. 8 No. 1 (Spring 1996).

24. See Alberic Braas and Charles Bralver, "How Bank Trading Rooms Really Make Money," *Journal of Applied Corporate Finance*, Vol. 2 No. 4 (Winter 1989).

25. Miller (1989), cited earlier.

4. MICHAEL JENSEN, WILLIAM MECKLING, AND THE ROCHESTER SCHOOL OF CORPORATE CONTROL

1. Branko Milanovic, *Global Inequality* (Harvard University Press, 2018), as cited in Steven Pinker, "Inequality and Progress," reprinted from *Enlightenment Now: The Case for Reason,*

Science, Humanism, and Progress, in *Journal of Applied Corporate Finance*, Vol. 33 No. 3 (Summer 2021).

2. See Phil Gramm, John Early, and Robert Ekelund, *The Myth of American Inequality: How the Government Biases Policy Debate*, Rowman & Littlefield, 2022. What's more, and contrary to what one continues to read in the popular press, even somewhat left-leaning journalists like David Leonhardt of the *New York Times* report that official U.S. childhood poverty rates have been cut in half since 1993. (See "Poverty, Plunging," *New York Times* Sept. 14, 2022.)

3. This account of Berle relies heavily on Nicholas Lemann's in his 2019 book, *Transaction Man: The Rise of the Deal and Decline of the American Dream* (Farrar Straus, and Giroux), about which more to come.

4. Meckling was the Dean of the University of Rochester's Simon School of Business, who in the late '60s had persuaded Jensen to follow his example in leaving the University of Chicago and joining him in Rochester.

5. See John Cassidy, "The Greed Cycle: How the Financial System Encouraged Companies to Go Crazy," *New Yorker* (September 23, 2002),

6. Michael Jensen, "The Agency Costs of Free Cash Flow: Corporate Finance and Takeovers," *American Economic Review* (1986).

7. Michael Jensen, "Eclipse of the Public Corporation," *Harvard Business Review* (Sept-Oct 1989). Mike in several conversations with me expressed his dissatisfaction with the title of this *HBR* piece, which he claimed was foisted on him by "the editors" and which he found "not just melodramatic, but plain wrong."

8. Communicated by Mike in both private discussions with, and public presentations witnessed by, this writer.

9. As this book was going to press (at the end of the first quarter of 2024), the total annual return to the S&P 500 during the nearly 45-year run since the start of 1980 had averaged a remarkable 12 percent.

10. For an account of the response of UK private equity to the COVID pandemic, and its role in filling an investment vacuum left by UK public companies, see Shai Bernstein and Josh Lerner, "Evidence from the UK of PE Performance During the COVID Crisis," *Journal of Applied Corporate Finance*, Vol. 31 No. 3 (Summer 2020).

11. Steven Rattner, "Trump is Wrong about the General Motors Bailout," *New York Times* (Sept. 18, 2018).

12. https://www.theguardian.com/business/2009/jun/01/general-motors-bankruptcy-chapter-11

13. I'm embarrassed to confess the number of times I've read, and continue to be astonished by, Ron Chernow's biography of Hamilton, a man that Ben Bernanke has identified as America's "foremost economic administrator," and whose biography he commended to his friend Mario Draghi when the latter was President of the European Central Bank and attempting to unify the divided European states—much as Hamilton was forced to do with the U.S. colonies.

14. Charles Calomiris and Stephen Haber, *Fragile by Design: The Origins of Banking Crises and Scarce Credit* (Princeton University Press, 2014).

15. Restrictions on interstate banking were not fully lifted until 1994. For an account of car dealerships, https://files.stlouisfed.org/files/htdocs/publications/review/03/07/Strahan.pdf

16. For a longer, more detailed account of who knew what about the mortgages at the time of the Global Financial Crisis, see my article, "The Economic (not Literary) Offenses of Michael Lewis: The Case of *The Big Short*," *Journal of Applied Corporate Finance*," Vol. 32 No. 4 (Winter 2022).

17. Even nearly a decade after the crisis, we had yet to learn the extent of the actual losses on the toxic mortgages. See Peter Wallison, *Hidden in Plain Sight: What Really Caused the World's Worst Financial Crisis and Why It Could Happen Again*," Encounter Books, 2016.

18. See, in what has become the most cited of *JACF* articles, Michael Jensen, "The Corporate Objective Function: Stakeholder Value vs. Value Maximization," *Journal of Applied Corporate Finance* (Fall, 2001).

5. STEWART MYERS AND THE MIT SCHOOL OF REAL OPTIONS AND CAPITAL STRUCTURE

1. Stewart C. Myers, "Finance, Theoretical and Applied," *The Annual Review of Financial Economics*, Vol. 7 (2015), pp. 1–34. The rest of this chapter draws liberally on this source. And unless otherwise identified, verbatim comments by Stew should be assumed to come from this source. They are used with the permission of the *Annual Review*'s publisher at MIT.

2. "Finance, Theoretical and Applied," cited in note 1.

3. As my partner Joel Stern never grew tired of telling people, when he first came to the University of Chicago in the early '60s to do his MBA, the words "nothing matters" were uttered with such frequency and fervor that "he thought he was in the wrong place; he thought he'd come to Berkeley."

4. George Eastman, when CEO of Eastman Kodak, viewed the use of debt financing as one of the most lethal of the seven corporate deadly sins.

5. See Alexander Robichek and Stewart Myers, "Valuation of the Firm: Effects of Uncertainty in a Market Context," *Journal of Finance*, May 1966; and "Problems in the Theory of Optimal Capital Structure," *Journal of Financial and Quantitative Analysis*, June 1966.

6. "Finance, Theoretical and Applied," cited in note 1.

7. See Stewart Myers, "The Capital Structure Puzzle," *Journal of Finance* (June 1984). The now ubiquitous figure first appeared in Robichek and Myers, "Problems in the Theory of Optimal Capital Structure," *Journal of Financial and Quantitative Analysis*, June 1966, p. 21.

8. See Robert Hagstrom, *The Warren Buffett Way* (Wiley, 2013).

9. See John Lintner, "Optimal Dividend Policy and Corporate Growth and Uncertainty," *Quarterly Journal of Economics*, Vol. 77 (1985), p. 65.

10. See Robichek and Myers, "Conceptual Problems in the Use of Risk-Adjusted Discount Rates," *Journal of Finance*, December 1966. Stew and Alex in turn have acknowledged their debt to Ezra Solomon, a highly regarded Stanford GSB professor.

11. Stewart Myers, "Interactions of Corporate Financing and Investment Decisions: Implications for Capital Budgeting," *Journal of Finance* (March 1974). The original M&M analysis presented a "somewhat murky" view of the cost of capital, one that was effectively "backed out" from observable valuation multiples. "The necessary conditions for the use

of WACC," as Stew said in his retrospective, "were not well understood in those days, and M&M did not provide much guidance." M&M's costs of capital were really capitalization, or "cap," rates, which they defined as ratios of expected average future cash flow or income to present value. Such cap rates could be used as estimates of expected rates of return only in the case of level perpetuities for, as Stew explained in his 1974 paper, "errors creep in when taxes are introduced and assets have irregular cash flows and limited lives."

12.   Miller later argued that higher personal taxes on investors' debt versus equity income could offset the value of corporate interest tax shields. Stew here assumes that the same personal tax rates apply to income from both debt and equity.

13.   For what Stew identifies as the correct formula, see Miles & Ezzell (1980). For a more complete explanation of the proper use of WACC and M&M Proposition 2, see Brealey, Myers & Allen (2020), chapter 19.

14.   See "Finance Theory and Financial Strategy," *Interfaces*, January-February 1984. Reprinted in A.C. Hax, ed., *Readings on Strategic Management*, Cambridge, MA: Ballinger, 1984.

15.   Stew's more recent work with Jamie Read on corporate real options and capital structure, which appeared in the *Critical Finance Review* and later the *JACF*, reinforces this argument by viewing both real calls and puts as different combinations of leverage with the underlying asset or business opportunity. Whereas corporate growth or expansion options involve the use of positive "leverage" that works to crowd out and limit corporate borrowing—since companies need to have the cash and capital ready to exercise their growth options when the time comes—abandonment options provide companies with what amounts to "negative leverage" that has the effect of enlarging their debt capacity. The abandoned asset or business effectively provides a new source of capital that management can draw on when appropriate. What's more, because the leverage built into growth options works to displace actual or explicit debt, reported corporate debt ratios were and are not nearly as low as they seemed, a point that Stew regrets not having made "30 years ago."

16.   Stewart Myers and Nicholas Majluf, "Corporate Financing and Investment Decisions When Firms Have Information That Investors Do Not Have," *Journal of Financial Economics* (June 1984).

17.   For among the most widely cited, see Paul Asquith and David Mullins, "Seasoned Equity Offerings: An Empirical Investigation," *Journal of Finance* (1986).

18.   More technically, the goal of such a scheme is to allocate the amount of capital to each of the business lines in such a way that *their marginal default values* end up all being *equal to one other, and to the MDV of the entire firm.*

6. CLIFFORD SMITH, RENÉ STULZ, AND THE THEORY AND PRACTICE OF *CORPORATE* RISK MANAGEMENT

1.   The key to understanding the tax benefits of hedging is to recognize "asymmetries" in the tax code that cause rising marginal tax rates, the alternative minimum tax, and the tax shields provided by depreciation allowances and tax-loss carryforwards to all work together to impose higher effective tax rates on more variable levels of reported income, including lower percentage rebates for ever larger losses. By limiting the variability of

taxable income, hedging effectively ensures that companies will be able to make the fullest possible use of *all* their tax shields, including loss carryforwards.

2. For one of the clearest and most compact expositions of Cliff's basic approach to analyzing and pricing derivatives, see Clifford Smith, Charles Smithson, and Sykes Wilford, "Managing Financial Risk," *Journal of Applied Corporate Finance*, Vol. 2 No. 4 (Winter 1990).

3. As one example, in 2003 General Motors announced its plan to sell a $10 billion bond issue whose proceeds would be used to buy other companies' bonds to shore up GM's plan deficit, then estimated at over $19 billion. GM's underwriter and financial adviser on the transaction was Morgan Stanley, which I joined the following year.

4. See Robert Merton, "Allocating Shareholder Capital to Pension Plans: A Talk," *Journal of Applied Corporate Finance*, Vol. 18 No. 1 (Winter 2006).

5. Ludger Hentschel and Clifford Smith, "Risk and Regulation in Derivatives (or Why Derivatives Are a Blessing, Not a Curse)," *Journal of Applied Corporate Finance*, Vol. 7 No. 3 (Fall 1994).

6. René Stulz, "Rethinking Risk Management," *Journal of Applied Corporate Finance*, Vol. 9 No. 3 (Fall 1996).

7. René Stulz, "How Companies Can Use Hedging to Increase Shareholder Value," *Journal of Applied Corporate Finance*, Vol. 27 No. 3 (Summer 2014).

8. Nevertheless, in what I choose to view as a piece of good news, Exxon recently announced the formation of a new energy unit whose traders are expressly forbidden to take speculative positions on energy prices.

9. Clifford Smith, "The Economics of Ethics: The Case of Salomon Brothers," *Journal of Applied Corporate Finance*, Vol. 32 No. 1 (Winter 2021).

7. JENSEN REDUX, STEVE KAPLAN, AND THE REMARKABLE SUCCESS OF U.S. PRIVATE EQUITY

1. This statement appears in the edited versions of both Jensen's and Greenspan's testimonies that were published in the *Journal of Applied Corporate Finance*, Vol. 2 No. 1 (Spring 1989).

2. Michael Jensen, "Eclipse of the Public Corporation," *Harvard Business Review*, 1989.

3. Michael Jensen and Kevin Murphy, "CEO Incentives: It's Not How Much You Pay, But How," *Harvard Business Review* (May-June 1990).

4. Robert Kidder, in "CEO Roundtable on Corporate Structure and Management Incentives," *Journal of Applied Corporate Finance*, Vol. 3 No. 3 (April 18, 1990).

5. James Birle, in "The Role of Corporate Boards in the 1990s," *Journal of Applied Corporate Finance* (Vol. 4 No. 3) February 29, 1992.

6. Davis, S. J., Haltiwanger, J., Handley, K., Jarmin, R., Lerner, J., & Miranda, J. (2014). Private Equity, Jobs, and Productivity. *American Economic Review*, 104(12), 3956–90. Here are links to the papers on SSRN: https://papers.ssrn.com/sol3/papers.cfm?abstract_id=2460790 https://papers.ssrn.com/sol3/papers.cfm?abstract_id=3465723

7. Quentin Boucly, David Sraer, and Dennis Thesmar (2011), "Growth LBOs," *Journal of Financial Economics*, 102(2), 432–453.

8.   Steve Kaplan and Jeremy Stein, "The Evolution of Buyout Pricing and Financial Structure in the 1980s," *Quarterly Journal of Economics*, Volume 108 (May 1993), 313–358.

9.   For Jensen's explanation of PE's boom-and-bust cycle, which he saw operating in all financial markets, particularly real estate, see Michael Jensen, "Active Investors and The Politics of Corporate Control," *Journal of Applied Corporate Finance*, Vol. 4 No. 2 (Summer 1991).

10. Ferenbach was credited by Mike Jensen himself with having "taught him everything he knew about private equity," and whom he regularly asked to "team-teach" the PE portion of his consistently oversubscribed "coordination and control" (or CCMO) course at Harvard Business School. See "Morgan Stanley Roundtable on Private Equity," *Journal of Applied Corporate Finance*, Vol. 23 No. 4. (Fall 2011). What's more, while working at Morgan Stanley from 2004–2013, I can't tell you how many HBS-trained investment bankers told me that Jensen's was their most memorable course.

11. Carl Ferenbach, as a participant in "Morgan Stanley Roundtable on Private Equity," see footnote above.

12. "Morgan Stanley Roundtable on the State of Global Private Equity," *Journal of Applied Corporate Finance*, Vol. 23 No. 3 (Summer 2011).

13. Ibid.

14. Steve Kaplan, Paul Gompers, and Vladimir Mukharlyamov, "What Do PE Firms Say They Do?," *Journal of Financial Economics*, 2016.

15. The Davis et al. (2019) study cited earlier finds that although public-to-private firms increase productivity as much as other buyouts, the increase is not statistically significant.

16. Robert Harris, Steve Kaplan, and Tim Jenkinson, "Private Equity Performance: What Do We Know?" *Journal of Finance* (2014).

17. Anti Ilmanen, Swati Chandra, and Nicholas MacQuinn, "Demystifying Illiquid Assets—Expected Returns for Private Equity," *The Journal of Alternative Investments*, Vol. 22 No. 3. (2019).

18. Ibid. "Return smoothing" refers to the ability of PE firms to avoid having to mark down the value of their portfolio companies in years when the S&P 500 goes down, which enables LPs to report higher values as well. In other words, the institutional investors were either assumed to be taken in by the illusion, or to place a high value on maintaining the fiction, of the low volatility of PE returns, an illusion perpetuated by the fact that, because PE portfolio firms were not publicly traded and had no fluctuating stock prices, they were somehow less risky than their public counterparts. But also worth pointing out here is that, when evaluating the performance of PE funds for their LPs during the period between 2009 and 2019, the S&P 500 had one of its strongest performances ever, making relative performance comparisons with PE particularly challenging.

19. Gregory Brown and Steven Kaplan, "Have Private Equity Returns Really Declined?" *Journal of Private Equity*, 2019.

20. See Greg Brown, Bob Harris, and Shawn Munday, "Capital Structure and Leverage in Private Equity Buyouts," *Journal of Applied Corporate Finance*, Vol. 33 No. 3 (Summer 2021).

21. The academic literature on this is inconclusive, with betas typically ranging from 1.0 to 1.3.

22. Reinforcing this possibility, a study by Arthur Korteweg called "Risk Adjustment in Private Equity Returns" published in the *Annual Review of Financial Economics* in 2019

provides the suggestion that buyout returns most closely resemble the "value" segment of S&P 500 companies. Pursued to its logical conclusion, this finding suggests that PE buyouts impose no greater market and "factor" risks on well-diversified investors than those associated with holding the S&P 500.

23. David Robinson and Berk Sensoy, "Cyclicality, Performance Measurement, and Cash Flow Liquidity in Private Equity," *Journal of Financial Economics* Vol. 122 No. 3 (2016).

24. Robinson and Sensoy (2015).

25. As another possible conflict of interest, Robinson and Sensoy provide evidence of "kinks" in the partnership agreement—points in time where the "accelerated-carry" portion of the GPs' carry kicks in—and they find that distributions increase dramatically at that point. Also, partnership agreements that call for step-downs in management fees as assets are sold have been shown to lead GPs to put off their asset sales until later in the fund's life.

26. See Shai Bernstein and Albert Sheen, "The Operational Consequences of Private Equity Buyouts: Some Evidence from the Restaurant Industry," *Review of Financial Studies* (2016).

27. J. Cohn, N. Nestoriak and M. Wardlaw, "Private Equity Buyouts and Workplace Safety," *Review of Financial Studies* (2021)

28. R. Agrawal and N. Tamber (2016).

29. C. Fracassi, A. Previtero, and A. Sheen,"Barbarians at the Store: Private Equity, Products, and Consumers," *Journal of Finance* (2022)

30. C. Eaton, S. Howell, & C Yannelis, "When Investor Incentives and Consumer Interests Diverge: Private Equity in Higher Education." *National Bureau of Economic Research* (2018).

31. R. Pradhan, R. Weech-Maldonado, J. Harman, & K. Hyer, "Private Equity Ownership of Nursing Homes: Implications for Quality," *Journal of Health Care Finance*, 42(2) (2014).

32. In these cases, the authors point to a kind of "arbitraging" of nursing home regulations and registered nurse classifications that effectively encourages excessive reliance on highest-skilled (Level I) and minimally skilled Level (III), with too little use of higher-paid, mid-tier (Level II) caregivers. See Atal Gupta, Sabrina Howell, Constantine Yanellis, and Abhinav Gupta, "Does Private Equity Investment in Healthcare Benefit Patients: Evidence from the Nursing Industry," NYU Stern School of Business (2020).

33. See Ashram Gandhi, YoungJun Song, and Prabhavan Updrshti, "Have Private Equity-Owned Nursing Homes Fared Worse Under COVID-19?," Duke University working paper (2020).

34. Pilar Garcia-Gomez, Ernst Maug and Stefan Obernberger, "Private Equity Buyouts and Employee Health," European Corporate Governance Institute working paper, (2022).

35. Shai Bernstein and Josh Lerner, "Private Equity and Portfolio Companies: Lessons from the Global Financial Crisis," *Journal of Applied Corporate Finance*, Vol.32 No. 3 (Summer 2020).

36. See Steve Kaplan's widely cited "The Staying Power of Leveraged Buyouts," *Journal of Financial Economics* (1991), which showed that roughly 60 percent of the '80s LBOs were still independent private companies in 1990, as contrasted with the roughly 15 percent that had returned to public ownership and another 25 percent that had been sold to other companies.

37.   For an account of the rise of "unicorns," see Keith Brown and Ken Wiles, "The Growing Blessing of Unicorns," *Journal of Applied Corporate Finance*, Vol. 32 No. 3 (Summer
2021).

38.   See Steven Kaplan and Paul Gompers, *Advanced Private Equity* (Edwin Elgar, 2022), p. 10.

39.   Steve Kaplan and Bengt Holmstrom, "The State of U.S. Corporate Governance," *Journal
of Applied Corporate Finance*, Vol. 14 No. 2 (Spring 2003).

40.   See Ronald Gilson and Jeff Gordon, "The Rise of Agency Capitalism and the Role of
Shareholder Activism in Making it Work," *Journal of Applied Corporate Finance*, Vol. 31
No. 1 (Winter 2019).

41.   Ibid.

42.   Ibid.

43.   Cliff Holderness, "The Effect of Shareholder Voting on Equity Issuance Around the
World," *Journal of Applied Corporate Finance*, Vol. 31 No. 1 (Winter 2019).

44.   Marco Becht, Andrea Polo, and Stefano Rossi "Does Mandatory Shareholder Voting Prevent Bad Acquisitions: The Case of the UK," *Journal of Applied Corporate Finance*, Vol. 31
No. 1 (Winter 2019).

8. THE RISE AND FALL OF STERN STEWART'S EVA FINANCIAL MANAGEMENT SYSTEM

1.   The concept was presented by Mike Jensen to the legions of MBA students who took his
"Coordination and Control of the Corporation" class first at the University of Rochester's Simon School of Business and later at Harvard Business School. The introduction of
the term "the three-legged stool of corporate governance" has been attributed to Professor Ron Schmidt, one of Jensen's colleagues at Rochester. But for the earliest exposition
of the concept, see a lesser-known article by Jensen and Meckling called "Specific and
General Knowledge, and Organizational Structure," which was reprinted in *Journal of
Applied Corporate Finance*, Vol. 8 No. 2 (Summer 1996).

2.   The best known of these is Alfred D. Chandler, *The Visible Hand: The Managerial Revolution in American Business* (1977). But if Chandler's *Visible Hand* is the most forceful
account of the reign of professional managerialism during the era of controlled capitalism, students of economic history are also urged to read Richard Langlois's new book,
The Corporation and the Twentieth Century (Princeton University Press, 2023), which shows
the vulnerabilities of the large, centralized, mid-twentieth century corporation giving
rise and way to shareholder activism, while offering suggestive evidence of the supe-
riority of markets over managers, especially when responding to the forces of global
competition unleashed during the 1970s.

3.   Alfred Chandler, in "Continental then how or where does it get recorded—and how or
where does it make itself known? Bank Roundtable on Corporate Strategy in the 1990s,"
Journal of Applied Corporate Finance, Vol. 6 No. 3 (Fall 1993).

4.   See Jerry Zimmerman's wonderfully simple and readable account of these internal conflicts in his article, "Transfer Pricing and the Control of Internal Corporate Transactions," *Journal of Applied Corporate Finance*, Vol. 8 No. 2 (Summer 1996).

5.   See Gordon Donaldson, "The Corporate Restructuring of the 1980s and Its Import for
the 1990s," *Journal of Applied Corporate Finance*, Vol. 6 No. 4 (Winter 1994).

6.   For an account of what went wrong and its remediation, see Gordon Donaldson, "Voluntary Restructuring: The Case of General Mills," *Journal of Applied Corporate Finance* Vol. 4 No. 3 (Fall, 1993).

7.   See Peter Waldman, "New RJR Chief Faces a Daunting Challenge at Debt-Heavy Firm," *Wall Street Journal*, March 14, 1989.

8.   Peter Magowan, "Continental Bank Roundtable on Performance Measurement and Management Incentives," *Journal of Applied Corporate Finance*, Vol. 4 No. 3 (Fall 1993).

9.   For a much more elaborate and detailed discussion of the EVA financial management system, readers are strongly encouraged to go straight to the horse's mouth and get a copy of Bennett Stewart's inimitable book, *The Quest for Value: A Guide for Senior Managers* (HarperCollinsPublishers, 1991).

10.   Steve O'Byrne, "Why EVA Failed," *Journal of Applied Corporate Finance*, Vol. 28 No. 3 (2019).

9. THE PERENNIAL PROBLEM OF U.S. CEO PAY AND STEVE O'BYRNE'S QUEST FOR THE PERFECT PAY PLAN

1.   TPF&C is now part of Willis Towers Watson and its executive pay practice is now a separate company, Pay Governance.

2.   Alfred P. Sloan, Jr., *My Years with General Motors*, Doubleday, New York, NY, 1963.

3.   Stephen F. O'Byrne and S. David Young, "The Evolution of Executive Pay Policy at General Motors," *Journal of Applied Corporate Finance*, Vol 29, No 1 (Winter 2017).

4.   Sloan, *My Years with General Motors*, 418. The number of managers covered by the Bonus Plan had grown to 14,000 by 1963, the final year surveyed in *My Years with General Motors*.

5.   As Steve has also pointed out, despite the roller coaster ride of the company's fortunes from the establishment of the program in 1918 through the 1950s, GM's directors went to great lengths—including several bouts of innovative (and often quite complicated) problem-solving—to achieve their compensation objectives while maintaining such fixed-share bonuses. As just one example, early in the 1920s, the GM board invited senior bonus plan participants to buy stock in a special entity that made a leveraged purchase of GM stock and to transfer their bonus awards to the special entity for up to seven years to pay down the stock purchase debt. This leveraged stock purchase was tremendously successful and boosted management stock ownership. But during a later stock purchase plan started in 1930, the bonus awards fell off sharply during the Depression years, leaving the special entity struggling to repay the debt. The board responded decisively and salvaged the program by offering debt forgiveness based on the original stock value. About half the participants surrendered their stock in the exchange; the other half saw a small gain when the program ended in 1937.

6.   John Calhoun Baker, "Incentive Compensation Plans for Executives," *Harvard Business Review* 15 (Autumn 1936): 44–61.

7.   Stephen F. O'Byrne and Mark Gressle, "How 'Competitive Pay' Undermines Pay for Performance (and What Companies Can Do to Avoid That)," *Journal of Applied Corporate Finance* 25 (Spring 2013).

8.   Arch Patton, "Current Practices in Executive Compensation," *Harvard Business Review* 29 (Jan. 1951): 56.

9.   Steve O'Byrne and David Young, "Six Factors That Explain Executive Pay (and Its Problems)," *Journal of Applied Corporate Finance*, Vol 22, No 2 (Spring 2010).

10. Arch Patton, "Top Executive Pay: New Facts & Figures," *Harvard Business Review* 44, no. 5 (1966), p. 96.

11. Dana Canedy, "Arch Patton, 88; Devised First Survey of Top Executives' Pay," *The New York Times*, 30 November 1996.

12. The falling off of GM's relative market performance and value during the 1980s was so precipitous that Bennett Stewart, with his well-known (and freely conceded) weakness for overstatement, once titled an article, "GM Has Destroyed More Value than the Roman Empire Created."

13. O'Byrne, Stephen F., "Say on Pay: Is It Needed? Does It Work?," *Journal of Applied Corporate Finance*, Winter 2018. Relative pay is CEO pay divided by market pay. Realizable or mark-to-market CEO pay captures changes in the value of unvested equity compensation. Mark-to-market pay for a measurement period values equity compensation based on the stock price at the end of the measurement period.

14. Stephen F. O'Byrne and S. David Young, "What Investors Need to Know about Executive Pay," *Journal of Investing*, Spring 2010.

15. Corey Rosen and John Case, *Ownership: Reinventing Companies, Capitalism, and Who Owns What*, Barrett-Koehler Publishers, Inc., Oakland, CA, 2022, p. 81.

16. U.S. Census Bureau, Franchising Is More Than Fast Food, press release, 1 Dec 2021.

17. *The Economist*, "To neutralize populism, give more people more control," 14 Jan 2020 [for Mongradon] and Rosen and Case, p. 91 [for worker cooperatives].

18. Pay leverage is the slope of the trendline relating cumulative relative pay to cumulative relative shareholder wealth (using log scales). It's easier to calculate than wealth leverage because it doesn't require projections of expected future pay. It also becomes a better proxy for wealth leverage over time because expected future pay falls to zero as an executive approaches retirement. For Steve, it turned out to be a very fruitful proxy for wealth leverage in the sense of leading him to a pay plan with perfect wealth as well as perfect pay leverage.

19. When industry performance raises the stock price, the number of grant shares is reduced. The plan aims to rewards management performance, not industry performance.

20. The vesting multiple is equal to $1/(1 +$ the industry return from the date of grant). Since the stock value is equal to stock price at grant x $(1 +$ total return$)$ = stock price at grant × $(1 +$ relative return$)$ × $(1 +$ industry return$)$, the vested stock value is equal to stock price at grant x $(1 +$ relative return$)$. The perfect performance share plan adjusts for industry, but not for cost of capital, while the EVA bonus plan adjusts for cost of capital, but not for industry. Both plans can be modified to adjust for both cost of capital and industry.

21. See O'Byrne & Gressle, "How 'Competitive Pay' Undermines Pay for Performance (and What Companies Can Do to Avoid That)," *Journal of Applied Corporate Finance*, Vol 25, No 2, Spring 2013, pp. 36–38.

22. The sharing percentage is the ratio of cumulative market pay to expected shareholder wealth based on industry performance, that is, beginning market equity x $(1 +$ the cumulative industry return$)$. See Stephen F. O'Byrne, "Three Versions of Perfect Pay for Performance (or the Rebirth of Partnership Concepts in Executive Pay)," *Journal of Applied Corporate Finance*, Vol 26, No 1, Winter 2014, p. 35.

23. For growing companies with positive EVA, FGV would typically reflect a constant EVA return on capital combined with an expectation of capital growth. But for turnarounds with negative EVA, FGV often reflects an expectation of a substantial increase in return on capital, but with no capital growth.

24. Stephen F. O'Byrne, "EVA and Shareholder Return," *Financial Practice and Education*, Spring/Summer 1997.

25. John Cassidy, "The Greed Cycle: How the Financial System Encouraged Corporations to Go Crazy," *The New Yorker* (September 23, 2003)

26. Michael C. Jensen and Kevin J. Murphy, "CEO Incentives—It's Not How Much You Pay, but How," *Harvard Business Review*, May-June 1990, pp. 138–153.

27. Steve O'Byrne, "Linking Management Performance Incentives to Shareholder Wealth," *Journal of Corporate Accounting and Finance*, Autumn 1991, pp. 91–99.

28. Pay leverage, as we noted earlier, is the slope of the trendline relating cumulative relative pay to cumulative relative shareholder wealth (using log scales). It is a backward looking, "fact-based" calculation using 5–10 years of historical data that is far more readily accepted by investors, directors, and proxy advisors than wealth leverage. Pay leverage usually overstates wealth leverage because it ignores changes in expected future pay, which usually have little sensitivity to performance thanks to competitive pay policy.

29. Alex Edmans, Xavier Gabaix, Tomasz Sadzik, and Yuliy Sannikov, "Dynamic CEO Compensation,"*Journal of Finance*, Vol LXVII, No 5 (October 2012).

30. Satya, according to Steve, was underpaid 36 percent relative to Microsoft's relative return over the trailing five years, adjusted for his pay leverage. See Steve O'Byrne, "Measuring and Improving Pay for Performance," chapter 39, *Handbook of Board Governance*, 3rd Edition, Richard LeBlanc, editor, Wiley & Sons, 2023.

31. Alignment here is r-squared, not correlation. The pay premium range is -25 percent to +33 percent. We use -25 percent at the low end because it requires +33 percent to get back to market. Alignment and pay premium are measured separately for the CEO, the other top four executives and the corporate directors. "Half of the time" is calculated treating each five year period for each of these three groups as one case.

32. This deficiency can be seen most clearly in Steve's finding that although the median alignment of U.S. CEO mark-to-market pay with stock price performance is nearly 80 percent, it's only 6 percent for grant date pay.

10. MARTIN FRIDSON, THE EXTRAORDINARY SUCCESS OF THE HIGH-YIELD BOND MARKET, AND THE LEVERAGING OF CORPORATE AMERICA

1. For readers looking for recent historical parallels to the U.S. S&L crisis, the interest rate mismatch at the core of that crisis might be thought of as a thousandfold magnification (in terms of numbers of banks) of the failure of Silicon Valley Bank in 2023.

2. Marty confided to me his suspicion that he may have significantly advanced the firm's understanding of and predisposition to take risk when he made a presentation to Salomon's head of fixed income trading in which he made the very basic point that losses

on defaulted issues did not typically result in 100 percent loss of face value, but instead averaged only about a 60 percent loss.

3.   See Edward I. Altman, "Financial Ratios, Discriminant Analysis and the Prediction of Corporate Bankruptcy," *Journal of Finance*, Vol. 23, No. 4 (September 1968), pp. 589–609.

4.   I received much the same counsel in 2004 from my boss at Morgan Stanley, Linda Riefler, former head of Global Research and director of Content and Client Services, when the firm hired me and purchased the *Journal of Applied Corporate Finance* from my fellow partners at Stern Stewart & Co.

5.   See Lee Wakeman, "The Real Function of Bond Rating Agencies," *Chase Financial Quarterly*, Vol. 1 No. 3 (Fall 1981).

6.   The Morgan Stanley colleagues were Rick Bookstaber and David Jacob. For the bond valuation model, see Robert C. Merton, "On the Pricing of Corporate Debt: The Risk Structure of Interest Rates," *Journal of Finance* (May 1974). The research firm KMV achieved considerable success by commercializing the model based on Merton's contingent claims analysis and was ultimately acquired by Moody's.

7.   Yet another of Marty's contributions to high-yield research was his analysis of the value of covenant protection to high-yield bondholders. As one example, after quantifying the expected impact (measured in basis points) on the bonds of companies that releveraged their balance sheets, Marty then showed how investors might go about estimating the value of including strong "anti-releveraging" covenants in a contemplated new bond issue.

8.   Drexel, to its credit, never denied that Milken made the offer, but then almost certainly destroyed any lingering vestige of popular good will by pointing out—as if it thought this an act of virtue—that the firm "never tried to hinder the book's publication. See "Stop! In the Name of Money," *Time* (March 21, 1988).

9.   Further reinforcing this high-yield euphoria was the recognition that the actual annual default rates on investment-grade bonds had in fact been understated because such bonds rarely defaulted while still rated investment-grade, thus making the case for high yield appear even stronger.

10.   Peter Passell, "Economic Scene; The $12 Billion Misunderstanding," *New York Times* (July 19, 1989), p. D2.

11.   Martin Fridson, "High Yield Origins: Legend versus Fact," *Financial History* (Summer 2022), pp. 24–27.

12.   TheStreetStaff, "What Was the Savings & Loan Crisis? How Did It Affect Investors?" *TheStreet* (October 7, 2022).

13.   Kenneth J. Robinson, "Savings and Loan Crisis: 1980–1989," *Federal Reserve History* (November 22, 2013).

14.   Paul Asquith, David W. Mullins Jr., and Eric D. Wolff, "Original Issue High Yield Bonds: Aging Analysis of Defaults, Exchanges, and Calls," *Journal of Finance* (Vol. 44, Issue 4, September 1989), pp. 923–952. Mullins and Wolff had been associated with Harvard Business School, which provided funding for the research.

15.   John Paul Newport, Jr., Reporter Associate Edward C. Baig, "Junk Bonds Face the Big Unknown," *Fortune* (May 22, 1989).

16.   Again, see Jensen's theory of "LBO Overshooting," which he saw at work in all variety of markets, notably real estate and oil and gas partnerships, where the sponsors operate

largely with other people's money. Michael Jensen, "Corporate Control and the Politics of Finance," *Journal of Applied Corporate Finance*, Vol. 4 No. 2 (Summer 1991).

17. Stuart Gilson, "Workouts vs. chapter 11: The Case of 3(A)2 Exchange Offers," *Journal of Applied Corporate Finance*, Vol. 19, No. 4 (Winter 2008).

18. The occasion was a roundtable discussion I organized and moderated while working at Morgan Stanley. For an edited transcript thereof, see "Morgan Stanley Roundtable on Managing Financial Trouble," *Journal of Applied Corporate Finance*, Vol. 19, No. 4 (Winter 2008).

19. Marshall E. Blume, Donald Keim, and Sandeep A Patel, "Returns and Volatility of Low-Grade Bonds: 1977–1989," *Journal of Finance*, 1991, Vol. 46, Issue 1, pp. 49–74.

20. The devastation wrought by telecom defaults can be demonstrated by the fact that, between 1996 and 2000, the face amount of the high-yield index's telecom sector increased by almost 400 percent versus 45 percent for the non-telecom sector. But during the period 2000 to 2003, whereas telecom outstandings shrank by over 40 percent, non-telecom outstandings almost doubled.

21. Such growth seems all the more impressive in light of the stiff competition that the high-yield market has been facing from the leveraged loan market to supply capital to speculative-grade companies. The loan market's growth has been fueled by expansion of investor demand for collateralized loan obligations, or CLOs, which give institutional investors ready access to diversified portfolios of secured debt with floating-rate coupons.

22. Merton Miller, "The Modigliani-Miller Propositions After Thirty Years," *Journal of Economic Perspectives* (1988).

23. Merton Miller, "Leverage," *Journal of Applied Corporate Finance*, Vol.4 No. 2 (Summer 1991)

24. Miller also wryly described the proper punishment for one of Milken's main "felonies"— aiding takeover investors like Ivan Boesky and Carl Icahn by "parking" their stock—as a "parking ticket."

25. W. Braddock Hickman, "Corporate Bond Quality and Investor Experience," National Bureau of Economic Research. Princeton, NJ: Princeton University Press. 1958.

11. CARL WALTER AND EXPOSING THE BRITTLE FAÇADE OF CHINESE CORPORATE AND PUBLIC FINANCE

1. Fraser Howie and Carl Walter, *Red Capitalism: The Fragile Financial Foundation of China's Extraordinary Rise* (John Wiley, 2010). This second of Carl's books, and the keynote speech, drew heavily on his first book, *Privatizing China: Inside China's Stock Markets* (John Wiley, 2005).

2. Shang Ming, Editor, *XinZhongguo jinrong 50 shinian* (50 years of New China's banking), (Beijing, Zhongguo caizheng jingji chubanshe, 1999), p. 307.

3. Carl Walter, "Was Deng Xiaoping Right? An Overview of China's Equity Markets," *Journal of Applied Corporate Finance*, Vol. 26 No. 3 (Summer 2014).

4. Jay Ritter, "Is Economic Growth Good for Investors?" *Journal of Applied Corporate Finance*, Volume 24, Number 3 (Summer 2012).

5. See Michael Brantley, "China's Economy is Not Overtaking the U.S.," *Journal of Applied Corporate Finance*, Vol. 31 No. 2 (Spring 2019).

6.   Some of it featured in the *JACF* as early as 2014. See Carl Walter, "Was Deng Xiaoping Right? An Overview of China's Equity Markets," *Journal of Applied Corporate Finance*, Vol. 26 No. 3 (Summer 2014).

7.   What's more, Carl himself disputes the characterization of "The Big Push" as in any important sense "government-orchestrated." As we will see below, he attributes the Chinese economic miracle almost entirely to the government's decision to open the country to direct foreign investment, and to the rise of and investment by private (non-state) Chinese entrepreneurs that resulted from mostly Western DFI.

8.   For the best exposition of this idea I've come across, see Daron Acemoglu and James Robinson's prize-winning NY Times bestseller, *Why Nations Fail: The Origins of Power, Prosperity and Poverty* (Crown Publishers, 2012).

9.   Randall Morck and Bernard Yeung, "Corporate Governance in China," *Journal of Applied Corporate Finance*, Vol. 26 No.3 (Summer 2014).

10. For 2018 GDP, the estimates run from 23 percent to 28 percent. See "Zhang, Chunlin, 2019, "How Much Do State-Owned Enterprises Contribute to China's GDP and Employment," World Bank, Washington, DC. © World Bank. https://openknowledge .worldbank.org/handle/10986/32306 License: CC BY 3.0 IGO; for 39 percent of 2015 GDP Carston A. Holz, see "The Unfinished Business of State-owned Enterprise Reform in the People's Republic of China, *Journal of Economic Literature*, December 2, 1018, https:// carstenholz.people.ust.hk/CarstenHolz-PRC-SOEreforms-2Dec2018.pdf

11. Insurance products, savings bonds, and mutual funds are not attractive given low yields, and the trust plans and bond market used mainly by institutional investors are not open to retail.

12. *Wall Street Journal*, October 4, 021, https://www.wsj.com/articles/evergrande-china-real -estate-debt-debacle-empty-buildings-cities-beijing

13. Kenneth S. Rogoff and Yuanchen Yang, "Has China's housing production peaked?" China and the World Economy (21) 1, p. 3; https://scholar.harvard.edu/rogoff/publications /peak-china-housing

12. JAMES SWEENEY AND MICRO-BASED ATTEMPTS TO MAKE MACRO RELEVANT

1.   America's public debt, however large and growing, represents much less of a cost burden than China's to its current and future citizens and taxpayers. Thanks to a per capita income six times that of China's, the U.S. not only has more surplus wealth to pay down its debts, but also enjoys lower interest rates from the dollar's status as the world's reserve currency, whose estimated benefit to all U.S. debtors is a $100 billion reduction in *annual* interest payments.

2.   Beckley, Michael *Unrivaled: Why America Will Remain the World's Sole Superpower*. (Ithaca, N.Y.: Cornell University Press, 2018).

3.   Diane Coyle, *GDP: A Brief But Affectionate History* (Princeton, NJ: Princeton University Press, 2014).

4.   Conference Board. 2019. "Total Economy Database."

5. Jorgenson, Dale W., Mun S. Ho, Jon D. Samuels. "Educational Attainment and the Revival of US Economic Growth" in Hulten and Ramey, *Education, Skills, and Technical Change: Implications for Future US GDP Growth*, (2019).

6. Dinny McMahon, *China's Great Wall of Debt: Shadow Banks, Ghost Cities, Massive Loans, and the End of the Chinese Economic Miracle* (Houghton Mifflin Harcourt, 2018).

7. Chi, Guanghua, Yu Liu, Zhengwei Wu, and Haishan Wu, "Ghost Cities' Analysis Based on Positioning Data in China." *Big Data Lab*, Baidu Research (2015); and Wade Shepard, *Ghost Cities of China* (London: Zed Books, 2015).

8. Most recent: https://www.credit-suisse.com/about-us/en/reports-research/global-wealth -report.html

9. James Sweeney, "Rethinking Macro Measurement, *Journal of Applied Corporate Finance*. (Vol. 32 No. 4) Fall 2020. The question was posed in my editor's intro to the issue.

10. Ibid. The question was posed in my editor's intro to the issue.

11. In fact, the 2023 book by Phil Gramm, Robert Ekelund, and John Early cited earlier, after adjusting official government statistics for benefits and more realistic measures of inflation, reports substantial increases in both real average hourly wages and median household income in the past half century. Phil Gramm, John Early, and Robert Ekelund, *The Myth of American Inequality: How the Government Biases Policy Debate*, Rowman & Littlefield, 2022.

12. Evidence for this claim is also provided by Gramm, Ekelund, and Early in their 2023 book, just cited.

13. Robert Gordon, *The Rise and Fall of American Growth* (Princeton, NJ: Princeton University Press, 2016).

14. http://www.nber.org/chapters/c6064.pdf

15. The term is attributed to psychologist James J. Gibson

16. And more recent financial history shows much the same relationship at work. For 15 emerging markets during the 24-year period from 1988 to 2011—including the BRIC countries of Brazil, Russia, India, and China—the reported correlation was a remarkably similar −0.41. See Jay Ritter, "Is Economic Growth Good for Investors?" *Journal of Applied Corporate Finance*, Volume 24, Number 3 (Summer 2012).

EPILOGUE: SUSTAINABLE FINANCIAL MANAGEMENT (AND THE PROMISE AND PITFALLS OF ESG INVESTING)

1. Michael Jensen, "The Corporate Objective Function: Stakeholder Value vs. Value Maximization," *Journal of Applied Corporate Finance* (Fall, 2001). The article was a reworking, prepared with Mike's oversight and encouragement, of an earlier version published in the *Business Ethics Quarterly*, Vol. 12 No. 2 (2002).

2. Jensen and his colleague Bill Meckling once wrote an article (eventually published in the JACF) that they titled "The Nature of Man," and whose account of human strengths and limitations begins with Plato.

3. Which, again, might be identified as the animating spirit behind and informing this book. Though many will recognize Smith as the author of *Wealth of Nations*, published in 1776,

fewer are likely to recall Smith's earlier book, *The Theory of Moral Sentiments*, and his position at the University of Glasgow as Professor of Moral Philosophy. Fewer still are likely to be aware that *Wealth of Nations* was long required reading for Columbia University undergraduates until the onset of the Great Depression seemed to discredit all productions of the Enlightenment.

4.   In this last statement, Jensen was surely aware of, if not consciously echoing, Milton Friedman's famous 1970 *New York Time's Magazine* op-ed article. "The Social Responsibility of Business is to Increase Its Profit." In revisiting these questions three decades later, Mike is restating Friedman's case for long-run value maximization, but in ways that shift the emphasis toward the search for even greater (though still positive-NPV) investment in stakeholders of all variety.

5.   Many have accused Jensen and Meckling of holding out an excessively pessimistic view of both human nature and the possibilities for collaboration and collective enterprise. But Mike himself, both in his writings and private conversations, dismissed this view as a complete misreading. As he liked to say, "the corporate managers and Harvard students I talk to all the time are not depressed, but excited, by agency cost theory. What excites them is *not* the pervasiveness of conflicts of interests within large organizations created by the reality of human self-interest. What excites them is the potential to create efficiencies and value by recognizing and effectively managing such conflicts."

6.   Literary types will recognize one of my favorite lines from the great French writer Albert Camus's greatest of novels, *The Plague*, sales of which skyrocketed during the pandemic.

7.   When WalMart announced, in January 2024, the most recent of its series of major increases in workers' and store managers' pay, its stock price increased by over $2, or more than 1 percent of its total market cap. And if part of this reaction can be attributed to the "signaling" or "information" effect of such an announcement, surely another part can be construed as investor approval of such corporate profit- and wealth-sharing.

8.   Steve Lydenberg, "A Taxonomy of Socially Responsible Investors," *Journal of Applied Corporate Finance*, Vol. 25 No. 3 (Summer 2014).

9.   Dan Hanson, "ESG Investing in Graham and Doddsville," *Journal of Applied Corporate Finance*, Vol. 25 No. 3 (Summer 2014).

10.   George Serafeim, "Integrated Reporting and Investor Clientele," *Journal of Applied Corporate Finance*, Vol. 26 No. 2 (Spring 2016).

11.   Alex Cheema-Fox, Bridget La Perla, Huy (Stacie) Wang, and George Serafeim, "Corporate Resilience and Response to COVID-19," *Journal of Applied Corporate Finance*, Vol.33 No. 2 (Spring 2021).

12.   Patrick Bolton, Marcin Kaperczyk, Zachary Halem, "The Financial Cost of Carbon," *Journal of Applied Corporate Finance*, Vol. 34 No. 2 (Spring 2022).

13.   Although the recent flurry of very large oil and gas acquisitions, like Exxon's purchase of Pioneer Resources, and Chevron's of Hess, might appear to contradict the idea of shrinking E&P exploration budgets, it's important to recognize that these transactions are driven not by the perception of expanded growth opportunities, but rather by the industry's need to consolidate in response to a market that is perceived to have to shrink over time.

14.   See Baruch Lev and Feng Gu, *The End of Accounting and the Path Forward for Investors and Managers*, cited earlier in chapter 3.

15. See David Denis and Stephen McKeon, "Rising Intangibles, Negative Cash Flows, and Corporate Funding Practices," 2022, cited earlier, who report finding that whereas the 10 percent of so of U.S. public company with negative operating cash flow in the 1970s were viewed as "zombies" and carried market-to-book ratios well below 1.0, in the most recent decade, the median market-to-book of today's bumper crop of U.S. money-losing companies is a remarkably buoyant 1.6.

16. The ShareAction living wage resolution is the main subject of the lead article, by London Business School's sustainability expert Tom Gosling, in the Spring 2023 JACF sustainability issue. High among the reasons for the proposal's failure, it appears to have been developed by ShareAction without any consultation with Sainsbury's management and bore no relation to any new strategy designed to produce greater employee commitment, higher productivity, or lower turnover. As Gosling also notes in the article, the vast majority of Sainsbury's employees were *already* receiving a "living wage," and the resolution failed Gosling's (and the London Business School's) three-part test for determining whether investors should initiate (or support) a given ESG issue: (1) Can it be demonstrated to have a materially (positive) long-run effect on a company's performance and value? (2) Are the company's actions likely to prove effective in bringing about the desired social end? (More pointedly, is Sainsbury's action alone likely to improve (or harm) the lot of its average workers? (3) Do Sainsbury's and its investors have any notable "comparative advantage" relative to, say, government policymakers who in the UK actually set the minimum wage for most industries, in bringing about such change?

17. Although today you have to own just $25,000 worth of a single stock to be allowed to propose a vote, before 2020 you could submit a resolution while owning as little as $1,000.

18. Kate Parrot and Brian Tierney, "Sustainability and The Case of American Electric Power," *Journal of Applied Corporate Finance*, Vol. 24 No. 2 (Spring 2012).

19. Ibid.

20. Carl Ferenbach and Chris Pinney, "Toward a 21st-Century Social Contract." *Journal of Applied Corporate Finance*, Vol. 24 No. 2 (Spring 2012). This was the lead article in the first of what has become our annual series of spring sustainability issues. And in the interest of full disclosure, Carl Ferenbach has been the financial backer, and our partner and co-owner, of the *JACF* since my Associate Editor John McCormack,and I left Morgan Stanley in 2013.

21. For possibly the most comprehensive account (by a profoundly sympathetic believer in big government) of the systematic failure of the U.S. federal government to carry out its functions in a cost-effective way, see Peter H. Schuck, *Why Government Fails So Often— And How It Can Do Better*, Princeton University Press, 2014.

22. See Paul Krugman, "Full Employment is Good for Society," *New York Times*, January 16, 2024.

INDEX

137–139; psychology of, xiii; of public companies, viii, 5–7; risk management for, 112–113; shareholders and, xiii–xiv, 145; in U.S., 14; WMPs, 230–231. *See also* *specific topics*

Mandelker, Gershon, 39–40

Manitowoc, 168

Manne, Henry, 273n4

Mao Zedong, 220, 224

marginal default values, 92–93

markets: capital, 8; in CAPM, 90; in Chicago School theory of value, 35–37, 45–46; for corporate control, xi–xiv, 3, 275n15; after COVID, 6, 141; market rate of interest formula, 27; market-to-book ratios, 83; regulation of, 10; in Rochester School of Corporate Control, 56–58, 61; in U.S., xvi. *See also efficient markets*

Markowitz, Harry, 24

Martin, John, 46

Maug, Ernst, 140

Mayers, David, 98–102, 104–108, 112

MBA students, 33

MBS. *See* mortgage-backed securities

McConnell, John, 45

McKeon, Steve, 47–48, 290n15

McKinsey & Co., 21

Means, Gardiner, 54

Meckling, William: Jensen and, 3–4, 52–56, 71, 78, 81–82, 124, 289n2; reputation of, ix, xii–xiiv, 58, 276n4, 290n5. *See also* Rochester School of Corporate Control

media, 208–209

Merrill Lynch, 5–6, 204–205, 210, 212–213

Merton, Robert, 3–4, 83–84, 108–109, 114–115, 203

microeconomics, 240–242, 242

Microsoft, 191–192, 196, 267, 285n30

Milken, Michael: at Drexel Burnham Lambert, 198–200, 210–212, 217–219, 286n8; Fridson and, 5–6, 205–206, 213, 217–218

Miller, Merton: on bankruptcy, 106; Bernstein, P., and, 24–25; career reflections from, 33–34, 51; colleagues of,

49; on corporate investment decision-making, 16–17; on economics, 2–3; education of, 23–24; in Japan, 45, 52; on leverage, 196, 216–217; Modigliani and, 29–32, 71–75, 75, 79–80, 277n11; observations from, 12–13, 18, 50; on pay-for-performance, 15; scholarship from, 23–24; stock market indicators, 16; on taxes, 277n12; theories of, 14. *See also* Chicago School theory of value

minimal equity ownership, xiv

MIT school of real options: APV in, 79–81, 90; capital structure in, 87–89; CAPM in, 78–79; collaboration in, 89–90; on corporate borrowing, 81–84; DCF in, 75–79, 84–85, 90; information costs and, 86–87; option pricing theory in, 84–85; philosophy of, 70–74; on risk capital, 91–93; trade-off theory in, 74–75, 75; WACC in, 79–81, 90, 178n13, 277n11

M&M. *See* Chicago School theory of value

Modern Corporate and Private Property, The (Berle and Means), 54–55

modern corporate risk management, 98–99

"Modern Industrial Revolution, The" (Jensen), 52–53

Modigliani, Franco, 2–3, 23–24, 29–32, 71–75, 75, 79–80. *See also* Chicago School theory of value

"Modigliani-Miller Propositions After Thirty Years, The" (Miller), 33–34

Moody's, 194–195, 203, 206, 210, 216, 286n6

Morck, Randall, 224–226

Morgan, J. P., x, 123

Morgan Stanley, 5–6, 67, 119–120, 201–205, 221, 286n18

mortgage underwriting standards, 92

mortgage-backed securities (MBS), 73, 119, 231

Mullins, David, 209–210

Murphy, Kevin, 125, 189–190, 193

Muscarella, Chris, 45

Musk, Elon, 251–252

Myers, Stewart: Brealey and, 89–90; on capital structure, 70–74, 87–88, 94; on corporate strategies, 84–85; criticism